AMTA Monograph Series

AMERICAN
MUSIC
THERAPY
ASSOCIATION

Effective Clinical Practice in Music Therapy:
Early Childhood and School Age Educational Settings

Marcia Earl Humpal, Monograph Editor
Cynthia Colwell, Series Editor

IBSN: 1-884914-16-0

Monograph Editor: **Marcia Earl Humpal**
                                Cuyahoga County Board of Mental Retardation and
                                Developmental Disabilities
                                Cleveland, Ohio

Series Editor: **Cynthia Colwell**
                                University of Kansas
                                Lawrence, Kansas

Copyright Information: **© by American Music Therapy Association, Inc., 2006**
                                8455 Colesville Rd., Suite 1000
                                Silver Spring, Maryland 20910 USA
                                www.musictherapy.org
                                info@musictherapy.org

                                No part of this book may be reproduced in any form without
                                prior written permission from the Executive Director of the
                                Association.

Technical Assistance: **Wordsetters**
                                Kalamazoo, Michigan

Cover Design & Typesetting: **Angie K Elkins, MT-BC**

Printed in the United States of America

List of Contributing Authors

Ruthlee Figlure Adler, MT-BC
The Ivymount School
Rockville, Maryland

Nicole Allgood, MSEd, MT-BC
Giant Steps Illinois, Inc.
Burr Ridge, Illinois

Amelia Greenwald Furman, MM, RMT
Minneapolis Public Schools
Minneapolis, Minnesota

Marcia Earl Humpal, MEd, MT-BC
Cuyahoga County Board of Mental Retardation and Developmental Disabilities
Cleveland, Ohio

Ronna Kaplan, MA, MT-BC
The Cleveland Music School Settlement
Cleveland, Ohio

Beth McLaughlin, MS, LCAT, MT-BC
Wildwood School
Schenectady, New York

Jean M. Nemeth, MA, MT-BC
Cheshire, Meriden and Wallingford Public Schools
Berlin, Connecticut

Elizabeth K. Schwartz, LCAT, MT-BC
Alternatives for Children
Suffolk County, New York

Angela M. Snell, MT-BC
Monroe County Intermediate School District
Monroe, Michigan

Elizabeth Swaney, MS, MT-BC
Trinity School
Cincinnati, Ohio

Rebecca Tweedle, MEd, MT-BC
Cuyahoga County Board of Mental Retardation and Developmental Disabilities
Cleveland, Ohio

Acknowledgments

Special thanks to the following who contributed to this publication through sharing of their materials and expertise:

Marcia Behr, MT-BC
Augusta, Missouri

Kathleen Coleman, MMT, MT-BC
Grapevine, Texas

Jane Hughes, MA, MT-BC
Tallahassee, Florida

Betsey King, MMT, MT-BC
Rochester, New York

Myrna Mandlawitz, Esq.
Washington, D.C.

Brenda Robbins Rice, MME, MT-BC
Tallahasee, Florida

Judy Simpson, MHP, MT-BC
Silver Spring, MD

Glenn Sonoda, MA, RMT
Norton, Ohio

Brian Wilson, MM, MT-BC
Kalamazoo, Michigan

Contents

Section IV: **Implementation Techniques, Methods, and Effective Clinical Practice**

Section V: **Resources**

Appendices

Chapter 1

Introduction and Brief History
Marcia E. Humpal, MEd, MT-BC

This monograph is one of a series of "Effective Clinical Practice" resources produced by the American Music Therapy Association (AMTA) to disseminate information on specific targeted populations. *Effective Clinical Practice in Music Therapy—Early Childhood and School Age Educational Settings* focuses on current traditional yet state-of-the-art practices used by clinicians who work on a daily basis with students and young children. While the information and practices contained and described herein are based on research, much of the material presented is the result of years of patient doing, revising, observing, discussing, and discovering what really works with the children and students with whom we work.

The information within is organized by section. Each section (and the chapters therein) represents a different aspect of effective delivery of music therapy services based on an education model. Section I presents a brief history of the development of music therapy in education and early childhood settings, then defines and portrays characteristics of individuals served in these settings. Section II describes eligibility and assessment processes as well as the legal aspects that influence music therapy service delivery. Section III breaks down the educational setting into two parts: school age and early childhood. Chapters in this section look at typical goals and treatment objectives, the settings themselves, and service delivery models. Working as part of an interdisciplinary team also is examined in this section. Section IV offers techniques, tips, methods, suggestions for adaptation and augmentation, technology information, and examples of actual successful strategies that the authors have used in their own sessions. Section V gives readers a myriad of resources and information.

The authors whose works and ideas are found in the following chapters are experts in their field. They bring years of experience to this publication, yet none has become stagnant in the delivering of music therapy services. New and creative plans and projects are a part of each person's professional world. All of us welcome comments or questions from readers. One of the true joys of being a clinician is the ever-present excitement of learning from and sharing with others. We hope you can take some of this information into your clinical settings as you develop your own effective clinical best practice in music therapy.

Background and Historical Information

The use of music as a therapeutic intervention with individuals with special cognitive needs or developmental disabilities has been well documented since the 1950s (Weigl, 1959). Initial studies of this time noted that children with mental retardation evidenced an emotional response to music similar to that of normal children. Other early studies examined the use of music to reinforce, organize and focus attention upon the learning experience. Increasingly, music was used for socialization, building inner strength, intrusion on fantasy, stimulation, and gratification (Lathom, 1968). In the 1960s, music therapy internships with this population were established and increased research activity supported music therapy's effectiveness (Bennis, 1969; Isern, 1964; Kessler, 1967; Lathom, 1964; Leland, 1964; Steele, 1968).

School Setting

In the 1970s, the emphasis changed from a medical model to an educational model (due in part to passage of federal legislature regarding the education of *all* students). Music therapy was used to support special and regular services in the school by assisting with needed behavioral changes, decreasing inappropriate behaviors that interfered with learning, and increasing desired behaviors (Lathom, 1979). Music therapy also was used to teach adaptive and vocational skills and to reinforce goals from other interdisciplinary areas (e.g., speech training, the teaching of writing). At this time, music therapy goals often emphasized behavioral rather than psychoanalytical goals. Music was used as a reinforcer of desired behavior (such as increasing attention span), as an aid to acquiring and maintaining "appropriate behavior" (for instance, if hands are busy playing a drum, they will not be hitting another child) or emotional adjustment (Steele, Vaughan, & Dolan, 1976). During this decade, Nordoff and Robbins (1971) published their landmark book, *Music Therapy in Special Education*. Music therapy was being recognized as an effective treatment for those with severe disabilities (Alley, 1977) and in special education settings (Steele, 1979).

In the 1980s, Eagle, in his annotated bibliography *Music Therapy for Handicapped Children and Youth* (1982), cites approximately 100 entries dealing with the topic of music therapy and mental retardation. By this time, music therapists were using music therapeutically as a carrier of information, a reinforcer, a background for learning, a physical structure for the learning activity, and as a reflection of skills or processes to be learned (Boxill, 1985; Eagle, 1982). Madsen (1981) expanded on these topics in his book *Music Therapy: A Behavioral Guide for the Mentally Retarded*. The *Project Music Monograph Series*, edited by Lathom and Eagle and published in 1982 by the National Association for Music Therapy, provided pertinent information for using music therapy with a vast array of other developmental disabilities. This project was developed to supply information for in-service providers attempting to obtain music therapy services for persons with disabilities (Smith & Hairston, 1999).

In the 1990s and into the 21st century, music therapy began to gain recognition as a viable related service in educational settings with much music therapy research conducted with children and youth with disabilities (Jellison, 2000). AMTA mounted an intensive advocacy effort that resulted in a letter from the Director of the U.S. Office of Special Education Programs stating that while music therapy is not directly named as a related service, it may indeed be considered as such under IDEA (Simpson, 2002). The ramifications from the passage of updated legislation such as IDEA 2004, the Individuals with Disabilities Education Act (see Chapter 3), have yet to be seen. Additional advocacy efforts included the development of a fact sheet, *Music Therapy in Special Education*. This resource is included in the *Resource Section* of this monograph.

A survey of music therapy assessment areas (Chase, 2004) lists current areas of assessment described by music therapists working in school settings. These categories often become the targeted goal areas for clinical practice. The following is a list of the top five areas described in the Chase study as well as representative examples that reflect the underpinnings of past research:

1. *Motor*—Holloway (1980) reviewed the effects of both active and passive music reinforcement to increase pre-academic and motor skills for children and adolescents with significant delays. Furthermore, music therapy can be an effective adjunct to sensory stimulation, often a goal area unto itself (James, Weaver, Clemens, & Plaster, 1985).

2. *Communication*—Many studies substantiate the positive effects of music therapy as a complementary therapy to speech therapy. In 1974, Galloway compiled a comprehensive bibliography of studies validating the use of music to develop as well as remediate communication skills.

3. *Social/Emotional*—Jellison, Brooks, and Huck (1984) structured small groups and music reinforcement to facilitate positive interactions and acceptance of students with severe handicapping conditions in the regular music classroom.

4. *Cognitive, Academic or Pre-academic*—Fraser (1961) noted that employing music therapy techniques helped children learn to write; Dorow (1976) found that music helped children achieve correct mathematical responses.

5. *Music*—Steele (1984) used both a behavioral and a sequential program of musical development intervention methods to teach music skills to students with learning disabilities.

Music therapists working in school settings today may address not only targeted areas discussed above but also needs the student may exhibit in sensory processing, as well as adaptive or vocational skills attainment. For an in-depth discussion of theoretical issues and models of music therapy interventions in schools and educational environments, see AMTA's *Models of Music Therapy Interventions in School Settings* (Wilson, 2002). This book includes information on both school age and early childhood settings. Additional helpful information may be found in AMTA's *Music in Special Education* (Adamek & Darrow, 2005).

In the 1990s and into the twenty-first century, music therapy began to gain recognition as a viable related service in educational settings with much music therapy research conducted with children and youth with disabilities. (Jellison, 2000)

Early Childhood

For over 30 years, music therapists have noted the positive effects of music therapy on their youngest clients. Steele and Jorgenson (1971) studied contingent socio-music listening periods in a preschool setting and reported that music therapy was an effective solution to problems in related disciplines. Kramer (1978) examined how music may be used as a cue in maintaining hand washing in preschool children. Gunsberg (1988) developed a system of improvised musical play as a strategy for fostering social play between preschool children with developmental delays and their typical peers. Witt and Steele (1984) reported a case study of music therapy with an infant and parent. Darrow (1987) investigated the effect of hearing impairment on the music aptitude of young children. Other investigators noted music therapy's effects on speech, language and verbalization of young children (Cartwright & Huckaby, 1972; Galloway & Bean, 1974; Harding & Ballard, 1983; Hoskins, 1988).

Prior to 1990, however, most music therapy research studies did not differentiate between age levels of children. Examples in the literature that supported the use of music for cognitive development, motor development, communication and social integration often incorporated early childhood into assumptions about music's effects on children in general (Humpal, 1990). Furthermore, beyond the scope of *music professionals*, little had been written concerning the very powerful force that music plays in educating the young learner with special needs. Since then, inclusion has become the norm nationwide, and in some cases, was facilitated by early childhood inclusive music therapy pilot programs (Davis, 1990; Furman & Furman, 1996; Hughes, Robbins, MacKenzie, & Robb, 1990; Humpal, 1991; Humpal & Dimmick, 1996).

Since the early 1990s, more studies have been conducted that herald music therapy's positive effects specifically for infants and young children in many different settings. Though more and more journals in related fields are publishing works by music therapists, historically, most music therapy research has been reported within the pages of its own three professional journals: *Journal of Music Therapy, Music Therapy,* and *Music Therapy Perspectives.* See the Resource section for an annotated bibliography of articles from music therapy journals between 1990 and 2005 specifically relating to music therapy for young children in educational settings

Through these journals and other published resources, AMTA has promoted much research that explores the benefits of utilizing music therapy with young children. In addition, the association has demonstrated a commitment to furthering information dissemination about music therapy and young children. Since 1993, an Early Childhood Roundtable has been a part of each national conference. An *Early Childhood Newsletter* has been published annually as part of the mission of AMTA's Early Childhood Network; editions have been posted on the Members Only section of the AMTA website since 2003. The *Music Therapy and the Young Child Fact Sheet,* compiled with input from countless music therapy practitioners, was completed in 1999 (see *Resource Section* of this monograph). As testimony to heightened interest in the early childhood population, two early childhood institutes have been held at AMTA conferences, affording continuing education opportunities to music therapists in this specialized area.

Trends

The benefits of music therapy for young children are being recognized and acclaimed by other professional agencies. Media attention is focusing on our profession, and music therapists are being invited to speak at conferences and to be a part of national summit meetings. Alliances are being formed with other organizations so that the message "music should be a part of all children's lives" can be sent forth loudly and clearly. Music therapists were included in Sesame Workshop's symposium on music and young children and the subsequent production of their multimedia kit, *Music Works Wonders* (Sesame Workshop, 2001). The profession also was represented at the *Start the Music* initiative held in Washington, DC, sponsored by Texaco, MENC, and the U.S. Department of Education (Texaco, 2000). *Early Childhood Connections*, the journal of music- and movement-based learning, devoted its entire Spring 2001 issue to "Music Therapy and Young Children."

Likewise, the number of music therapists who speak at state, regional, and national conferences of music education, general education associations as well as organizations devoted to specific categories of disabilities is increasing. Professional journals refer to music therapy more and more frequently, and the impact of the Internet (which has introduced music therapy to numerous individuals and organizations) grows each day. The Internet also offers opportunities to explore how music therapy is being utilized in educational settings throughout the world. *Voices: A World Forum for Music Therapy*, a free online web-journal may be accessed at http://www.voices.no/. The World Federation of Music Therapy sponsors an e-magazine, *Music Therapy Today* that may be found at http://www. musictherapyworld.de/.

A 1999 study that investigated current practices in school settings (Smith & Hairston, 1999) reported four categories of employment for music therapists working in educational venues. The majority of respondents were employed by school districts. Other categories included self-employed, employed by an agency which provided services for school-based settings, and employed in other school-related settings (such as intermediate schools, boards of mental retardation and developmental disabilities, state residential schools, private schools). To be hired by a school district in some states, music therapists must hold valid teaching licenses or certificates. This requirement may be a factor in the increasing numbers of music therapists hired under other job titles.

The increase in inclusive instructional environments may be influencing the number of music therapists who (1) are hired as consultants to help music educators create meaningful musical experiences for their students with exceptionalities, or (2) are called upon to develop strategies for classroom teachers that use music for the attainment of nonmusical goals. Moreover, adapting to the ever-changing special education scene, some school districts are utilizing a program-based consultative music therapy model of service delivery. This model combines features of both the direct service and consultative approaches (Chester, Holmberg, Lawrence, & Thurmond, 1999).

The AMTA Member *Sourcebook* (AMTA, 2004) reported that school-related facilities and self-employment appear to be the major growth areas for newly created jobs in 2003. Interestingly, one of the populations most often listed as being served by private practice music therapists in 2002 was that of children with developmental disabilities (Wilhelm,

2004). Early intervention and children's day care/preschool also showed an increased number of new music therapy jobs (AMTA, 2004).

•

Food for Thought

Throughout the remaining pages of this monograph, authors will describe how they are effectively using music therapy in early childhood and school-age educational settings as the 21st century unfolds. Determining "effective clinical practices" is a process that is never complete; it is an ongoing, dynamic course of action that requires constant investigation, examination, and reevaluation so that our practices do, indeed, remain the best that they can be in response to reauthorizations of existing public laws and as new clinical protocols are developed through practice and research.

Determining "effective clinical practices" is a process that is never complete; it is an ongoing, dynamic course of action that requires constant investigation, examination and reevaluation so that our practices do, indeed, remain the best that they can be in response to reauthorization of existing public laws and as new clinical protocols are developed through practice and research.

•

References

Adamek, M., & Darrow, A. (2005). Music in special education. *Silver Spring, MD: American Music Therapy Association.*

Alley, J. M. (1977). Education for the severely handicapped: The role of music therapy. Journal of Music Therapy, *14(2),* 50–59.

American Music Therapy Association (2004). AMTA Member Sourcebook 2000. *Silver Spring, MD: Author.*

Bennis, J. A. (1969). The use of music as a therapy in the special education classroom. Journal of Music Therapy, *6(1),* 15–18.

Boxill, E. H. (1985). Music therapy for the developmentally disabled. *Austin, TX: Pro-Ed.*

Cartwright, J., & Huckaby, G. (1972). Intensive preschool language program. Journal of Music Therapy, *9(3),* 137–146.

Chase, K. (2004). Music therapy assessment for children with developmental disabilities: A survey study. Journal of Music Therapy, *41(1),* 28–54.

Chester, K., Holmberg, T., Lawrence, M., & Thurmond, L. (1999). A program-based consultative music therapy model for public schools. Music Therapy Perspectives, *17(2),* 82–91.

Darrow, A. A. (1987). An investigative study: The effect of hearing impairment on the music aptitude of young children. Journal of Music Therapy, *24(2),* 88–96.

Davis, R. (1990). A model for the integration of music therapy within preschool classrooms for children with physical disabilities or language delays. Music Therapy Perspectives, *8,* 82–84.

Dorow, L. (1976). Televised music lessons as educational reinforcement for correct mathematical responses with the educable mentally retarded. Journal of Music Therapy, *13(2),* 77–86.

Eagle, C. (1982). Music therapy for handicapped children and youth: An annotated and indexed bibliography. *Washington, DC: National Association for Music Therapy.*

Fraser, L. (1961). The use of music in teaching writing to the retarded child. Proceedings of the National Association for Music Therapy, *10,* 86–89.

Furman, A., & Furman, C. (1996). Music therapy for learners in a public school early education center. In B. Wilson (Ed.), Models of music therapy interventions in school settings: From institution to inclusion *(pp. 258–276). Silver Spring, MD: American Music Therapy Association.*

Galloway, H. (1974). A comprehensive bibliography of music referential to communicative development, processing, disorders, and remediation. Journal of Music Therapy, *11(4),* 202–207.

Galloway, H., & Bean, M. (1974). The effects of action songs on the development of body-image and body-part identification in hearing impaired preschool children. Journal of Music Therapy, *11(3),* 125–134.

Gunsberg, A. (1988). Improvised musical play: A strategy for fostering social play between developmentally delayed and nondelayed preschool children. Journal of Music Therapy, *24(4),* 178–191.

Harding, C., & Ballard, K. (1983). The effectiveness of music as a stimulus and as a contingent reward in promoting the spontaneous speech of three physically handicapped preschoolers. Journal of Music Therapy, *20(2),* 86–101.

Holloway, M. (1980). A comparison of passive and active music reinforcement to increase preacademic and motor skills in severely retarded children and adolescents. Journal of Music Therapy, *17(2),* 58–69.

Hoskins, C. (1988). Use of music to increase verbal response and improve expressive language abilities of preschool language delayed children. Journal of Music Therapy, *25(2),* 73–83.

Hughes, J., Robbins, B., MacKenzie, B., & Robb, S. (1990). Integrating exceptional and nonexceptional young children through music play: A pilot program. Music Therapy Perspectives, 8, 52–56.

Humpal, M. (1990). Early intervention: The implications for music therapy. Music Therapy Perspectives, 8, 31-34.

Humpal, M. (1991). The effects of an integrated early childhood music program on social interaction among children with handicaps and their typical peers. Journal of Music Therapy, 28(3), 161–177.

Humpal, M., & Dimmick, J. (1996). Music therapy for learners in an early childhood community interagency setting. In B. Wilson (Ed.), Models of music therapy interventions in school settings: From institution to inclusion, (pp. 277–311). Silver Spring, MD: American Music Therapy Association.

Isern, B. (1964). Music in special education. Journal of Music Therapy, 1(4), 139–142.

James, M., Weaver, A., Clemens, P. & Plaster, G. (1985). Influence of paired auditory and vestibular stimulation on levels of motor skill development in a mentally retarded population. Journal of Music Therapy, 22(1), 22–34.

Jellison, J. (2000). A content analysis of music research with disabled children and youth (1975–1999): Applications in special education. In American Music Therapy Association (Ed.), Effectiveness of music therapy procedures: Documentation of research and clinical practice. Silver Spring, MD: American Music Therapy Association.

Jellison, J., Brooks, B., & Huck, A. (1984). Structuring small groups and music reinforcement to facilitate positive interactions and acceptance of severely handicapped students in the regular music classroom. Journal of Research in Music Education, 32, 322–333.

Kessler, J. (1967). Therapeutic methods for exceptional children. Journal of Music Therapy, 4(1), 1–2.

Kramer, S. (1978). The effects of music as a cue in maintaining handwashing in preschool children. Journal of Music Therapy, 15(3), 136–144.

Lathom, W. (1964). Music therapy as a means of changing the adaptive behavior level of retarded children. Journal of Music Therapy, 1(4), 132–134.

Lathom, W. (1968). The use of music with retarded patients. In E. Gaston (Ed.), Music in therapy. New York: Macmillan.

Lathom, W. (1979). The use of music in the treatment of retarded children. Address at the American Association for Mental Deficiency, Miami, FL.

Lathom, W., & Eagle, C. (1982). Project Music Monograph Series. Lawrence, KS: National Association for Music Therapy.

Leland, H. (1964). Adaptive behavior as related to the treatment of the mentally retarded. Journal of Music Therapy, 1(4), 129–131.

Madsen, C. (1981). Music therapy: A behavioral guide for the mentally retarded. Lawrence, KS: National Association for Music Therapy.

Nordoff, P., & Robbins, C. (1971). Music therapy in special education. New York: John Day.

Sesame Workshop. (2001). Music works wonders. New York: Author.

Simpson, J. (2002). Increasing access to music therapy: The roles of parents, music therapists and AMTA. In B. Wilson (Ed.), Models of music therapy interventions in school settings (pp. 3–14). Silver Spring, MD: American Music Therapy Association.

Smith, D., & Hairston, M. (1999). Music therapy in school settings: Current practice. Journal of Music Therapy, 36(4), 274–292.

Steele, A. L. (1968). Programmed use of music to alter uncooperative problem behaviors. Journal of Music Therapy, 5(4), 103–107.

Steele, A. L. (1979). A report on the first World Congress on Future Special Education. Journal of Music Therapy, 16(1), 43–47.

Steele, A. L. (1984). Music therapy for the learning disabled: Intervention and instruction. Music Therapy Perspectives, 1(3), 2–7.

Steele, A. L., & Jorgenson, H. (1971). Music therapy: An effective solution to problems in related disciplines. Contingent socio-music listening periods in a preschool setting. Journal of Music Therapy, 8(4), 131-145.

Steele, A. L., Vaughan, M., & Dolan, C. (1976). The school support program: Music therapy for adjustment problems in elementary schools. Journal of Music Therapy, 13(2), 87–100.

Texaco. (2000). Citing music's multiple benefits to a child's development, summit recommends earlier, better and more programs. Online press release, July 25, 2000. Retrieved from http://www.chevrontexaco.com/news/archive/texaco_press/2000/pr7_25.asp

Weigl, V. (1959). Functional music: A therapeutic tool in working with the mentally retarded. American Journal of Mental Deficiency, 63, 672–678.

Wilhelm, K. (2004). Music therapy and private practice: Recommendations on financial viability and marketing. Music Therapy Perspectives, 22(2), 68–83.

Wilson, B. (Ed.). (2002). Models of music therapy interventions in school settings. Silver Spring, MD: American Music Therapy Association.

Witt, A., & Steele, A. L. (1984). Music therapy for infant and parent: A case example. Music Therapy Perspectives, 1(4), 17–19.

Chapter 2

Definitions and Characteristics of Individuals Served in Early Childhood and School Age Settings
Angela M. Snell, MT-BC

The Individuals with Disabilities Education Act (IDEA) emphasizes education in the least restrictive environment (LRE). (Read Chapter 3 for detailed information about IDEA as well as additional legislation affecting educational settings.) LRE initiatives have broadened the role of health care and special education providers to include community-wide education, networking, and advocacy on the behalf of children and adults with exceptional conditions. As a result, there is a larger, more diverse audience in need of information about disabling conditions and the types of services available. This chapter includes the legal definitions of exceptional conditions referred to in IDEA and gives an overview of the accompanying characteristics. It is meant to complement the information in this book to assist music therapists and others who are investigating the role of music therapy in special education. It is important for those entering careers in early childhood and school-age settings to know that the range of conditions and abilities will be wide. Music therapists have been delivering services in school settings since (and in some cases, before) the inception of P.L. 94-142 (Education for All Handicapped Act of 1975 - predecessor of current IDEA) and are uniquely qualified to address the individual and group needs for students, staff, and community members within the LRE model.

•

Definitions

IDEA defines a general list of disabilities eligible for services under the law. However, the list is not exhaustive; placement and services are based on individual educational needs rather than a diagnostic or special education label. A diagnostic or special education label still may be useful, however, in that each label represents a range of conditions service providers need to look for and treat. States are required to develop eligibility procedures to guide local districts in creating federally compliant programs. Therefore, each state may have different terminology regarding qualifying conditions. Additionally, there are separate service provisions for infants and toddlers, preschool children, and school-age students resulting in further differences in terminology and program designs from state to state. The end result is an Individualized Education Program (IEP) or an Individualized Family Service Plan (IFSP) based upon individual needs rather than a disability label.

The following pages list disability definitions mentioned in IDEA, giving the reader an overview of the types of conditions one may encounter in the early childhood and school settings. Other chapters in this publication address eligibility, exceptional conditions, and effective clinical practices in more detail.

•

Early Childhood

Under Part C of IDEA, *infants and toddlers with disabilities* are defined as children "under three years of age who need early intervention services" because they

(1) Are experiencing developmental delays, as measured by appropriate diagnostic instruments and procedures, in one or more of the following areas:

(i)   cognitive development;

(ii)   physical development, including vision and hearing;

(iii)   communication development;

(iv)   social or emotional development; and

(v)   adaptive development; or

(2) Have a diagnosed physical or mental condition that has a high probability of resulting in developmental delay and may also include, at a State's discretion, at-risk infants and toddlers.

Note: the definition now also includes preschoolers whose families opt to continue Part C services.

(IDEA 2004, Reg. Sec. 300.25) (Authority: 20 U.S.C. 1401(16) and 1432(5)).

A *diagnosed physical or mental condition* would include:

•   chromosomal abnormalities;

•   genetic or congenital disorders;

•   severe sensory impairments, including hearing and vision;

•   inborn errors of metabolism;

•   disorders reflecting disturbance of the development of the nervous system;

•   congenital infections;

•   disorders secondary to exposure to toxic substances, including fetal alcohol syndrome; and

•   severe attachment disorders.

A state can also opt, but is not required, to include a third group of "children from birth through age two who are at risk of having substantial developmental delays if early intervention services are not provided" (IDEA 2004, Reg. Sec. 300.25) (Authority: IDEA 2004, 20 U.S.C. 1432(5)). This refers to infants and toddlers who fall in the "at risk" category for developmental delay based upon factors such as low birth weight, respiratory distress, lack of oxygen, brain hemorrhage, infection, nutritional deprivation, and a history of abuse or neglect. They need not be identified as having a disability or as having a developmental delay. In this type of case, the evaluators can choose to qualify the child via their informed clinical decision based on the "at-risk" factors.

THREE WAYS CHILDREN QUALIFY as "INFANTS & TODDLERS with DISABILITIES"		
(1) Developmental Delay	(2) Diagnosed or Established Condition	(3) "At-Risk" Factors (AN OPTIONAL CATEGORY)
a) A condition is not diagnosed or established	a) A diagnosed condition is established & labeled	a) A condition is not diagnosed or established,
AND	AND	b) A developmental delay is not documented,
b) A delay in one or more areas of functioning is documented	b) The condition has a high probability of causing a developmental delay	AND
		c) Informed clinical decision for qualification is based on "at-risk" factors that have a high probability of causing developmental delay

Figure 1. "Infants and Toddlers with Disabilities" Qualifying Factors (adapted from Early On, 2004).

Part C of the law emphasizes the development of strong family-centered programs in the approach to treating the child (303.1; 303.3). Service programs are to actively include the parents or caregivers to help them develop new or adaptive parenting skills to support their child beyond the limited minutes of weekly interventions. The law requires interagency coordination and collaboration efforts aimed to empower parents to access available programs and to give them options that best suit their child's needs. This means that service providers also will need skills in (a) relating to and supporting parents who have issues directly and indirectly related to their child, and (b) communicating and collaborating with other professionals and agencies. Additionally, with the push for services in the natural environment, one can expect to see children who are nondisabled, such as siblings or neighbors, in early childhood groups. Typically developing children can also enter service programs through collaborative partnerships with other child service agencies. Professionals working within this framework need to have wide-ranging skills in addressing (a) exceptional conditions, (b) abnormal developmental conditions, (c) varied-ability group dynamics, (d) parent issues related directly and indirectly to the child, (e) and professional collaboration. See Figure 2 for the four subgroups of people who, in addition to the infant or toddler with a disability, are impacted by this family oriented model.

SUBGROUPS IMPACTED BY FAMILY COORDINATED INFANT/TODDLER PROGRAMS			
(1) Parents/Care Givers	*(2) Intra-Agency Staff*	*(3) Inter-Agency Staff*	*(4) Children with Typical Development*
Conditions: • *Emotional support* • *Possible economic stress* • *Possible physical stress* • *Coaching on adaptive parenting strategies* • *Possible myriad of other issues*	*Conditions:* • *Multidisciplinary collaboration & consultation* • *Transdisciplinary creative programs* • *Diverse assessment perspectives* • *Resource sharing*	*Conditions:* • *Multidisciplinary collaboration & consultation* • *Transdisciplinary creative programs* • *Diverse assessment perspectives* • *Resource sharing*	*Conditions:* • *Normal developmental emotional & physical issues* • *Possible underlying issues* • *May need adaptive interaction strategies to interact with child with disabilities*

Figure 2. Subgroups Impacted by Family Coordinated Infant/Toddler Programs.

•

School Age

Once a child reaches age 3, he or she can be considered for services under Part B of IDEA. Inclusive environments remain a priority. The focus is to assist the child to access his or her education through the regular curriculum to the greatest extent possible. A gradual shift in what is considered age-appropriate least restrictive environments (LRE) begins at age 3. As a child goes through the preschool years and then on to older stages, appropriate learning environments begin to include many more experiences beyond the home, with increasing independence from family and caregivers. Frequently children with developmental delays will need to learn adaptive strategies to participate in more mature learning experiences so they can have the opportunity to generalize skills across LRE settings. Expressive language skills and cooperative group skills become more important as students progress through their school years. Parents' and family members' actions of support for the child remain important, but also begin to shift to help support independence. The emphasis upon independence and educational inclusion helps shape IEP outcome expectations, services, and program placements.

As in Part C, the disabilities recognized and defined in relation to Part B are not an exhaustive list (Bateman & Linden, 1998; Siegel, 2001). Program and service options are based on individual education needs, not the educational classification or diagnosis. In order to receive services, there must be evidence that the disability has a negative affect on the student's educational performance (Siegel, 2001). In reading the overview of disability definitions outlined below, one should consider the many different ways these conditions can manifest and the possible learning hurdles they may cause in relation to *access to curriculum in the least restrictive environment.*

The following definitions are found in IDEA with regard to Part B 300.8: *Child with a disability* is defined as a child having

> *mental retardation, a hearing impairment (including deafness), a speech or language impairment, a visual impairment including blindness, serious emotional disturbance (referred to in this part as emotional disturbance), an orthopedic impairment, autism, traumatic brain injury, an other health*

impairment, a specific learning disability, deaf-blindness, or multiple disabilities, and who, by reason thereof, needs special education and related services.

However, for children who are ages 3 through 9, the definition for *child with a disability* is more broadly based. It is defined with the following two criteria:

1.   a child who has a developmental delay in one or more of the following areas: cognitive development, physical development, communication development, social or emotional development, or adaptive development (the degree of developmental delay is defined by each individual state's rules and regulations);

2.   the child needs special education and related services.

Siegel (2001) reports the following list of disabling conditions as identified in IDEA:

- hearing impairments, including deafness;
- speech or language impairments, such as stuttering or other speech production difficulties;
- visual impairments, including blindness;
- multiple disabilities, such as deaf-blindness;
- orthopedic impairments caused by congenital anomalies, such as a club foot;
- orthopedic impairments caused by diseases, such as polio;
- orthopedic impairments caused by other conditions, such as cerebral palsy;
- learning disabilities;
- serious emotional disturbance;
- autism;
- traumatic brain injury;
- mental retardation;
- other health impairments that affect a child's strength, vitality, or alertness, such as a heart condition, rheumatic fever, nephritis, asthma, sickle cell anemia, hemophilia, epilepsy, lead poisoning, leukemia, diabetes, attention deficit disorder (ADD), attention deficit hyperactivity disorder (ADHD).

The IDEA 2004 definition of "other health impairments also includes Tourette Syndrome.

These disabilities are further defined under IDEA section 300.8 and are included in the Disability Charts on the following ten pages. The charts list:

(a)   Possible Manifestations,

(b)   Adaptive Modification Considerations, and

(c)   Samples of Possible Music Therapy Supports.

The lists are provided to present a brief overview of each disability. They are not intended to be complete, nor are the lists meant to apply in their entirety to each individual.

Conditions manifest in different combinations for each individual and require prescribed modifications and therapy by trained professionals. It is recommended that the reader refer to further material in this book, as well as other applicable resources, for more information.

AUTISM		
Disability & Legal Definition	Possible Manifestations	Adaptive Modification Considerations
A developmental disability significantly affecting verbal and nonverbal communication and social interaction, generally evident before age three that adversely affects a child's educational performance. Other characteristics often associated with autism are engagement in repetitive activities and stereotyped movements, resistance to environmental change or change in daily routines, and unusual responses to sensory experiences. Autism does not apply if a child's educational performance is adversely affected primarily because the child has an emotional disturbance (71 Federal Register 156 (to be codified at 34 CFR Part 300) Section 300.8 (c) (1), 2004). A child who manifests the characteristics of autism could be identified as having autism if the criteria above are satisfied.	• uneven, inconsistent abilities in communication, motor skills, sensory functioning, and functional, pragmatic use of skills/70% have IQ below 70 • can be nonverbal, echolalic, and/or verbal with impaired ability to understand & apply language • compulsive & ritualistic behavior • impaired ability to decode social cues and interactions • self-stimulation and/or self-injurious behavior • avoidance of eye contact • difficulty interacting with people, objects, & events • difficulty self-modulating motor actions & moods • difficulty tolerating change	• provide for a predictable environment • incorporate adaptive communication systems prescribed by the speech and language pathologist, frequently involving picture or written schedules and cues, as well as gestures • use positive behavior management • provide for multi-sensory approaches and experiences • provide information in small segments using few words • provide opportunities for choice • provide clearly defined rules • be able to adjust task expectations to the immediate emotional and physical needs

Sample of Possible Music Therapy Supports:
» use of musical elements prescriptively to support predictability and positive associations
» establish musical supports for beginnings, endings, & changes
» couple music with visual representations of commands, feelings, places, schedule sequences, and social stories
» use of music to support generalization, functional use of skills, social give & take, and acceptance of change in least restrictive environments
» use of music to support self-organization, cooperation, sustained use of skills, and social skills
» use of music to support development of an expanded repertoire of expressive modes
» use of a variety of sound colors, textures, and musical sensory experiences appropriate to immediate and long-term needs
Figure 3. Disability Chart — Autism

DEAFNESS AND HEARING IMPAIRMENT		
Disability & Legal Definition	Possible Manifestations	Adaptive Modification Considerations
DEAFNESS: *A hearing impairment that is so severe that the child is impaired in processing linguistic information through hearing, with or without amplification, that adversely affects a child's educational performance (Section 300.8 (c) (3)/2004).* *HEARING IMPAIRMENT:* *An impairment in hearing, whether permanent or fluctuating, that adversely affects a child's educational performance but this is not included under the definition of deafness in this section* *(Section 300.8 (c) (5), 2004).*	• *behavior & speech can range from normal to impaired* • *inattentive during group discussions* • *slow to answer questions or responds inappropriately to simple inquisitions* • *inattentive/can appear to be a behavior problem* • *may have defective speech, minimal expressive vocabulary, and inadequate language structure & volume* • *turns head to one side* • *normal intelligence ranges* • *may function below ability level* • *difficulty with peer interaction* • *most have at least some level of hearing ability*	• *become knowledgeable about and honor the selected method of communication, such as speech reading, sign language, or total communication* • *be sure to face the child when speaking & eliminate extra noise in the room* • *avoid standing with a bright light or sunny window behind you as you speak* • *speak clearly, but do not exaggerate articulation or volume* • *avoid lengthy verbal lectures, use written backup* • *use visual, auditory, & tactile forms of learning* • *use technological supports as necessary*

Sample of Possible Music Therapy Supports:

» *use of music to support communication needs, especially in relation to language development*

» *use of musical elements to prescriptively support development of good communication habits, including rhythm, intensity, duration, accents, pitch, and intonation*

» *use of musical engagement to mediate communication by organizing people into interactive behavior*

» *adapts music therapy procedures to the learning characteristics and communication styles of the deaf and hard-of-hearing*

» *use of music therapy techniques to support academic (including music education), motor, social, and emotional skills*

Figure 4. Disability Chart — Deafness and Hearing Impairment

EMOTIONAL DISTURBANCE		
Disability & Legal Definition	Possible Manifestations	Adaptive Modification Considerations
A condition exhibiting one or more of the following characteristics over a long period of time and to a marked degree that adversely affects a child's education performance: a) An inability to learn that cannot be explained by intellectual, sensory, or health factors. b) An inability to build or maintain satisfactory interpersonal relationships with peers and teachers. c) Inappropriate types of behavior or feelings under normal circumstances. d) A general pervasive mood of unhappiness or depression. e) A tendency to develop physical symptoms or fears associated with personal or school problems. (Note: This term includes schizophrenia. It does not include children who are socially maladjusted, unless they have been identified as having an "emotional disturbance.") (Section 300.8 (c) (4), 2004.)	• hyperactivity, impulsiveness • inconsistencies of behavior • short attention span • low frustration tolerance • acting out behavior, fighting • inappropriate social skills • inability to form satisfactory relationships w/ peers and adults • abnormal mood swings • poor coping skills • immaturity • exaggerated or flat affect • learning problems • unfocused • distorted thinking • excessive anxiety • unusual or bizarre motor acts • withdrawal from interaction • verbal manipulation of both adults and peers • low self-esteem or inflated self-esteem	• clearly defined rules and consequences, limit of 3 to 5 • provide a structured defined environment • provide consistency in following established rules and in follow-through on promises made • establish a positive rapport • reinforce positive behavior • employ positive behavior management techniques • be sensitive to signs of emotional difficulty or crisis and provide for a pre-established physical safe space • develop/be aware of activities which calm and provide emotional success and security • be familiar with the child's file and behavior plans

Sample of Possible Music Therapy Supports:

» use of music to provide nonverbal positive reinforcement and break negative attention cycles

» engage the child in the musical process to change and/or stabilize mood

» use of music to support development of productive expressive modes, exploration of feelings, and appropriate social skills

» use of music as a reinforcer for the development of academic skills

» use of music to develop coping strategies

» specific use of musical elements, such as rhythm, melody, and harmony, to provide support for immediate physical and emotional security

Figure 5. Disability Chart — Emotional Disturbance

MENTAL RETARDATION		
Disability & Legal Definition	Possible Manifestations	Adaptive Modification Considerations
Significantly subaverage general intellectual functioning, existing concurrently with deficits in adaptive behavior and manifested during the developmental period, that adversely affects a child's educational performance *(Section 300.8 (c) (6), 2004).* Level IQ Scores *Mild* *50-55 to ~70* *Moderate* *35-40 to 50-65* *Severe* *20-25 to 35-40* *Profound* *Below 20-25* *(American Psychiatric Association, 1994.)*	• short-term memory impairment • difficulty forming generalizations, impaired pragmatic skills • immature social behavior • delayed and/or impaired speech and language skills • uses/understands a limited vocabulary • has difficulty with abstract concepts, including time • difficulty understanding nonverbal cues, such as body language, facial expressions, & tone of voice • expressive/receptive language impairments, emotional frustration • learned helplessness • slow/delayed responses/ processing • difficulty with transitions • spacial awareness and coordination deficits • need for assistance and adaptations increases significantly for those in lower mental retardation levels	• provide a structured, predictable environment • provide concrete experiences using a variety of media, including movement and visuals • develop age-appropriate lessons & experiences in natural environments • incorporate communication adaptations as outlined in the child's education plan • breakdown tasks into small segments • repetition is important • design tasks for success • include lessons in peer interaction, cooperation, work skills, & functional skills • require use of skills across environments

Sample of Possible Music Therapy Supports:

» use of live music prescriptively to stimulate multisensorial responses important in learning development

» use of music to provide concrete supports and experiences for abstract concepts

» provide repetition enhanced by musical variety and change to support self-motivation and interest

» use of musical elements to provide immediate or simultaneous nonverbal positive reinforcement

» prescribed use of music to improve learning, response time, accuracy, memory, cooperation, attention span & length of on-task behavior

» use of music to create age-appropriate learning experiences and environments

» therapeutic use of music to develop social skills, emotional management skills, and to elicit child's orientation to self, space, and time

» use of music to support functional use of skills in least restrictive environments

Figure 6. Disability Chart — Mental Retardation

ORTHOPEDIC AND OTHER HEALTH IMPAIRMENTS		
Disability & Legal Definition	Possible Manifestations	Adaptive Modification Considerations
ORTHOPEDIC IMPAIRMENT: *A severe orthopedic impairment that adversely affects a child's educational performance. The term includes impairments caused by congenital anomaly, impairments caused by disease (e.g., poliomyelitis, bone tuberculosis, etc.), and impairments from other causes (e.g., cerebral palsy, amputations, and fractures or burns that cause contractures)* *(Section 300.8 (c) (8), 2004).* *OTHER HEALTH IMPAIRMENT:* *Having limited strength, vitality or alertness, including a heightened alertness to environmental stimuli, that results in limited alertness with respect to the educational environment, that-* *a) Is due to chronic or acute health problems such as asthma, attention deficit disorder or attention deficit hyperactivity disorder, diabetes, epilepsy, a heart condition, hemophilia, lead poisoning, leukemia, nephritis, rheumatic fever, sickle cell anemia; and Tourette Syndrome;* **and** *b) Adversely affects a child's educational performance* *(Section 300.8 (c) (9), 2004).*	• *disturbances in gait and mobility, use of arms or hands* • *muscle tone problems* • *spasms, seizures, involuntary movements* • *impairments in sight, hearing, or speech* • *cognitive abilities range from gifted or normal to learning disabled or developmentally impaired* • *abnormal sensations or perceptions* • *short attention span* • *hyper- or hypo-responsiveness to people and the environment* • *isolated and/or generalized weaknesses* • *difficulty with fine and/or gross motor skills* • *medication side effects, including lethargy, hyperactivity, confusion* • *impaired social skills* • *limited expressive outlets* • *self-esteem can range from good to poor*	• *arrange room to accommodate crutches, walkers, or wheelchairs* • *watch for and prevent moments of isolation* • *be familiar with assistive devices & allow child to use them functionally* • *be alert to physical and emotional strengths & weaknesses* • *allow information to be tape recorded* • *allow extra time for responses* • *provide several options for self-expression* • *incorporate peer interaction* • *assist peers to understand the child's disability (in keeping with confidentiality laws and student dignity)* • *uphold high expectations while creatively adjusting demands to the child's immediate needs*
Sample of Possible Music Therapy Supports:		
» *use of specific properties of music to develop improved stamina, physical functioning (gross and fine motor skills), and sensorimotor responses (eye-hand coordination)* » *provide music therapy experiences to elicit appropriate social skills and adaptive strategies* » *provide specially designed group music experiences to expose child's strengths to peer groups* » *apply therapeutic music elements to support expanded expressive outlets, self-management, and access to the academic curriculum*		

Figure 7. Disability Chart — Orthopedic and Other Health Impairments

SPECIFIC LEARNING DISABILITY		
Disability & Legal Definition	Possible Manifestations	Adaptive Modification Considerations
A disorder in one or more of the basic psychological processes involved in understanding or in using language, spoken or written, that may manifest itself in an imperfect ability to listen, think, speak, read, write, spell, or to do mathematical calculations, including conditions such as perceptual disabilities, brain injury, minimal brain dysfunction, dyslexia, and developmental aphasia. The term does not include learning problems that are primarily the result of visual, hearing, or motor disabilities, of mental retardation, of emotional disturbance, or of environmental, cultural, or economic disadvantage (Section 300.8 (c) 10), 2004).	• intelligence scores are significantly higher than academic performance in one or more areas • mixed dominance, directional confusion, poor motor control • sequencing problems, retrieval difficulties • disorganized, poor attention span, easily distracted, impulsive • inability to copy, reversals • poor verbal and written skills • no concept of time, difficulty performing or understanding math concepts • poor body image • few age-appropriate social-cognitive abilities • difficulty with abstract concepts • problems with attitude, motivation, behavior, social interaction • low self-esteem • auditory processing problems • excessive mood variation • hyperactive, fidgety, low frustration threshold	• be familiar with the unique set of symptoms and conditions the child is dealing with • incorporate the child's learning modality (be it visual, auditory, kinesthetic, or other) • provide a well-structured environment • break down information into smaller units • provide several different options to demonstrate knowledge • allow use of assistive devises and adaptive strategies • use a multi-sensory approach • design success oriented experiences • give immediate and positive feedback • incorporate motivators • support social skills development and cooperative peer interactions

Sample of Possible Music Therapy Supports:

» provide specially designed 1:1 and group music experiences to expose child's strengths to self and peer groups

» therapeutically support active music engagement to stimulate the combined use of motor and thinking skills

» prescriptively apply the inherent order of music to set behavioral expectations, provide reassurance, support the child in experiencing sustained use of skills in cooperative peer groups, and practice self-organization

» prescriptive use of music to improve academic learning, response time, accuracy, memory, attention span & length of on-task behavior

» therapeutic use of music to develop social skills, emotional management skills, and to elicit child's orientation to self, space, and time

Figure 8. Disability Chart — Specific Learning Disability

SPEECH OR LANGUAGE IMPAIRMENT		
Disability & Legal Definition	Possible Manifestations	Adaptive Modification Considerations
A communication disorder, such as stuttering, impaired articulation, a language impairment, or a voice impairment, that adversely affects a child's educational performance. *(Section 300.8 (c) (11), 2004).* *(NOTE: Both language and speech deficits fall in this category. A speech deficit only refers to impairments in communication expression. A language deficit refers to difficulties with both expression of ideas and reception of language.)*	• *voice, articulation, or fluency difficulties* • *impaired auditory processing skills, difficulty following oral directions* • *difficulty with pragmatic use of language* • *limited vocabulary & expressive options* • *complexity of sentence structure below age level* • *consistent poor grammar with little or no improvement* • *problems with sequences and recall* • *poor social skills or ability to follow rules of conversation* • *may exhibit frustration, isolation, discouragement, and possible outbursts of anger*	• *provide a stimulating and supportive environment* • *allow child time to answer, do not attempt to hasten the child's speech* • *consult with the speech & language pathologist to understand the child's condition* • *become familiar with and incorporate the chosen approach, including adaptive language programs* • *provide multi-sensory experiences in language & peer interaction* • *be aware of and support the child's emotional needs* • *incorporate child's strengths into language experiences* • *provide language experiences across settings to support generalization* • *support development of various forms of expressive outlets* • *understand that cognitive skills are usually not impaired unless other disabling conditions co-exist*

Sample of Possible Music Therapy Supports:

» *knowing that music development parallels language development AND that it processes through both brain hemispheres, therapists assess and apply specific musical elements, such as rhythm, cadence, and pitch/melody, to support remediation of speech/language skills.*

» *apply use of musical elements therapeutically to stimulate and give expressive meaning to cognitive functions through meaningful nonverbal media (music), use of music to support development of an expanded repertoire of expressive modes*

» *provide experiences linking vocal/verbal and gestural expressions to meaningful language sequences and their functional applications*

» *use of music to provide concrete supports and experiences for abstract concepts, couples music with visual representations of thoughts and feelings*

» *therapeutically support active music engagement to stimulate the combined use of motor, thinking, and social skills*

Figure 9. Disability Chart — Speech or Language Impairment

TRAUMATIC BRAIN INJURY		
Disability & Legal Definition	Possible Manifestations	Adaptive Modification Considerations
An acquired injury to the brain caused by an external physical force, resulting in total or partial functional disability or psychosocial impairment, or both, that adversely affects a child's educational performance. The term applies to open or closed head injuries resulting in impairments in one or more areas, such as cognition; language; memory; attention; reasoning; abstract thinking; judgement; problem-solving; sensory, perceptual, and motor abilities; psychosocial behavior; physical functions; information processing; and speech. The term does not apply to brain injuries that are congenital or degenerative, or to brain injuries induced by birth trauma (Section 300.8 (c) (12), 2004).	• speech, vision, and other sensory disadvantages • motor coordination problems • muscle spasticity • paralysis on one or both sides of the body • seizures • short- and long-term memory impairments • impaired judgement • possible impaired or uneven academic skills • mood swings, depression, low self-esteem • emotion- and impulse-control problems • social and emotional problems • short attention span • difficulty with spacial orientation • impaired sequencing skills	• provide repetition and consistency • demonstrate new tasks, state instructions, provide examples to illustrate ideas and concepts • avoid figurative language • reinforce lengthening periods of attention to appropriate tasks • probe skill acquisition frequently, provide repeated practice • teach compensatory strategies for increasing memory • be prepared for students' reduced stamina, provide rest breaks as needed • keep environment as distraction free as possible • understand child's unique combination of impairments • develop strategies to help child manage emotions, self-concept • use multisensory approaches, focus on child's strengths • support positive social interaction strategies

Sample of Possible Music Therapy Supports:

» provide specially designed music experiences to expose child's strengths to self and peer groups

» therapeutic use of music to develop social skills, emotional management skills, and to elicit child's orientation to self, space, and time

» prescriptive use of music to improve academic learning, response time, accuracy, memory, attention span & length of on-task behavior

» prescriptively apply the inherent order of music to set behavioral expectations, provide reassurance, support the child in experiencing sustained use of skills in cooperative peer groups, and practice self-organization

» design music experiences to stimulate multiple senses to involve the child at many levels and to facilitate many developmental skills

» apply specifically designed musical elements to motivate and or calm the child according to his/her immediate needs

» use of music to provide concrete supports and experiences for abstract concepts, and to facilitate productive communication strategies

Figure 10. Disability Chart — Traumatic Brain Injury

VISUAL IMPAIRMENT INCLUDING BLINDNESS		
Disability & Legal Definition	Possible Manifestations	Adaptive Modification Considerations
An impairment in vision that, even with correction, adversely affects a child's educational performance. The term includes both partial sight and blindness. (Section 300.8 (c) (13), 2004).	• developmental conditions depend upon severity, type, age of onset, and overall functioning level of the child • intelligence is not related to person's ability to see • may hold body/head in unusual fashion to attempt better vision • frequent headaches • difficulty grasping abstract concepts that depend on visual stimuli • physical appearance of eyes may look different, such as a blank eye gaze or disfigurement • mobility and orientation difficulties • difficulty perceiving social nuances, such as facial expressions, causing difficulty developing social skills	• understand academic strengths and weaknesses • provide for access and use of recommended adaptive and technological devices • be familiar with adaptive forms of reading/writing being used by the child, such as braille, large-print, magnification, computer software allowing child to hear what has been written • orient peers to conditions of visual impairment, teach them how to properly assist child with impaired vision • promote independence • provide multi-sensory experiences • promote development of social skills, cooperative interactions, and problem solving

Sample of Possible Music Therapy Supports:

» design music experiences to stimulate multiple senses to involve the child at many levels and to facilitate many developmental skills

» apply specifically designed musical elements to support generalization of mobility, orientation, and adaptive skills

» use of music to provide concrete supports and experiences for abstract concepts

» design music and elemental supports to facilitate quality experiences in the structure and timing of social interaction

» therapeutically support active music engagement to stimulate the combined use of motor, thinking, and social skills

» prescriptively apply the inherent order of music to set behavioral expectations, provide reassurance, support the child in experiencing sustained use of skills in cooperative peer groups, and practice self-organization

» specifically designed music experiences to support development of strengths and weaknesses

Figure 11. Disability Chart — Visual Impairment Including Blindness

DEAF-BLINDNESS AND MULTIPLE DISABILITIES		
Disability & Legal Definition	Possible Manifestations	Adaptive Modification Considerations
DEAF-BLINDNESS: *Concomitant hearing and visual impairments, the combination of which causes such severe communication and other developmental and educational needs that they cannot be accommodated in special education programs solely for children with deafness or children with blindness* *(Section 300.8 (c) (2), 2004).*	• *both hearing and vision are impaired* • *defective speech, minimal expressive vocabulary, and inadequate language* • *difficulty grasping abstract concepts that depend on visual and auditory stimuli* • *significant limits in interaction* • *various combinations of deficits (see Deafness, Hearing Impaired, & Visual Impairment)*	• *requires multisensory adaptive approaches & supports* • *give concentrated efforts in developing adaptive interaction, expressive, & emotional skills* • *incorporate creative combinations of adaptive approaches relative to the presenting disabilities (see Deafness, Hearing Impaired, & Visual Impairment)*
MULTIPLE DISABILITIES: *Concomitant impairments (such as mental retardation-blindness, mental retardation-orthopedic impairment, etc.), the combination of which causes such severe educational needs that they cannot be accommodated in special education programs solely for one of the impairments. The term does not include deaf-blindness* *(Section 300.8 (c) (7), 2004).*	• *various combinations of disabilities* • *behaviors/conditions include any number of manifestations presented in indicated disabilities (see other disability listings)* • *cognitive abilities range from profound to normal* • *may present complex communication, interaction, and behavioral issues*	• *requires multisensory adaptive approaches & supports* • *give concentrated efforts in developing adaptive interaction, expressive, & emotional skills* • *incorporate creative combinations of adaptive approaches relative to the presenting disabilities (see other disability listings)*

Sample of Possible Music Therapy Supports:

» *design music experiences to stimulate multiple senses to involve the child at many levels and to facilitate many developmental skills*

» *apply specifically designed musical elements to motivate and or calm the child according to his/her immediate needs*

» *use of music to support self-organization, cooperation, sustained use of skills, and social skills*

» *use of music to support development of an expanded repertoire of expressive modes*

» *adapts music therapy procedures to the immediate and long-term learning and communication styles/needs*

» *use of music to support development of an expanded repertoire of expressive modes*

» *use of specific music experiences to provide age-appropriate learning situations, meaningful interactions, and adaptive skills*

» *use of any combination of prescribed supports appropriate to the presenting disabilities and emotional states (see other disability listings)*

Figure 12. Disability Chart — Deaf-Blindness and Multiple Disabilities

●

Other Identified and Unidentified Conditions

Music therapists may encounter conditions that are not specifically listed. Some of the identifiable conditions (such as cerebral palsy, Down Syndrome, and attention-deficit disorder) are common. Others (such as Williams Syndrome and Rubenstein Tabi) are rare. Furthermore, there are conditions for which there appear to be no diagnoses yet clearly have developmental consequences. We can learn about these conditions through literature reviews, networking, and consulting with other disciplines to make informed treatment decisions.

•

General Characteristics

Many of the characteristics found among the different disabilities overlap and manifest behaviorally in similar fashion. For example, cerebral palsy (CP) involves nerve and muscle dysfunctions that affect body movement and muscle control. Depending upon the degree of involvement with the central nervous system, the physical barriers can significantly impede a child's ability to explore, interact, and learn from his or her surroundings. The result could be impaired motor abilities, delayed social skills, and delayed cognitive skills. A completely different disability, such as autism, involves significant disturbances in physical, social, and language skills. Autism also causes barriers to the child's ability to explore, interact, and learn from his or her surroundings. The result could be impaired motor abilities, poor social skills, as well as delayed cognitive skills, but for very different reasons. Both children may benefit from group experiences designed to support goals in the three areas of motor, social, and cognitive skills. The teacher or related service personnel may need to apply different individually tailored supports for each child. Below is a brief overview of general characteristics found in early childhood and school environments, illustrating the skills needed in assessment, educational treatment planning, facilitating of group dynamics, and knowledge of exceptional and typical development (see Figure 13).

BRIEF OVERVIEW GENERAL CHARACTERISTICS FOUND IN EARLY CHILDHOOD & SCHOOL AGE SETTINGS	
Reasons for Range of Behavioral Manifestations	Range of Behavioral Characteristics
• *normal developmental stages* • *physical impairments, including motor skills, deformities, CP, paralysis, orthopedic impairments* • *visual impairments* • *hearing impairments* • *health issues, including seizures, sickness, medication side effects, chronic issues (heart, lungs, pain, muscles, circulation, etc.)* • *cognitive impairments* • *cognitive abilities* • *sensory processing deficits* • *learning disabilities* • *communication disorders, including difficulties processing language, receptive and expressive deficits, autism, articulation problems* • *emotional impairments* • *normal personality traits*	• *short attention spans* • *off-task behavior* • *poor self-organization* • *appears to not grasp physical boundaries* • *appears to not grasp social boundaries* • *hyperactivity, fidgety, restless, in and out of seat* • *hypoactivity, appears limp, non-responsive* • *misunderstands directions, concretely interprets abstract concepts* • *inability to follow group directions/instructions* • *inattentive eye contact* • *inattentive or odd body posture* • *self-stimulatory or self-injurious behaviors* • *negative attention seeking* • *eager to please, over-dependence on praise* • *noncompliant, defiant, destructive* • *mobility difficulties* • *over-dependence on adult assistance* • *poor social skills, unable to positively interact or cooperate with peers* • *emotional swings, anxious, irritable, withdrawn, detached from reality, immature behavior* • *unpredictable behavior*

Figure 13. General Characteristics Found in Early Childhood and School Age Settings.

The Impact of LRE Initiatives

Current trends support placing children with disabilities in group learning environments that include same age peers and/or resemble typical situations. Bateman and Linden (1998) state, "The inclusionist movement has resulted in increased numbers of children with disabilities being placed full-time in regular classes" (p. 13). Siegel (2001) reports the *1997 Reauthorization of IDEA* added another provision to require access to the regular curriculum for children not placed in regular classrooms. It is true that IDEA does not mandate education in the regular classroom; however, it clearly indicates a preference for LRE education in regular settings with nondisabled peers (Batement & Linden, 1998; Seigel, 2001). Individual needs are considered by the IEP to determine LRE for each student (see Figure 4 for possible scenarios for LRE service delivery).

CONTINUUM OF SERVICE DELIVERY -- INFANTS AND TODDLERS			
May be considered MOST RESTRICTIVE ---			*May be considered* LEAST RESTRICTIVE
1:1 Service Clinical Setting	1:1 Service Home Setting	Service in Home with Family	Service in Neighborhood Settings
• *in isolation* • *with parents, family, caregiver present*	• *in isolation* • *with parents, family, caregiver present*	• *with parents, family, caregiver participating* • *with parents, family, caregiver, peer neighbor participating*	• *with parents, family, caregiver participating* • *play group members participating*
CONTINUUM OF SERVICE DELIVERY -- SCHOOL AGE CHILDREN			
May be considered MOST RESTRICTIVE ---			*May be considered* LEAST RESTRICTIVE
Homebound/ Residential Setting	Center-Based School Setting	Regular Education School Setting	School Setting
• *1:1 service in isolation* • *service with parents, family, caregiver present* • *service with visiting peer(s)*	• *1:1 service in isolation* • *service in small peer group* • *service in categorical classroom* • *service in groups including non-disabled peers* • *service in other typical environments, groupings, events*	• *1:1 service in isolation, consult with teacher* • *service in small peer group* • *service in regular ed. classroom* • *service in other typical environments and groupings/events*	• *1:1 service in isolation* • *service in small/large peer group* • *service in regular ed classroom* • *service in other typical environments and groups/events*

Figure 14. Continuum of Service Delivery.

Transition services are formally mandated on the first in effect IEP when the child turns 16 and include instruction, related services, community experiences, employment and other post-school adult living objectives, and if appropriate, acquisition of dailly living skills and a functional vocational evaluation. Transition services are gaining importance due to court rulings that found school district transition practices to be minimal and noncompliant with IDEA (Bateman & Linden, 1998). "Access to the community" is a noticeable theme throughout the language in IDEA. This has created an increase in group learning approaches where multiple-ability levels present themselves, thereby bringing unique learning opportunities and challenges.

●

Conclusion

There are many types of disabilities and there are many more variables in the ways conditions manifest in individual cases. LRE initiatives continue to influence educational program designs. It is important to be knowledgeable about the conditions and etiologies involved with the various disabilities. One must continually remain current with research and methodologies specific to exceptional conditions.

Music therapists are uniquely qualified to positively impact the emotional and structural complexities currently facing educational settings. The music medium provides a unique avenue for communication, interaction, and learning when typical teaching methods do not work. Gordon (as reported by Valerio, Reynolds, Bolton, Taggart, and Gordon, 1998) finds that musical aptitude is not necessarily dependent upon cognitive or physical ability. Music therapists' educational and clinical backgrounds prepare them to assess and treat disabling conditions using musical elements to support a wide range of strengths and weaknesses in communication, academic, motor, emotional, and social functioning areas. Because music is ability-ordered, the music therapist is able to facilitate learning in typical settings and provide support for multiple-ability levels simultaneously.

For more thorough information, the reader is referred to the material and references in subsequent chapters of this book and *Models of Music Therapy Interventions in School Settings* (Wilson, 2002), a helpful reference specific to music therapy in school settings. Its chapters include such topics as research on mainstreaming, music therapy assessment, models of service delivery, and music therapy with specific disabilities, including severe and profound disabilities, autism, learning disabilities, deaf/hard-of-hearing, and early childhood conditions. Additionally, those working with school-age children can remain informed by monitoring the American Music Therapy Association (AMTA) journals, publications, and website (www@musictherapy.org), the Certification Board for Music Therapists (CBMT, 2004) (www@cbmt.org), as well as current research on music in health and education, exceptional conditions, normal development, and educational methodologies.

Music therapists' educational and clinical backgrounds prepare them to assess and treat disabling conditions using musical elements to support a wide range of strengths and weaknesses in communication, academic, motor, emotional and social functioning areas.

●

References

Bateman, B. D., & Linden, M. A. (1998). Better IEPs: How to develop legally correct and educationally useful programs (3rd ed.). Longmont, CO: Sopris West.

Certification Board for Music Therapists (CBMT). (2004). Scope of practice language analysis. Downingtown, PA: Author.

Individuals with Disabilities Education Improvement Act of 2004, Final regulations, Federal Register 71(156) (2006).

Individuals with Disabilities Education Act of 1997, Pub. L. No. 105-17. Federal Register, 64(48) (1999).

Siegel, L. M. (2001). The complete IEP guide: How to advocate for your special ed child (2nd ed.). Berkeley, CA: Nolo.

Valerio, W. H., Reynolds, A. M., Bolton, B. M., Taggart, C. C., & Gordon, E. E. (1998). The early childhood music curriculum guide for parents, teachers and caregivers: Music play. Chicago: GIA Publications.

Wilson, B. L. (Ed.). (2002). Models of music therapy interventions in school settings. Silver Spring, MD: American Music Therapy Association.

●

Resources

American Psychiatric Association. (1994). Diagnostic and statistical manual of mental disorders *(4th ed.).* Washington, DC: Author.

Duquette, C. (2001). Students at risk: Solutions to classroom challenges. *Markam, Ontario, Canada: Pembroke Publishers.*

Nielsen, L. B. (2002). Brief reference of student disabilities . . . with strategies for the classroom. *Thousand Oaks, CA: Corwin Press.*

Sheldon, C. F., & Pollingue, A. B. (2000). The exceptional teacher's handbook: The first-year teacher's guide for success. *Thousand Oaks, CA: Corwin Press.*

Sousa, D. A. (2001). How the special needs brain learns. *Thousand Oaks, CA: Corwin Press. www.earlyonmichigan.org*

Chapter 3

Eligibility and Legal Aspects
Elizabeth K. Schwartz, LCAT, MT-BC

Throughout the last 100 years, children born in this country have gained increasing rights and privileges through passage of laws and the institution of government-funded and administered programs. The right to a free, public education for children and youth under 21 is now firmly established in the United States. Within the last 30 years, educational opportunities for all children, including those with special needs, have been supported in law, regulation, and practice.

Music therapists working with children will need to work with the educational system either directly or indirectly. Even children placed in residential or hospital settings or in Early Childhood programs will remain under the jurisdiction of governmental education regulations and authority. It is therefore critical for music therapists working with children to be familiar with those regulations and standards in order to assure access to services for the children as well as to funding sources for the provision of music therapy services.

•

Special Education Law and Regulation

The early years of this century saw a struggle in defining the types of children who should benefit from publicly funded education. Some children were shut out from the system completely; others were placed in institutional or segregated settings. Despite this, music was an important component of these programs, primarily for children who were deaf, hard-of hearing, blind, or mentally retarded (Adamek, 1996).

By the mid 1950s, parents and advocates of children with special needs looked to racial discrimination cases decided in federal courts as a model for the rights of children with special needs to be included in public education. In 1963, federal legislation extended the list of children who could be served to include those with more severe disabilities including emotional, speech, vision, hearing, and other health impairments as well as mental retardation (Adamek, 1996).

Landmark legislation defining the rights of all children with special needs to a public education was passed in 1975. The Education for All Handicapped Children Act (Public Law 94-142) had a number of significant components including:

- All children with disabilities from 5 to 21 had the right to a free public education.
- The education must be provided in the least restrictive environment.
- The education must be appropriate to the individual needs of the child.
- Families had the right to have input into the child's educational program.

In 1986, Public Law 99-457 extended these same educational benefits to children with special needs from ages 3 to 5. The law also established programming for children under 3, commonly referred to as Early Intervention.

In 1990, passage of Public Law 101-476 once again expanded the scope of regulations affecting children with special needs in the educational setting. This law was named the Individuals with Disabilities Education Act (IDEA). In addition to increasing the range of disabilities covered, IDEA emphasized access to regular educational curriculum for children with disabilities. It also contained an expanded list of supportive related services, which should be made available to children in order for them to benefit from placement in a free, appropriate public education. This list of related services included many of the more established therapies such as speech and physical therapy. However, regulatory clarifications affirmed that the list of services was not meant to be all-inclusive. Under IDEA 1990, many music therapists were able to demonstrate the need for music therapy as a related service in the child's program and were successful in providing access to music therapy for these children. In addition, the focus of IDEA 1990 to assure access to the regular curriculum gave music therapists the opportunity to develop music programs specific to children with special needs as part of access to typical curriculum.

IDEA was legislatively reauthorized in 1997 and again in 2004 with a renewed emphasis on the requirement to provide services in the least restrictive environment for children ages 3 to 21. Placement on a continuum of services from segregated self-contained settings to full inclusion in typical educational settings must be considered. The child is required to be placed in the most typical environment in which he or she can continue to benefit from placement in public education. For many children, this meant a move from segregated settings to the local public school. IDEA 1997 provided for involvement of regular education staff in the child's educational plan. For children in Early Intervention (ages birth to 3), the focus is on providing services in community-based settings or in the most typical setting such as the home.

IDEA 1997 called for the development of measurable outcomes for the goals listed on the child's educational plan (Individualized Family Service Plan—IFSP or Individualized Education Program—IEP). Reporting on progress toward these goals must be with the same frequency as regular education. This provision has been continued in 2004.

Children receiving services under IDEA 2004 must also be included in educational assessment programs sponsored by the states or districts, although IDEA allowed for testing modifications and alternative assessments. IDEA 1997 and 2004 include specific guidelines for discipline for children in special education with the requirement of providing both behavioral assessments and behavioral intervention plans when necessary.

The IDEA specifically provides for related services necessary for children to benefit from their educational placement. As in earlier versions of the law, the list of approved related services for children ages 3 to 21 is not meant to be exhaustive, but the language of the law did not specifically state the term *music therapy*. Discussion on the Regulations pertaining to IDEA 1997 and 2004 included the following comments:

> *As under prior law, the list of related services is not exhaustive and may include other developmental, corrective, or supportive services (such as artistic and cultural programs, art, music, and dance therapy) if they are required to assist a child with a disability to benefit from special education in order for the child to receive FAPE [Free Appropriate Public Education]. Therefore it is determined through the Act's evaluation and IEP requirements that a child with a disability requires a particular supportive service in order to receive FAPE, regardless of whether that service is included in these regulations, that service can be considered a related service under these regulations, and must be provided at no cost to the parents. (64 Federal Register 48, 12548 (1999))*

> *Section 300.34(a) and section 602(26) of the Act state that related services include other supportive services that are required to assist a child with a disability to benefit from special education. We [U.S. Department of Education] believe this clearly conveys that the list of services in § 300.34 is not exhaustive and may include other developmental, corrective, or supportive services if they are required to assist a child with a disability to benefit from special education. (71 Federal Register 156, 46569 (2006))*

As further clarification, in June of 2000, the American Music Therapy Association received a letter from Mr. Kenneth P. Warlick, Director of the Office of Special Education Programs in the United States Department of Education. The letter states in part:

> *We continue to support our prior position that for some children, art, music, or dance therapy is to be identified in their IEPs as a related service if the IEP team, which includes the child's parents, determines that the particular therapy would be necessary for the child to benefit from special education and to receive FAPE. (K. P. Warlick, personal communication, June 9, 2000)*

Beginning with IDEA 1997, greater numbers of children have been able to receive music therapy as part of their educational and therapeutic program. In addition to provision as a related service, the emphasis in the IDEA on access to regular education and appropriate supportive services has opened the door for music therapy as a programmatic part of the child's overall educational and therapeutic plan.

In contrast, the list of approved services and providers for Early Intervention (birth to 3) is specific and does not include music therapy. A number of state and municipal agencies, however, have chosen to include music therapy on the IFSP level. Many music therapists do work in Early Intervention and have found creative ways to fund their services either through IDEA or other grant funds, program operating funds or private pay. Music therapy has been the therapeutic treatment in the following types of programs, which are on the list of services offered in Early Intervention:

- Developmental Groups
- Respite Care
- Transdisciplinary Treatment
- Parent Training

(It should be noted that in areas where music therapy is not recognized, the music therapist must work with an approved provider or be dually certified in an approved service.)

IDEA 2004 continues the right to education for children with disabilities as supported in previous legislation. The law states in part:

> *(1) Disability is a natural part of the human experience and in no way diminishes the right of individuals to participate in or contribute to society. Improving educational results for children with disabilities is an essential element of our national policy of ensuring equality of opportunity, full participation, independent living, and economic self-sufficiency for individuals with disabilities. (Public Law 108-446.)*

While maintaining the basic principals of IDEA 1997, IDEA 2004 maked some fundamental changes in both practice and philosophy including:

- New definitions and requirements for providing "highly qualified" special education teachers;
- Reductions in paperwork and noneducational activities;
- Greater focus on minority and homeless populations;
- "Early intervening services" aimed at reducing the need for special education;
- Greater coordination with other educational laws such as the *Elementary and Secondary Education Act (No Child Left Behind)*;
- Authority to serve infants and toddlers under Part C beyond the age of 2;
- Procedural changes in due process and discipline issues;
- Creation of the National Center for Special Education Research (Title II). (Apling & Jones, 2005)

While federal law outlines program requirements and parameters, it is the responsibility of state, regional and local agencies to implement, evaluate, and contribute to funding for these programs. The governing structure of the United States draws a line between state and federal responsibilities. Therefore, each state has the opportunity to interpret and add to federal law and regulations. The Education Department of each state thus has its own set of rules and guidelines that must be adhered to by programs and providers operating in that state. While state and local agencies must follow the federal law, there are many areas in which they can and do create their own regulations. For instance, occupational regulations are the jurisdiction of the states. Program funding is also a state level function.

As in the past, laws and regulations pertaining to special education will continue to evolve and change. These laws translate directly into access to music therapy for children and families and funding for music therapists to provide programming. It is essential for music therapists to be aware of changes and new requirements as they come along. Information can be accessed through the American Music Therapy Association (www.musictherapy.org) or through local, state, or federal education sites such as www.ed.gov/osers or by searching for a particular state's Education Department on the Internet.

●

Funding and Reimbursement

While the laws and regulations pertaining to special education are clearly articulated, the issue of funding these programs is often complex and difficult to navigate. Funding in support of IDEA flows from the federal government to the states, which then distributes it to the local level in a variety of methods. The federal government has never authorized full funding necessary to support IDEA programs. Special education programs are then partially supported by state funds as well as local school taxes or property taxes.

It is essential for music therapists in school settings to understand the source of their funding for salary as well as for equipment and program support. Many music therapists are supported by IDEA grants, which are distributed through the states to local programs. Governance of these monies is often subjected to a series of local and regional rules. Grants often must be renewed on a yearly basis. Some music therapists are funded through program operating funds, which also are partially supported by IDEA. Local authorities, such as district school boards or administrators often have significant influence over how this money is spent. Having administrators and parents who understand the importance of music therapy helps assure that funds will be available for music therapy.

It is important to note that when music therapy is listed as a related service on a child's IEP, it is a mandated service and must be provided as listed on the IEP. Funding for music therapy as a related service is assured the same as it is for any other approved related service.

Music therapists may seek funding from private grants to support school-based programs. Some music therapists are able to use research grants or respite funds. Music therapists must understand the process and be knowledgeable about the status of the music therapy program, regardless of where the money originates.

As noted above, music therapy is not currently an approved related service under the Early Intervention section of IDEA. However, states can and do approve programs in addition to those listed in IDEA. Any program funding is under the jurisdiction of that local or state agency. Several states do authorize music therapy under early intervention. To

In addition to provision as a related service, the emphasis in IDEA 1997 on access to regular education and appropriate supportive services opened the door for music therapy as a programmatic part of the child's overall educational and therapeutic plan.

check on the status in your state, visit the agency web site or consult with the Government Relations Representative from AMTA.

•

Eligibility

Preschool and School-Aged

Federal law (Part B of IDEA) delineates a specific process for determining eligibility for services for children with special needs, ages 3 to 21. In most instances, administration of this program is handled by the child's local school district. Services and evaluations are provided either by the school district itself or by a contracted agency. Since federal law does not yet require education for children under 5, most districts do not have the facilities or staff to provide early childhood or preschool services. This situation might change with the adoption of universal pre-kindergarten programming. Contracting agencies can be either for-profit or not for-profit. Some provide comprehensive programming and evaluations, and some provide specialty services such as a private music therapy agency. Funds generally flow from the federal to the state to the local school district level and then to the providing agency.

The school-aged portion of IDEA (3 to 21) requires that each child referred to the system receive a full and complete evaluation. This evaluation is the same whether or not the child received services under early intervention. A complete evaluation would include a social history, medical report, psychological testing, educational observation, and specific evaluations in the areas of concern. The parent must sign a consent for evaluation before any evaluations can take place. There is a specific time frame in place (60 calendar days or within a state-established timeframe) that spells out how long it should take from the parental consent for evaluation until receipt of the final reports. Decisions on eligibility are made in most cases by a district committee, which includes the child's parent. This committee is sometimes referred to as the CPSE (Committee on Preschool Special Education) or the CSE (Committee on Special Education).

If a child is found eligible for services by the CPSE or CSE, an IEP is generated. The IEP lists program length and duration, special education setting, related services needed, and outcome-based goals and objectives for each area approved. The IEP goals are reviewed annually. Re-evaluations are completed at least once every 3 years for children ages 5 to 21. Under the paperwork reduction pilot program of IDEA 2004, some states will be eligible to try multi-year IEPs.

This process for determining eligibility can include the music therapist at any point from initial identification to service provision to re-evaluation. The process is listed below as required by IDEA:

Special Education Process under IDEA
1. Child is identified as possibly needing service.
2. Child is evaluated.
3. Eligibility is decided.

4.   Child is found eligible/not eligible.

5.   IEP/IFSP meeting is scheduled.

6.   IEP/IFSP meeting is held and IEP or IFSP is written.

7.   Services are provided.

8.   Progress is measured and reported to parents.

9.   IEP is reviewed.

10.   Child is reevaluated.

IDEA also outlines who is considered to be an IEP team member. The IEP team includes the following members:

IEP Team Members

1.   Student (as appropriate)

2.   Parent/Guardian

3.   Regular education teacher

4.   Special education teacher

5.   School system representative

6.   A person who can interpret evaluation results

7.   Transition services representative (as appropriate)

8.   Others with special knowledge of child.

The contents of the IEP also are particular to each program or local agency, but the following items must be included according to IDEA:

Content of the IEP

1.   Current academic achievement and functional performance

2.   Measurable annual academic and functional goals

3.   Special education and related services

4.   Participation with nondisabled children

5.   Participation in state/district-wide assessments, including appropriate accomodations

6.   Dates and places

7.   Transition services

8.   Measurement of progress.

Eligibility for provision of music therapy as a related service under Part B of IDEA is the same as for any other approved related service. It must meet the test (as outlined in IDEA law) that music therapy is "required to assist a child with a disability to benefit from special education in order for the child to receive FAPE [Free Appropriate Public Education]."

Early Intervention

Under the Early Intervention portion of IDEA (Part C), responsible agencies vary according to local regulations. Parents who have concerns about their young infant generally contact a state authorized oversight agency. In some instances, significant birth history or a specific medical diagnosis will trigger an immediate referral in the first few weeks of life. The agency then will arrange for an evaluation of the child. The evaluation includes a social and medical history as well as specific evaluations in the areas of concern. Children deemed eligible for Early Intervention services will be appointed a service coordinator who acts as the child's advocate as well as serves as the team leader. Services to be provided and specific goals, objectives, and outcomes are then outlined on the IFSP and agreed to by the family, service coordinator, and service provider.

The emphasis in early intervention is on the family as well as the child. Most often services are provided in the child's most natural environment, which might be the home or day care setting. Emphasis is placed on modeling appropriate strategies and interventions for the parents or caregivers. Progress is monitored every 3 months and program eligibility is reviewed every 6 months.

Transition Planning

When a child in special education reaches the age of 16, the IEP team must begin to consider the skills the child will need to move to the world of work or the post-educational setting. IDEA requires that the IEP for children who reach this age address goal areas that will prepare them for a vocation as well as independent living and leisure time skills. This process is commonly called Transition Planning and services can include education, vocational training, supported employment, adult services, and independent living or community participation.

•

Documentation

Required documentation for school-based music therapists is dependent upon the manner in which they provide services. For music therapy provided as a programmatic element, required documentation is determined by the local agency as well as by the music therapist's own Code of Ethics and basic competencies. These might include individual or group goals and objectives, progress reports, session logs, observance of educational learning standards, and assessments and evaluations.

The documentation requirements for music therapy as a related service are the same as for any related service and are specifically listed in IDEA. Again, local and state agency requirements and professionalism will also play a role in thorough documentation. IDEA Related Service documentation includes:

IDEA Related Service Documentation
1.   Parent/Guardian signed consent for evaluation
2.   Measurable annual goals (IDEA 2004 deletes the term *benchmarks* or *short-term objectives,* except for children assessed on alternate assessments based on alternate education standards. However, "effective clinical practice" may indicate delineating goals into smaller measurable steps or segments.)
3.   Session logs
4.   Progress reports (same frequency as in typical education)
5.   Annual IEP review
6.   Annual/Triennial re-evaluation

7.   Transition planning (if appropriate).

•

Qualifications

Though IDEA seems to support the delivery of music therapy as an appropriate service for children with special needs, this federal law and the connected regulations do not specify who should provide the services. Occupational regulations are under the control of the states. Local authorities can also add their own requirements. Therefore, the issue of licensure or certification for music therapists practicing in schools is determined on a state and local level. The IDEA letter of clarification to AMTA from OSEP Director Kenneth Warlick states:

> . . . your inquiry raises several issues regarding the standards for, and type of, personnel who are qualified to provide music therapy as a related service. State and local educational agencies must ensure that students with disabilities receive appropriate instruction or services as reflected in their IEPs. 34 CFR&300.600. This means that any instruction or service for a child with a disability under Part B must be provided by personnel who meet appropriate State standards for qualified personnel, as that term is defined at 34 CFR & 300.23 if the Part B regulations.

> Part B requires States to have policies and procedures relating to the establishment and maintenance of standards for ensuring that personnel necessary to carry out the purposes of Part B are appropriately and adequately prepared and trained. (K. P. Warlick, personal communication, June 9, 2000)

IDEA 2004 addresses the issue of providing "highly qualified" special education teachers. The measure of "highly qualified" gives considerable weight to state licensure or certification. Currently the "highly qualified" standards apply only to teachers and not to related services personnel. However, rules, regulations and clarifications of IDEA 2004 in the coming years may alter the requirements and qualifications needed to practice music therapy and other related services in special education. Music therapists practicing in school-based settings have at their disposal the resources of their professional (AMTA) and certifying (CBMT) agencies if questions should arise on the issue of qualifications for providing music therapy.

●

References

Adamek, M. S. (1996). In the beginning: A review of early special education services and legislative regulatory activity affecting the teaching and placement of special learners. In B. L. Wilson (Ed.), Models of music therapy interventions in school settings: From institution to inclusion (pp. 15–24). Silver Spring, MD: American Music Therapy Association.

Apling, R. N., & Jones, N. L. (2005). Individuals with Disabilities Education Act (IDEA): Analysis of changes made by P.L. 108-446. Congressional Research Service, The Library of Congress.

Federal Register, 64(48). March 12, 1999. Rules and Regulations, p. 12548. Retrieved June 20, 2006, from http://www.ed.gov

Individuals with Disabilities Education Improvement Act of 2004, Final regulations, Federal Register 71(156) (2006).

●

Resources

American Music Therapy Association. (2001). Music therapy as a related service: How to get into the public schools (AMTA Institute Handbook, Pasadena 2001). Silver Spring, MD: Author.

Küpper, L. (Ed.). (2000). Guide to the Individualized Education Program: Jessup, MD: NICHCY Editorial Publications Center, U.S. Department of Education.

Mandlawitz, M. R. (2004). Comparisons of key provisions: IDEA and the IDEA as amended (IDEA 2004). Position Paper 2004.

Chapter 4

Assessment

The following authors contributed to this chapter: Ruthlee Figlure Adler, MT-BC; Nicole Allgood, MSEd, MT-BC; Marcia Behr, MT-BC; Amy Furman, MM, RMT; Marcia Humpal, MEd, MT-BC; Ronna Kaplan, MA, MT-BC; Beth McLaughlin, MS, LCAT, MT-BC; Jean Nemeth, MA, MT-BC; Elizabeth Schwartz, LCAT, MT-BC; Angela Snell, MT-BC; and Rebecca Tweedle, MEd, MT-BC

Assessment is an essential part of music therapy service delivery in educational settings. Federal, state, and local policies mandate assessment or evaluation to determine eligibility for receiving services. Furthermore, assessment guides the building of the student's program as noted on the IFSP or the IEP and provides ongoing information for determining the direction of future programming.

•

Music Therapy Assessment in an Educational Setting

Wilson and Smith (2000) investigated assessment for services delivered in school settings. Music therapists reported using assessments to compare information with data obtained from other assessment measures, to determine baseline behaviors, and to determine eligibility for services. The authors found that some music therapists used existing assessment tools, though many have developed their own assessments to meet their specific needs.

Individuals with Disabilities Education Act (IDEA) federal guidelines require that assessment material must:

- Include a variety of assessment tests or tools and strategies;
- Be given by trained and knowledgeable personnel;
- Not be used solely to determine intelligence;
- Accurately reflect the child's aptitude if there is impaired speaking or sensory skills;
- Assess all areas of suspected disability;
- Provide relevant information that will help determine the educational needs;
- Include other objective tests or subjective reports and observations by other professionals. (Siegel, 2001)

Styles of music therapy service delivery, laws, guidelines, standards, and philosophical considerations all play a part in determining what types of assessments music therapists develop. Bruscia (1987) elaborated on assessing the improvisation of music. Loewy (2000) described Psychotherapy Levels of Inquiry and a qualitative means of depicting them when assessing via structured and free flowing musical experiences to initiate the new relationship. Nordoff and Robbins (1977) looked at responses, relationships, and musical communicativeness. Wigram (2000) advocated including the range, the lack of, and the quality of responses as well as a comparison of the music responses to normal musical exploration in music therapy assessment. He also noted that a child's musical interaction could provide validation or nonvalidation of the presence of traits associated with exceptional conditions, like autism. Briggs (1991) explained that all children seem to pass through a developmental sequence for acquiring musical skills. Her model described four areas of musical milestones: auditory, vocal/tonal, rhythmic, and cognitive. Briggs further discussed how musical skill development could be divided into four phases: Reflex, Intention, Control, and Integration (see Chapter 12 for more information). Along more developmental lines, Boxill's (1985) *Music Therapy Assessment* addressed the nonmusical goal areas of motor, communication, cognitive, affective, social, as well as music as a goal area unto itself.

Chase (2004) examined and described the major skill areas and subcategories most frequently assessed by music therapists. She also explained how these areas are assessed, the common features of current assessment tools used by music therapists, and the positive and/or negative aspects of these tools. Chase's survey revealed that music therapists want standardized music therapy assessments designed for use in clinical practice to be easy to use, comprehensive, and adaptable. Chase (2002) also authored *The Music Therapy Assessment Handbook*. This resource gives an overview of various types of assessments and assessment processes for specific populations, as well as supporting background information.

Special issues of *Music Therapy Perspectives* and the *Journal of Music Therapy* (American Music Therapy Association, 2000a, 2000b) have been devoted to the topic of assessment. Readers are encouraged to refer to these resources for a more detailed review of this topic.

AMTA Standards of Clinical Practice

The American Music Therapy Association's *Standards of Clinical Practice* (AMTA, 2001) provides assessment guidelines that are very much in line with federal and state rules and regulations. The Standards support assessment of all areas so responsible interpretations, conclusions, and recommendations can be made for the benefit of the client. The Standards address communication, academic, motor, emotional, and social functioning areas, as well as responses to music, music skills, and preferences. They specify the use of methods appropriate to the client's age and functioning, coupled with observations from, in, and out of music situations. Furthermore, the document stresses professional interpretation of results and includes recommendations for other services.

CBMT Scope of Practice

The *Scope of Practice* (CBMT, 1998) of The Certification Board for Music Therapists lists approximately 23 different assessment skills music therapists are trained to employ. This document addresses many more skills in the use of music "to restore, maintain, and improve

Music therapists reported using assessment to compare information with data obtained from other assessment measures, to determine baseline behaviors and to determine eligibility for services.

skills, adaptation, and/or performance in" the following domains: cognitive, psychological/affective, social, physical/physiological/sensory/sensorimotor, communication, and behavior. This document provides "legally defensible" support for MT-BCs, validating their unique level of expertise in interpreting music therapy assessment information (as opposed to other special education professionals who incorporate music into their approaches) (CBMT, 2004). Furthermore, the *Scope of Practice* helps clarify that the music therapist is the only educational team member trained to assess music-related behaviors; interpret how these behaviors relate to nonmusical functioning; and use music prescriptively to impact behavior, learning, and emotional well-being. This document may be helpful for explaining why the music therapist may need to deliver the music in prescriptive situations until consultation can suffice.

●

General Assessment Information

In educational and early intervention settings, music therapy often is conducted as part of a team approach. Therefore, music therapists should be familiar with assessment tools used by other professionals who work in these settings. Often a battery of tests is administered, allowing various professionals to see the child or student in an array of settings. Kathy Wojciak, an early intervention specialist who teaches university courses on assessing young children, cautions that, in addition to knowing about characteristics of specific disabilities and assessments, it is crucial for those who work in special education settings to also have a thorough understanding of *normal* development (personal communication, November 30, 2004).

Tests may measure intelligence or achievement. They may compare the person to others of the same age, using a standardized tool. Other assessments may be dynamic in nature, examining the student's behavior in a natural environment. Additional behavioral information may be obtained through interviews with the students or the family. Some assessments are designed to determine if a child has characteristics of specific disabilities or where the child might fall on a spectrum (such as autism spectrum disorders). Other assessment tools are designed to discover information that can pinpoint potential goals and objectives.

Federal mandates influence the ways children will be assessed to determine eligibility for special education services. Norm and criterion references tools, along with observations and interviews may be required, depending upon the child's age. Very young children may be assessed with a play-based tool. These assessments must be conducted in a natural environment where the child feels comfortable (e.g., in the home or in an educational setting while using familiar toys). Play assessments combined with the formal testing yield valuable information about young children (Cohen & Spenciner, 1994; Linder, 1990).

For an excellent reference about existing standardized assessments, examine *The Special Educator's Book of Lists* (Pierangelo, 2003). One section of this book succinctly describes 123 assessment tools used in special education.

•

Types of Music Therapy Assessment in Educational and Early Childhood Settings

The types of music therapy assessments are distinguished by their purpose either to determine eligibility or to gather information. Within the second category, gathering information, there are multiple subcategories of assessment types including those intended to determine the present level of functioning and goal planning, determine ongoing information during treatment, gather global holistic information, complete diagnostic assessments and the use of surveys or interviews.

Assessment to Determine Eligibility

Public School

Music therapy may gain entry into a public school setting via two main routes. The first is by the decision of the school district. Music therapy service delivery thus may be programmatic in nature, considered part of educational enrichment, or provided as consultation to other educational personnel. In this scenario, assessment is not necessary for the student to receive services.

The other way by which music therapy may be admitted to a school system is by decision of the IEP committee. The parent or school district representative may request an assessment to determine if a particular student requires music therapy. The assessment needs to address *why* music therapy is needed. In order for music therapy to be recommended as a related service, the student must perform in a significantly different way on IEP goal-related behaviors and skills when music therapy strategies are implemented. Note that the assessing music therapist must carefully design the assessment music experiences to closely adhere to the nonmusical IEP tasks to which they are being compared (Coleman, 1999).

The music therapist who conducts the formal assessment for eligibility often does so under a separate contract (charging a set fee per assessment). If services are deemed appropriate, this music therapist might not be the one who will deliver services. In other situations, music therapists who are on the staff of an educational facility may assess for eligibility and also provide services.

Other members of the team may refer a student to determine if inclusion of music therapy would provide a unique motivation for the individual to benefit from the educational program. An Assessment Request Form may be required to access this service. This might be filled out by anyone on the child's educational team. The assessment process is individualized and designed with the IEP in mind. Given the rationale for the referral as indicated on the Assessment Request Form, checklists from the appropriate sections of the IEP could be developed to determine the suitability of music therapy and the direction the service might take.

See Chapter 5 for an in-depth look at the SEMTAP (Brunk & Coleman, 2000), an example of an assessment process designed to determine eligibility.

Early Intervention—Birth to 3

In most of the country, music therapy is not currently an approved service under Part C of IDEA. In some states, music therapists are not on the list of approved providers, and therefore are not technically allowed to provide service except under the guise of another approved provider. However, some facilities run billable groups called Developmental Groups or Parent/Child groups, partnering music therapists with another professional who is an approved provider. This provider is required to write all logs and progress notes, as well as perform ongoing assessments and attend all groups. In some instances, the music therapist may be dually certified and so can be the approved provider under the other certification or license.

Eligibility for the group is not based on a music therapy assessment but rather on a needs-based assessment decided by the IFSP team. The rationale for providing these groups, using music therapy as the intervention, is that the music environment and music therapy strategies most effectively address the goals of the group. The criteria (or assessment items) used in deciding if a family and child would benefit from the group closely follow the goals written into the IFSP (as decided by the IFSP team at the IFSP meeting).

Assessment to Gather Information

Present Level of Functioning and Goal Planning

Music therapists use assessment to measure students' levels of functioning at the onset of service, thereby aiding the development of appropriate goals, objectives, and directions for treatment. Some music therapists may use therapist-made tools; others may depend on checklists created for other fields or adapt tools presented by other professionals.

A checklist is a listing of skills that can be observed by the therapist. The music therapist, parents, paraprofessionals, or other staff involved with the student can document these lists. Because students often demonstrate different skills in different environments, completion of the checklist by various parties may yield a more valid picture of the student. Using skill checklists can help the music therapist fine-tune the focus of the therapeutic interventions.

Checklists may examine musical and nonmusical responses and skills in areas such as behavioral and psychosocial, language and communication, perceptual and sensory, motor, and cognitive. For example:

- *Behavioral and Psychosocial:* attending, compliance, decision making, leadership, engagement, participation, eye contact to person, eye contact to task, on-task responses, independence, positive verbal interaction with peers, transition between tasks, turn taking, levels of play, and emotional responses.
- *Cognitive:* general cognitive functioning; matching objects to objects; matching objects to pictures; matching pictures to pictures; matching colors, letters, shapes, and/or numerals; identifying or labeling colors, letters, shapes, and/or numerals; functional math (quantity and numbers); functional reading and pre-reading; problem solving; and memory/sequential memory.

Checklists may examine musical and non-musical responses and skills in areas such as behavioral and psychosocial, language and communication, perceptual and sensory, motor, and cognitive.

- *Music-related Behaviors:* tempo changes, phrasing, harmonic progressions, anticipated musical resolutions, musical surprises, tailored accompaniments (noting musical element used), dynamic changes, rhythmic patterns, accented sounds, or movements.

Ongoing

Assessment may be an ongoing component of the music therapy program that is highly worthwhile to the development of all the students, not only those whose progress would be adversely affected without the service. The music therapist may be able to address both general learning needs as well as specific skill deficits of individual children through this process of ongoing group assessment.

When conducting music therapy with young children, ongoing assessment may examine the child's level of play as well as specific skills evident in this play. First, the music therapist determines the stages or categories as well as the domains to be examined. For instance, examine the play on a cognitive as well as a social continuum. Determine goals accordingly, taking into consideration any factors that may influence a normal development of play skills (e.g., cerebral palsy, visual impairment). In a group setting, ascertain where each member of the group falls, so the activities and equipment can be arranged to bump up skills after enough practice has taken place. A play-based approach is not "just letting the children play." If conducted correctly, there is much planning before, after, and especially *during* activities (while following the child's lead), with constant ongoing assessment and evaluation taking place in order to make the therapy effective for all individuals concerned. For more in-depth information on stages of play, see Chapter 12.

Global

With young children, a specific music therapy assessment might not be conducted. The early intervention team may decide to obtain information via a formal play-based assessment conducted independently by the main service provider. The music therapist may provide suggestions for using musical play as part of the assessment process. Team members may share their observations after informally evaluating the child at play or in a more structured setting. Such assessments help the team determine holistic goals that address the needs of the whole child through developmentally appropriate practices.

Diagnostic Assessment

Music therapy diagnostic assessments may reveal unique information about the student's functioning level as well as strengths and weaknesses in core impairments. For example, Wigram (2000) described a method of music therapy assessment for the diagnosis of autism and communication disorders. Using Bruscia's (1987) *Improvisation Assessment Profile*, the assessment method identifies and analyzes musical events in improvisational music therapy. This information, paired with that acquired from a broader battery of assessments, may offer more clearly-defined treatment options.

Surveys or Interviews

Surveys or interview may yield considerable information about the student's behavior, abilities, and areas of need. Family members or other staff may complete these. Surveys or interviews might gather both or either music and nonmusic information. For an example from a music therapy assessment, see Figure 15.

PARENT INTERVIEW SECTION	
Interview with parent of:	(Child's name)
Date of interview:	
Child's favorite music:	
Instruments/Tape/Music videos at home:	
Family members that play instruments:	
Use of voice or objects in a musical manner:	
Spontaneous movement to music:	
Parent's goals for music therapy:	
Parent interested in home extension ideas:	(circle one) Yes No

Figure 15. Example from a Music Therapy Assessment (from Giant Steps Illinois, Inc.)

Furthermore, surveys and interviews may provide an avenue for students themselves to identify—either verbally or in writing—their favorite instruments, songs, and performers. Students might state how they use music in their lives and what they wish to gain from music therapy.

•

Examples From Clinicians

The final section of this chapter presents portions of assessment tools and/or processes that have been developed and used by clinicians across the United States. Sources for more detailed information as well as contributors' names are noted so that readers may examine the topic of assessment in more detail if they so desire.

Request for Assessment (Pre-assessment Checklist) for Eligibility

<table>
<tr><td colspan="4" align="center">**MUSIC THERAPY ASSESSMENT REQUEST CHECKLIST**
Used by permission of Marcia Behr, © 1999</td></tr>
<tr><td colspan="4">To determine if a student is a candidate for music therapy assessment, observe the student in a variety of locations and activities. Focus on behaviors observed with the presentation of live or recorded music compared to behaviors demonstrated without musical stimuli. In each case, consider the following questions and circle the most appropriate response:</td></tr>
<tr><td colspan="4" align="center">**Does the student demonstrate a _significant_ increased response to musical stimuli?**</td></tr>
<tr><td>**Cognitive/Academic Function**</td><td>Yes</td><td>No</td><td>Same</td></tr>
<tr><td>1.   Demonstrates increased attention and/or interest in the music environment e.g., instruments, technology, etc.</td><td></td><td></td><td></td></tr>
<tr><td>2.   Attends to task: how long?</td><td></td><td></td><td></td></tr>
<tr><td>3.   Demonstrates increased ability to follow directions</td><td></td><td></td><td></td></tr>
<tr><td>4.   Participates in/completes disliked or difficult task</td><td></td><td></td><td></td></tr>
<tr><td>**Communication Function**</td><td></td><td></td><td></td></tr>
<tr><td>1.   Initiates conversation; shares information about music</td><td></td><td></td><td></td></tr>
<tr><td>2.   Indicates musical preference</td><td></td><td></td><td></td></tr>
<tr><td>3.   Sings chorus of song</td><td></td><td></td><td></td></tr>
<tr><td>4.   Able to learn and sing an entire song</td><td></td><td></td><td></td></tr>
<tr><td>**Social/Behavior Function**</td><td></td><td></td><td></td></tr>
<tr><td>1.   Seeks out music staff</td><td></td><td></td><td></td></tr>
<tr><td>2.   Remains in group setting for increased duration</td><td></td><td></td><td></td></tr>
<tr><td>3.   Shares musical interest with peers</td><td></td><td></td><td></td></tr>
<tr><td>4.   Demonstrates increased motivation to complete directed tasks</td><td></td><td></td><td></td></tr>
<tr><td>5.   Demonstrates pride in musical accomplishments</td><td></td><td></td><td></td></tr>
<tr><td>**Communication**</td><td></td><td></td><td></td></tr>
<tr><td>1.   Assumes appropriate posture for instrument play</td><td></td><td></td><td></td></tr>
<tr><td>2.   Moves body in rhythm with music</td><td></td><td></td><td></td></tr>
<tr><td>3.   Able to play instruments bi-laterally</td><td></td><td></td><td></td></tr>
<tr><td>4.   Crosses midline</td><td></td><td></td><td></td></tr>
<tr><td colspan="4"></td></tr>
<tr><td colspan="4">Why do you believe music therapy is necessary for this student to benefit from his/her special education?

</td></tr>
<tr><td colspan="4">Please include additional comments on the back of this checklist.</td></tr>
<tr><td colspan="4">Observed by:</td></tr>
<tr><td colspan="4">Title:</td></tr>
<tr><td colspan="4">Date:</td></tr>
<tr><td colspan="4">Figure 16. Music Therapy Assessment Request Checklist.</td></tr>
</table>

Assessment for Eligibility Under the IEP

The Music Therapy Music-Related Behavior (MT-MRB) Assessment was developed by Angela M. Snell to effectively meet the music therapy assessment needs of students who receive special education services as mandated by IDEA, in Monroe County, Michigan. The MT-MRB Assessment requires a music therapist trained in skills outlined in the Certification Board for Music Therapists (CBMT) *Scope of Practice*. Its procedures follow the AMTA *Standards of Clinical Practice* and adhere to special education rules and regulations.

The purpose of the assessment is:

1. To evaluate music-related behaviors and interpret their relevance to nonmusical functioning;
2. To determine if music therapy interventions are necessary to the IEP;
3. To give assessment information obtained via the music medium that may help the team
    a) discover hidden deficits and abilities;
    b) provide support or nonsupport for other team members findings;
    c) give recommendations and suggestions for team approaches, including both musical and nonmusical suggestions as appropriate; and
4. Summarize conclusions and make recommendations to the IEP team for support or nonsupport of music therapy service.

The assessment is based on evidence gathered through the process. The approach uses individual music response indications to find evidence of deficits, abilities, and preferences (both musical and nonmusical) to form conclusions and make treatment decisions. This includes:

1. MT-MRB's relevance to nonmusical functioning;
2. the child's responses to on-the-spot prescriptive music interventions;
3. the child's present level of educational functioning with/without MT;
4. other team members' assessment results and observations; and
5. consideration of the educational needs in the least restrictive environment.

The MT-MRB provides an option to display behavioral results both with and without music therapy assistance. Results of the assessment provide:

1. a summary of student background;
2. current functioning levels and educational approaches;
3. music therapy's unique form of evaluation; and
4. conclusions and recommendations.

The MT-MRB Assessment affords a flexible approach that can apply to the wide range of ages, disabilities, and behavioral manifestations found in school settings. The report can be as lengthy or abbreviated as needed for the individual situation. MT-MRB information can frequently be obtained with one direct session and even producing important MT-MRB information during a seemingly "noncompliant" session. It allows music therapists to differentiate their unique assessment information from those of other disciplines (e.g., occupational or physical therapists), while remaining in line with the formats of their reports. Furthermore, the report reflects responses to musical elements (tempo, rhythm, melody, phrasing, etc.) and the impact of on-the-spot prescriptive use of those musical elements, rather than simply stating the titles of the songs used. It allows musical terms to be used and helps explain why (or why not) music therapy services need to be administered by a trained music therapist.

The MT-MRB Assessment works with both well-written IEPs and poorly written IEPs. In addition, it is designed to help parents, administrators, and other team members understand how and why a music therapist is needed or not needed to provide service.

For more information on this assessment process as well as examples of cases and forms, see pages 236–275 of *Models of Music Therapy Interventions in School Settings* (Snell, 2002).

Dual-Purpose Assessment

The following design submitted by Jean Nemeth may be effective for determining both level of general functioning and efficacy of music-based programming in promoting growth. The format consists of two individual music therapy sessions, conducted approximately one week apart and at different times of the day (e.g., one morning and one afternoon). Each session consists of a series of music activities delivered in a session that can last up to 1 hour (depending on the child's age, tolerance, etc.). Responses to the music-based programming are assessed in the following categories:

- Sensory Awareness/Responses (Visual/Auditory/Tactile/Kinesthetic);
- Motor Skills (Gross & Fine Motor);
- Communication (Expressive & Receptive);
- Social Awareness/Responses (self/others/environmental awareness, affect, attending, body language, social responses/reciprocation, etc.);
- Cognitive Skills (varies according to age/level of student—including areas such as cause/effect, choice making, concept formation, learning skills, and body awareness).

A simple checklist format is adapted as necessary to meet the needs of individual situations. A two-session approach is used because: (a) different times of day or week often seem to affect performance, and equally as important, (b) an increase in responsiveness to the music-based programming may take place from the first session to the second session. This potential increase bodes well for future progress and lends credence to the effectiveness of music therapy as an approach. The impetus is to get a picture of whether/how music can be effective with a particular child and to form a basis for a recommendation of service format, hours, and goal/objective areas. A formal report reflects all these areas.

Assessment to Determine Goals and Objectives

In the next example, students in the primary and intermediate age groups are included in music therapy classes as part of their overall program. The group sessions are a service that is provided with no referral or assessment required. However, goals and objectives are developed for each student to reflect needs in areas of management, academic, physical, and social development. In order to assess these needs, a checklist has been developed for each area of the IEP that outlines objectives describing a hierarchy of skills (checklist developed by Beth McLaughlin, MT-BC, and Mark Ahola, MT-BC). The skill areas are organized according to the *New York State Standards for Arts Education* and include the following:

Standard 1—Creating, Performing and Participating
- Music Therapy—Management

- Music Therapy—Academic/Instruments
- Music Therapy—Academic/Vocal
- Music Therapy—Physical/Movement
- Music Therapy—Physical/Instruments
- Music Therapy—Social
- Music Therapy—Independence
- Music Therapy—Piano
- Music Therapy—Guitar

Standard 2—Knowing and Using the Arts
- Music Performance

Standard 3—Responding to an Analyzing Art
- Music Comprehension

Standard 4—Understanding Contribution of Arts to our Culture
- Music—Cultural Awareness

Figure 17 is an example of the IEP Checklist that examines the targeted area of Management.

IEP CHECKLIST TARGETING MANAGEMENT	
Desired Behavior	**Level of Prompt**
will sit upon entering room	
will sit quietly during relaxation	
will sit appropriately during music with staff support	
will sit appropriately during music without staff support	
will participate in initial music activity as modeled	
will re-engage in activities upon redirection	
will stand up for turn to play music instrument	
will approach prop/instrument, grasp it, and carry it back to seat	
will use instruments appropriately	
will play hand-held percussion without dropping instruments	
will respond to a group direction by getting an instrument or putting it away	
will relinquish instruments appropriately	
will transition between activities with 1 re-direction	
will complete 4 activities in a 30-minute session without disruption	
will engage in activities chosen by therapist	
will put materials away when "finished" song is sung	
will use appropriate language to express frustration	
will maintain appropriate posture during mvt. & instrumental activities	
will stay with group during locomotor movement activity	
will perform partner dance sequences with appropriate motor control	
will perform group dances without dropping to the floor	
Levels of prompts: $+$ performs to criteria PC physical cue GC gestural prompt C co-active VC visual cue __ does not perform to criteria V verbal cue	

Figure 17. IEP Checklist Targeting Management. Source: Management Objectives from IEPKeeper (designed by Bill Sofko, www.vilaj.com), Wildwood School Music Therapy Data Base (2003), Beth McLaughlin, MT-BC, and Mark Ahola, MT-BC.

Play-based Checklist for Early Childhood

The *Music Therapy Assessment and Evaluations Checklist*, a multi-year format, developed by Marcia Humpal and Jacquelyn Dimmick, examines how the child explores his or her environment through such musical means as singing, sound play, moving, and listening. After researching the normalizing effect of music experiences for the young child and examining musical characteristics of, and program goals for, typically developing young children, a hierarchy of competencies was developed within each musical area as well as for nonmusical skills and stages of play. Creativity is noted throughout each area, as well as how participation and engagement levels reflect the child's stage of social play.

Space is provided for anecdotal information considering the child's social, medical, sensory, communication and motor abilities and/or needs. Additional room is given for team notes regarding progress made or adaptations needed, as well as for recording of the IFSP outcome or IEP objective and its attainment status (Dimmick & Humpal, 1994).

Input is gathered by direct observation, interactive play, and from the entire interdisciplinary team (including the family). A prototype of this *Music Therapy Assessment and Evaluations Checklist* may be found in *Models of Music Therapy Interventions in School Settings*, pages 421–424 (Humpal, 2002).

A Narrative Assessment Report

In comparison to the more checklist style of assessment, this is an example of a more narrative type report covering staff information, classroom observation, information obtained from a 1-to-1 music therapy evaluation, client educational needs, and concluding with an interpretation of evaluation results and recommendations for services.

ASSESSMENT REPORT

Birth date: _____
Grade: Early Childhood Special Education
Date: _____

Assessment: Classroom Observation — Music Therapy

Information Reported by Staff:

Staff report that since his implant and activation, B responds best when music is utilized. During group, he is more actively engaged and focused when music is used. This assessment will consider how music therapy strategies could improve B's acquisition of skills and facilitate meeting his IEP objectives, especially vocalization, listening skills, and imitation skills.

Classroom Observation:

In the classroom, B attends inconsistently to environment and speech sounds at this time. He does not consistently respond to his name. He makes a few sounds. His motor imitation is better with music. During group, he smiled and clearly appeared to be enjoying himself. While others were making sounds, B simply nodded his head. He required 4 prompts to produce an "mm" sound.

Music Therapy 1:1 Evaluation:

B immediately looked and smiled when he heard the music. During assessment, he had the opportunity to play a variety of instruments including bells, small maracas, rainstick, shaker eggs, cabasa, drums, and mallets. He held and played the instruments without throwing or dropping them. His attention to each activity was good: he willing engaged and refocused with each new activity that was introduced. B was able to work for 30 minutes. When his attention wandered, an instrument immediately brought his focus back. During a musical stop/go activity, B used the vocal approximation "op" 4 times. Given a rainstick and the model "oo," he used two descending pitches of about 1/2 step while watching the beads roll down. He then recreated this sound 2 times by himself and 2 more times with a model. With some of the motor actions, he watched and was cued by the movement. He appeared to do better when using items to imitate. Given a Barney paper plate, he copied 7/8 motions, with sticks 3/4 motions as compared with simple body movements such as clapping which was 3/5. B was also able to imitate "ha, ha," and an "eee" sound during music activities. He was attentive and had good eye contact. He is still learning cause and effect with his voice and sounds and needs 1:1 time to attach meaning to sounds. He showed interest and awareness of certain instruments by pointing to his ear and nodding his head. He showed preference for instruments like claves and a cabasa with a higher pitch.

Assessment: Observation   Date: _____

B received a cochlear implant in November, 2003, and was activated December 3, 2003. An observation of B was completed in order (1) to determine how B is using his hearing in the classroom throughout his day while engaging in various activities, and (2) to observe B's response to the use of music in various activities. B is beginning to respond to his name when called. He responds to environmental sounds when they are pointed out to him. He is aware of sounds he makes such as banging a toy upon the table or stamping his feet on the floor. In a group situation involving the use of recorded music and musical instruments, B remained actively engaged and on-task for up to 20 minutes. He participated in the activities and stayed with the group. He imitated the vowel sounds /a/ as in hot, /u/ as in who, and attempted /i/ as in me. His vocal quality was normal and unstrained. He was cooperative and an active participant. B also was observed in two different group activities that did not involve the use of music. While the teacher read a story to the group, Brian turned his body away, hung his head, and refused to look at the book. He stood up and left the area on two different occasions and was directed to come back to join the group. He shook his head no and pointed to the toy shelves. He could be redirected to sit with the group and attend to the story when props were used. However, he did not sustain attention while waiting for a turn. The other activity involved matching emotions/facial expressions and placing the pictured faces in a slot. Again, B sat with arms folded, body facing away from the group, refusing to participate. When the teacher began to sing, "If You're Happy and You Know It Clap Your Hands," B immediately turned and began to smile and clap along with the group.

Educationally Relevant Medical Information:

B was diagnosed with a profound sensorineural hearing loss in October, 2002, at the age of 2 years, one month. B received a cochlear implant November, 2003; the implant was activated in December, 2003.

Educational Needs:

Music therapy is the use of music and music-related strategies to assist or motivate a person towards specific nonmusical goals. A registered or board-certified music therapist provides these services. Music therapy is a related service as defined by the Individuals with Disabilities Education Act (P.L. 105-17). In order for music therapy to be recommended as a related service, it must be shown that the student performs in a significantly different way on IEP goal related behaviors and skills when music therapy strategies are implemented. In the classroom, B attends inconsistently to environment and speech sounds at this time. He is not consistently responding to his name. He makes a few sounds. His motor imitation is better with music. B needs to attach meaning to sounds and speech. He needs to begin to play with sounds and vocalizations.

Figure 18. Assessment Report (Completed by Amy Furman)

ASSESSMENT REPORT
Interpretation of Evaluation Results:
B's response to music and musical sounds is more consistent than his response to environmental sounds. B is more actively engaged and on-task during activities with music. During the assessment, B demonstrated an improved performance level on several areas of the IEP when music therapy approaches were used. These include increased vocalizations, motivation to try skills, attention span, and listening skills. Individual music therapy sessions are recommended to help B maximize his listening experiences and increase imitation and vocalization skills. In a group setting, the cues and opportunities go by too quickly for him to have time to generate sounds. As skills are acquired, they should be generalized to a group setting by the music therapist to assist in B developing group skills.
Recommendation:
Individual sessions 2 times a week for 20 minutes each with a switch to 1 individual and 1 group time when determined appropriate.

Figure 18. Assessment Report (Completed by Amy Furman)

•

References

American Music Therapy Association. (2000a). Journal of Music Therapy: *Special Issue on Assessment, 37(2).*

American Music Therapy Association. (2000b). Music Therapy Perspectives: Assessment in Music Therapy, *18(1).*

American Music Therapy Association. (2001). Standards of Clinical Practice/Code of Ethics. *Silver Spring, MD: Author.*

Boxill, E. (1985). Music therapy for the developmentally disabled. *Rockville, MD: Aspen Systems Corporation.*

Briggs, C. (1991). A model for understanding musical development. Music Therapy, *10(1), 1–21.*

Brunk, B. K., & Coleman, K. A. (2000). Development of a special education music therapy assessment process. Music Therapy Perspectives, *18(1), 59–68.*

Bruscia, K. (1987). Improvisational models of music therapy. *Springfield, IL: Charles C. Thomas.*

Certification Board for Music Therapists (CBMT). (1998). CBMT Scope of Practice. *Downington, PA: Author.*

Certification Board for Music Therapists (CBMT). (2004). Scope of Practice language analysis. *Downingtown, PA: Author.*

Chase, K. (2002). The music therapy assessment handbook. *Columbus, MS: Southern Pen Publishing.*

Chase, K. (2004). Music therapy assessment for children with developmental disabilities: A survey study. Journal of Music Therapy, *41(1), 28–54.*

Cohen, L. G., & Spenciner, L. J. (1994). Assessment of young children. *New York: Longman.*

Coleman, K. (1999). Thoughts about music therapy assessment. AMTA Early Childhood Newsletter, 5, 5–6.

Dimmick, J. A., & Humpal, M. E. (1994). Music therapy assessment and evaluations checklist: Early childhood. *Cleveland, OH: CCBMR/DD.*

Giant Steps, Illinois, Inc. (n.d.). Music Therapy Assessment: Parent Interview Survey. *Burr Ridge, IL.*

Humpal, M. E. (2002). *Music therapy for learners in an early childhood community interagency setting. In B. Wilson (Ed.),* Models of music therapy interventions in school settings *(pp. 389–428). Silver Spring, MD: American Music Therapy Association.*

IEPKeeper. (n.d.). Retrieved June 20, 2006, from http://www.vilaj.com/services/iepkeeper/index.html

Linder, T. (1990). Transdisciplinary Play-based Assessment. *Baltimore, MD: Paul H. Brookes.*

Loewy, J. (2000). Music psychotherapy assessment. Music Therapy Perspectives, *18(1), 47–58.*

Nordoff, P., & Robbins, C. (1977). Creative music therapy. *New York: John Day.*

Pierangelo, R. (2003). The special educator's book of lists. *San Francisco: John Wiley & Sons.*

Siegel, L. M. (2001). The complete IEP guide: How to advocate for your special ed child *(2nd ed.) Berkeley, CA: Nolo.*

Snell, A. M. (2002). *Music therapy for learners with autism in a public school setting. In B. Wilson (Ed.),* Models of music therapy interventions in school settings *(pp. 211–275). Silver Spring, MD: American Music Therapy Association.*

Wigram, T. (2000). A method of music therapy assessment for the diagnosis of autism and communication disorders in children. Music Therapy Perspectives, *18(1), 13–22.*

Wilson, B. L., & Smith, D. S. (2000). Music therapy assessment in school settings: A preliminary investigation. Journal of Music Therapy, *37(2), 95–117.*

Chapter 5

Development of a Special Education Music Therapy Assessment Process

Betsey King, MMT, MT-BC; Kathleen A. Coleman, MMT, MT-BC

Editor's Note: This chapter is an expansion of an article entitled, "Development of a Special Education Music Therapy Assessment Process" that was published in Music Therapy Perspectives, 18(1), 2000, pp. 59–68; and later in Models of Music Therapy Interventions in School Settings, Brian Wilson, (ed.), 2002. In addition to the SEMTAP, several authors in subsequent chapters in this book have described other assessment models and procedures that they use in their clinical practices.

Music therapy eligibility assessment in a public school setting is a comprehensive process that includes much more than the actual administration of a music therapy evaluation. Music therapists who want to work in the public schools need to: (a) understand the federal and state laws governing the provision of related services, (b) be able to articulate the role of music therapy in the public schools and distinguish it from other music-related activities, (c) set and maintain boundaries with parents and school staff, (d) work to build understanding and cooperation when music therapy is unfamiliar or misunderstood, and (e) know how to translate assessment results into reasonable and pragmatic recommendations. Through all of this, the music therapist must focus on the students—on their unique abilities and challenges, and on their individual educational needs.

Although many music therapy articles and presentations address the concern that music therapists need "standardized" assessment instruments, public school music therapists must ask whether such tools would be appropriate for special education evaluations. The special education population is diverse and, even within disability groups, skills and deficits vary widely. Some students require intense assistance with communication issues while being independent in their mobility. Others demonstrate severe physical limitations which can obscure cognitive strengths. Literature on music therapy assessment for children with special needs has focused on evaluating a child's cognitive developmental level through musical tasks (Rider, 1981); on identifying a child's unique skills and adaptive abilities through musical interaction (Grant, 1995); and on using music and music stimuli over several weeks to comprehensively evaluate a child's abilities in the motor, communication, cognitive, affective and social domains (Boxill, 1985). Some assessments are based on a particular therapeutic approach, such as improvisation (Bruscia, 1987). Other approaches suggest the integration

A music therapist conducting an assessment for a student in the public schools, however, must be concerned with only one thing: the impact of specific music therapy interventions in assisting that student to achieve the goals set in his or her Individualized Educational Program (IEP).

of information from standardized assessment tools used by other professionals (Gfeller & Baumann, 1988; Johnson, 1996). These assessment tools and procedures are all valid in certain situations. Assessments often are conducted for the purpose of choosing the best strategies for music therapy sessions, or to determine the level of musical skills in a person with disabilities. A music therapist conducting an eligibility assessment for a student in the public schools, however, must be concerned with only one thing: the impact of specific music therapy interventions on that student's ability to achieve the goals set in his or her Individualized Education Program (IEP).

Assessments and therapies that meet the standards of special education law parallel a student's IEP, addressing specific goals and objectives from that document. The members of an IEP team must demonstrate—first through assessment and then through implementation and documentation—that particular interventions are necessary for the student to achieve his or her IEP goals and objectives. A music therapist need not provide an overall assessment of a student's cognitive, behavioral, social, or physical abilities; other IEP team members (such as the diagnostician and classroom teacher) will have completed these evaluations. Likewise, a music therapist will not want to focus exclusively on a child's musical abilities (i.e., keeping a steady beat, matching pitch), as this does not show the team how music therapy would assist the student in achieving *non-*musical IEP goals, such as color identification, increased attention span, or independence in the community.

In this chapter, we describe the use of an individualized music therapy assessment *process* which allows each therapist to utilize his or her individual therapeutic methodology while providing a clear, convincing rationale for the inclusion of music therapy in a student's IEP. Known as the SEMTAP (Special Education Music Therapy Assessment Process), this process acknowledges each child's distinctive educational profile and highlights the role of the music therapist as a member of a transdisciplinary IEP team. It conforms to current special education law, resulting in recommendations that can be justified to both parents and administrators. It does not depend on a single standardized assessment instrument that may not address the unique needs of each child. Additionally, the SEMTAP can be an educational tool for music therapists working with school districts that are unfamiliar with music therapy.

This chapter will provide an outline and justification for the use of the SEMTAP by music therapists working in the public schools. We will (a) review the federal law that forms the basis of all special education procedure; (b) outline the assessment process (SEMTAP) that was developed in response to the law; (c) present an assessment case study; (d) describe the ways in which a music therapy assessment can be an educational tool for a school district unfamiliar with music therapy; and (e) review the results of 16 independent assessments that we conducted for school districts new to music therapy, reporting on administration and parental responses to our evaluation procedure.

Special Education Law

Music therapists become part of public school special education programs in a variety of ways. Some are hired to provide group music therapy to particular classrooms or programs (such as early intervention). Some assist music educators with the inclusion process for students with disabilities. For this article, we will not focus on these voluntary arrangements between a school district and a music therapist. Instead, we will concentrate on the federally delineated process by which music therapy is included or rejected for a particular student's Individualized Education Program, namely, the music therapy assessment.

Legislation

In 1973, in an amendment to the Rehabilitation Act referred to as Section 504, the United States Congress sought to recognize the civil rights of children with disabilities. Section 504 "prohibited recipients of federal financial assistance from excluding disabled students from participating in, or being denied the benefits of, the school programs offered to others" (Martin, 1991). In 1975, Congress passed additional amendments to existing legislation (The Education of the Handicapped Act—EHA) that came to be known as PL 94-142: the Education for All Handicapped Children Act. This legislation (which provided funding to assist schools with the costs of special education) also came with regulations; as summarized by Martin (1991), it stated that:

> *All children would have to be served, regardless of the nature or severity of their handicapping conditions. Parents would be given written notice of their rights and of actions proposed by the schools. Evaluation practices of schools would have to be reformed, and parents would have the right to seek an independent evaluation to contrast with the school's. Parents and school personnel would meet annually to put in writing the Individualized Education Program (IEP) plan that would govern services to the child. Schools would have to make available as needed related services such as physical therapy, occupational therapy, and school nursing services. Students with disabilities would be integrated with nondisabled students to the maximum extent appropriate. Finally, schools would have to agree to let an independent authority, an impartial hearing officer, rule on disputes and order needed changes in the school district's program. (p. 2)*

In 1990, after several small amendments to both Section 504 and EHA (made in response to judicial challenges), the EHA became the Individuals with Disabilities Education Act, or IDEA. In 1997 and 2004, further amendments were made to IDEA. Litigation on Section 504 and IDEA is common, and court rulings sometimes have resulted in changes that are recognized by schools and parents even though they are not part of the statutes.

One section of the 1997 IDEA amendments recognized that "the implementation of [PL-94-142] has been impeded by low expectations and an insufficient focus on applying replicable research on proven methods of teaching and learning," and adds that "20 years of research and experience has demonstrated that the education of children with disabilities can be made more effective by... providing appropriate special education and related services and aids and supports in the regular classroom to such children, whenever appropriate..." (*Individuals with Disabilities Education Act Amendments of 1997*, Chapter 2, Section 681, 4–5). This statement, and the definition of related services provided in the law (see below), are the basis for a parent's request for a related service such as music therapy.

•

Related Services

IDEA states that "the term 'related services' means transportation, and such developmental, corrective, and other supportive services... as may be required to assist a child with a disability to benefit from special education" (Section 602 (26), IDEA 2004). The Senate Report on PL 94-142 stated that the list of related services (which includes such diverse interventions as speech-language pathology, social work services, and rehabilitation counseling) is "not exhaustive and may include other developmental, corrective, or supportive services (such as artistic and cultural programs, and art, music, and dance therapy), if they are required to assist a child with a disability to benefit from special education" (cited in Bateman, 1998). Amendments to PL 94-142, including the most current 2004 IDEA amendments, do nothing to change the basic definition of related services or the original Senate Report's comments.

The key term in the definition of related services and the attached Senate Report is *required*. In assessing a child's need for music therapy as a related service, the public school music therapist must make his or her recommendation based on this standard. A key United States Supreme Court ruling (*Board of Education v. Rowley*, 1982) stated that a child's IEP "need only be procedurally correct, individualized, and reasonably calculated to allow the student to receive benefit' (cited in Bateman, 1998). Bateman refers to this as "a Chevrolet, not a Cadillac Standard" (p. 96) and agrees with a Vermont hearing officer who stated that "the IEP is not required to maximize the educational benefit to the child, nor to provide each and every service and accommodation which could conceivably be of some educational benefit" (1993, VT SEA, In re Child with Disabilities, 20 IDELR 314, cited in Bateman, 1998). However, related services, such as music therapy, must be provided by a school district only when they are *required* for a child to benefit from special education.

•

Assessments

Federal law has set forth specific guidelines for the evaluation of a student being considered for special education programming. These guidelines also are followed for assessments for related services. They are as follows:

1.   Evaluation must occur before programming can begin;

2. Parents must be included in the evaluation process;

3. The evaluation must be kept current, to respond to the student's changing needs;

4. The evaluation must be conducted by a recognized specialist;

5. Reevaluation is required at least every 3 years, but must also occur when the parent or teacher requests it;

6. Parents may procure an independent evaluation if they disagree with the school's evaluation, and that assessment must be considered in program decisions;

7. If a school refuses to conduct an evaluation, the parents are entitled to a written justification for the refusal (Martin, 1991, pp. 15–16).

When the federal guidelines for assessment are followed, and music therapy is recommended, a district cannot legally refuse to provide services. Therefore, music therapists who wish to introduce or maintain music therapy in a district need to understand the law's related service provisions and be able to articulate them to administrators and other members of an IEP team. They need an assessment process that determines if music therapy is "required" for a student to benefit from his or her education program, and considers the legal concept of "reasonable benefit" in making recommendations.

●

The Special Education Music Therapy Assessment Process

Background

The Special Education Music Therapy Assessment Process (SEMTAP) is the result of the authors' combined 20 years experience in working with children with special needs, and the school districts that serve them. During this time, we have attended over 300 IEP meetings and provided service to over 600 students. In developing the SEMTAP, we consulted with other music therapists throughout the United States on their special education assessment experiences. Speaking engagements in several states across the country gave us the opportunity to talk with parents about their experiences in obtaining related services for their children. Over a three-year period, we had the opportunity to provide 22 independent assessments for school districts that, in most cases, had little to no experience with music therapy. All this information has led us to develop a comprehensive, *individualized* assessment process that addresses both legal and practical issues in special education music therapy evaluations.

In developing the SEMTAP, we based each step on the guidelines for related service and assessment found in the federal statutes on special education. Many steps were included or adjusted after experiences with parents or school districts who were active in, or considering, legal actions due to disputes over music therapy. We also considered practical safeguards against conflict-of-interest issues over which some school districts expressed concern.

The SEMTAP is an eligibility assessment; its purpose is to determine whether or not music therapy is necessary as part of a student's IEP. The process is designed to have two results. First, the music therapist using the SEMTAP will be able to make a direct comparison of a student's performance on his or her IEP objectives—*with and without* the structure of music therapy strategies. Second, the music therapist will be able to justify a recommendation for or against music therapy in a way that will satisfy both parents and school district personnel. We believe that most confrontations between parents and school districts can be avoided if all parties understand the music therapy assessment process and its legal basis.

The Process

The SEMTAP contains the following steps, each of which is detailed in this section:

1. The formal request for assessment
2. The music therapy assessment process
    a. review of documentation
    b. interviews
    c. observation in a non-musical setting
    d. preparation of the assessment
    e. administration of the assessment
    f. preparation of the assessment report and documentation
3. Presentation of the report and recommendations

The formal request for assessment. A parent, or other member of the IEP team, can ask for a music therapy assessment at an annual IEP meeting or an IEP meeting called specifically to make the request. This is *not* a request for music therapy *services*; it is a request for an *assessment*. It is helpful if the person making the request has some anecdotal or documented evidence in hand (e.g., a student's response to songs sung in the classroom, reports from a private music therapist). Some music therapists provide IEP teams with short checklists or forms that can be used to structure the discussion about an assessment. Supportive informational materials on music therapy and its role as a related service may also be useful to the IEP team considering the request. Most importantly, an outline of the SEMTAP will demonstrate to the IEP team how a decision for or against service will be made.

We recommend that any music therapist who is contacted to conduct an eligibility assessment for an IEP team verify that the members of the team—especially the parents or guardians—are satisfied with the current IEP. Since the SEMTAP is based directly on the goals and objectives in the IEP, parents who feel that the objectives are far above or below their child's actual skills or do not address areas that they are concerned about are unlikely to be satisfied with a music therapy assessment recommendation based on those objectives.

It is our strong recommendation that a student's private music therapist NOT participate directly in the IEP meeting, nor offer his or her services for the assessment. In our experience, the appearance of a private music therapist at an IEP meeting has often

We believe that most confrontations between parents and school districts can be avoided if all parties understand the music therapy assessment process and its legal basis.

resulted in a district's perception that the music therapist is simply seeking additional work. Furthermore, since the private music therapist may have (rightly) evaluated and treated the student under broader, more liberal guidelines than those set forth in special education law, the district, parents or therapist may have difficulty making a distinction between the two. Because the relationship between a music therapist and a client's parents can be a close one, with the parties sharing months or years of struggles and successes, the school district may not feel that the private music therapist has the ability to conduct the assessment impartially. We recommend that the private therapist provide the names of other therapists in the area who can conduct an independent evaluation. If an independent assessor is not available locally, the district will have to bring in a music therapist from outside the area.

The school district may choose to contract with one music therapist to do assessments, and a second therapist to provide recommended therapy. This arrangement helps to ensure that recommendations for service are not based on a therapist's need for work. Some districts have utilized this system for a year or two and then, as personnel felt more comfortable with music therapy, moved to using one therapist for all parts of the process.

If the IEP team denies a parent's request for a music therapy evaluation, the parent has a right to receive a written response, detailing the reasons for the denial.

The music therapy assessment process. If an assessment is ordered by the IEP team, these are the steps we recommend as the SEMTAP:

1.   Review the student's current IEP and other records as necessary. Make sure that all confidentiality forms have been signed.

2.   Interview members of the IEP team, especially the classroom teacher and a parent. If the IEP focuses on a particular area of need (e.g., language acquisition), interview the related therapist (speech therapist). Ask particularly about areas of the IEP in which the student is not making expected progress. Provide each person interviewed with a transcript of their comments and have them sign it, indicating confirmation of their remarks.

3.   Based on the review of the IEP and interviews, target a specific number of IEP objectives on which the assessment will be based. Choose those objectives that can be addressed with music therapy strategies and include, if possible, those objectives mentioned as particular challenges in the interviews. The music therapist will want to look at the IEP objectives and make sure that they are specific and measurable. An objective such as "the student will improve classroom skills" does not provide enough information on which to create a music therapy strategy for the assessment. If some objectives are too vague, the music therapist may wish to have the team clarify its intentions in a *documented* meeting before proceeding. Target only those 4–6 objectives that could be addressed within one or two music therapy assessment sessions. (See Figure 19 for considerations in selecting objectives.)

4. Schedule and complete an observation of the student. Make an arrangement with teachers or therapists so that there is an opportunity to observe the student working on the targeted IEP objectives—in a NON-musical setting. Document the observations in real time through notes, audio recording or videotape.

5. Plan a music therapy assessment session that will address each of the targeted objectives. We recommend that the assessment occur in the form of a music therapy session, with opening and closing music, variety in the music strategies, and smooth transitions. The therapist may choose strategies from his or her own practice, from standardized tests, or from other music therapists' assessments. The sole requirement is that each music therapy strategy addresses a specific, targeted objective from the student's IEP—reflecting both the skill itself, and the skill level that the student is being asked to achieve. For example, a target objective from an IEP might state that the student will achieve 80% accuracy in one-to-one correspondence matching of printed numbers 1–5 with pictures of one to five familiar objects. A music therapy song in which the student "fills in the blank" with ordinal numbers as they are displayed on cards would not accurately measure this skill. Neither would a song that asks only for a verbal response to "How many do you see?"

6. When targeted objectives involve a student's ability to participate in a group, the music therapist may choose to conduct part of the assessment by leading the student and his classroom peers in one or more group music therapy strategies. We recommend that this take place on the same day as any one-on-one assessment session, so as to observe the student in a similar physical and emotional state.

7. Conduct the music therapy assessment in a quiet, enclosed space at the school that the student attends. Make real time observations through notes, audio recording, or videotape.

8. Before discussing the assessment session with anyone, study the observation and music therapy assessment documentation and make a direct comparison of the student's performance on targeted IEP objectives with and without the structure of the music therapy strategies.

9. Prepare a written report that documents each step of the assessment process, including the following items:
    a. the purpose of the assessment (an educational section that relates the assessment process to the needs of the student, and to the law);
    b. an outline of the assessment procedure;
    c. relevant information from the files reviewed (especially the targeted IEP goals and objectives);

d.   information from the interviews (be sure to indicate who made each statement, and note who has signed the transcripts of their remarks);

e.   summary of the observations of the classroom and/or other "non-musical" settings (specifically citing the student's performance on targeted objectives);

f.   description of the music therapy assessment setting and general student alertness/behavior on the day of the testing;

g.   detailed description of the music therapy assessment session (specifically citing the student's performance on targeted objectives);

h.   results of the music therapy assessment: a direct comparison of the student's performance of IEP skills *with and without* music therapy intervention;

i.   recommendations for or against music therapy service (which result in service provision and are legally binding);

j.   suggestions (which the district may consider voluntarily).

CONSIDERATIONS IN SELECTING OBJECTIVES FROM AN IEP FOR THE SEMTAP	
Objective	Considerations
Student will hop on one foot for ninety seconds.	Is there evidence in the literature that music therapy would be helpful in supporting this objective? Is this one of the more functional objectives on the IEP? Would working on this objective be the best use of time in music therapy?
Student will remain dry for the 2 hour period between supervised bathroom visits.	Is there evidence that music therapy could support this objective?
Student will decrease inappropriate behavior while in the classroom by 50%.	What constitutes inappropriate behavior? Does the IEP committee intend that the student do this independently, or can cues be provided to help the student? Should a concurrent increase in specified appropriate behaviors occur at the same time or will passivity be considered success?
Student will consistently imitate three vocalizations that include initial sounds for "b," "h," and "w."	Can music therapy strategies cue imitation of vocalizations? Is this an objective on which the student has had trouble? Are there other objectives (perhaps related to attention) that will have an impact on the student's ability to achieve this one?
Student will remain seated for the 30 minute "circle time" at the beginning of the school day.	Is there evidence that music therapy could support this objective? Is music used in the circle time? Is it used contingently to cue the students to attend? Can the music therapist participate in a circle time as part of the music therapy assessment?
Student will demonstrate the ability to proceed through the lunch line and into the cafeteria with minimal verbal cues.	Is music therapy effective in teaching sequencing for functional tasks? Is music therapy effective in helping with memorization and impulse control?

Figure 19. Considerations in Selecting Objectives from an IEP for the SEMTAP

Presentation of the report and recommendations. After the assessment is completed, an IEP meeting will be called to discuss the results and recommendations. The assessing music therapist should attend this meeting; it is not appropriate for the IEP team to review the music therapy assessment without the music therapist present. Since members of the IEP committee (including the parents) may disagree with the findings of the assessment, the music therapist must be prepared to verbally articulate all parts of the process and defend his or her recommendations.

If the assessment process shows that the student receives a significant assist or significant motivation from music therapy strategies to perform IEP skills, then music therapy may be recommended as a related service for that student. When recommending music therapy services, the music therapist may consider the following factors:

1. If the results of the assessment indicate that music is a primary learning modality for the student, then a recommendation for "direct service" is appropriate. "Direct service" means that the music therapist provides all recommended therapy, and usually implies that the music therapist will "pull" the student out of the classroom for individual or group sessions.

2. If the results of the assessment indicate that music therapy assists the student in performing tasks within the classroom (such as participating as part of a group, or completing tasks at a "listening center" or computer), then a recommendation for "consult-to-student" service should be considered. "Consult" service, as part of a student's IEP, means that that therapist will serve the student in the classroom (or as part of another therapy session, such as speech therapy), and provide information, advice, and materials to the classroom teacher (or therapist) that can be used when the music therapist is not present. This model requires strict documentation on the part of the teacher or therapist and that fact should be listed as a condition of the recommendation.

3. In some cases, a combination of direct and consult service may be recommended. In making any recommendation, however, the music therapist should take into consideration the legal standard of "reasonable" benefit. A school district is *not* required (under federal statutes) to provide the maximum amount of therapy possible, and a recommendation to that effect will increase the chances of conflict within the IEP team.

If recommending music therapy services, the music therapist must include goals and objectives. Objectives must be written before placement (Bateman, 1998, p. 156)

If music therapy is not recommended, the music therapy report should clearly indicate either (a) the lack of a significant difference in the student's performance of IEP tasks with and without music therapy structure, or (b) a student's superior performance without music therapy. If the music therapist explains the SEMTAP to the IEP committee (including parents) prior to conducting the assessment, the meeting at which the assessment results are reviewed will be more likely to proceed smoothly. Parents or other members of the team may disagree with the findings, and the parents have the right to ask for another, independent, assessment. Again, the music therapist must be able to articulate the rationale for his or her recommendations verbally, as well as in writing.

Rationale for Single-Session Assessment Sessions

Since the introduction of the SEMTAP in 1997, the most common question posed by therapists who are considering its use is, "How can I see if a student will benefit from music therapy in a single music therapy session?" Although we agree that additional sessions would provide more information on which to make a recommendation, we have designed the SEMTAP for one or two assessment sessions for two reasons. First, it is unlikely that a school district will pay for multiple assessment sessions, especially in the case of a district that does not employ a full-time music therapist. Most other members of the IEP team conduct their assessments in one or two sessions. In certain cases, multiple sessions might be more useful than in others, but a district will be reluctant to authorize, for example, four sessions for a particular assessment because once one student has been assessed this way, a precedent has been set and other parents will insist on the same standard.

Second, there are several indicators of a student's potential to benefit from music therapy that will appear in the very first session. Therapists can look for the following things that, in a student who responds to music therapy, will contrast with behaviors from the non-musical observation:

1. Increased eye contact with the therapist and musical objects.
2. Reaction to the interruption of music; responsiveness to music used contingently.
3. Changes in posture and movement during music therapy
4. Changes in affect
5. Increased vocalization, imitation of sounds and words, or increased use of language (verbal or augmentative communication)
6. Increased initiation
7. Decreased off-task behavior and verbalizations
8. Ability to recall information from newly presented musical material
9. Ability to sequence actions, words, pictures more readily.

Therapists working with a school district must remember the law when deciding on a recommendation. A student's general enjoyment of music without an observable and significant change in his or her ability to work on tasks from the IEP may be enough to recommend that student for private music therapy. It is not enough, however, to meet the IDEA standard for related services.

The SEMTAP as an Educational Tool

The SEMTAP report, which includes an individualized evaluation and a written explanation of its relationship to the student's IEP, can act as an educational tool—emphasizing the legitimate role of music therapy in special education. In 1977, Alley stated that music therapists must show that their services are "unique enough to be viewed as complementary to, but not overlapping with, standard educational disciplines . . . specific to educational . . . and competitive for available funding resources" (p. 50). This advice is still relevant today. A report written with this in mind will record in detail the process by which a recommendation for or against service was made, provide background information on music therapy and music therapy strategies, and make a point-by-point comparison of the student's responses with and without music therapy intervention.

As district personnel become more familiar with music therapy, and as music therapy becomes an accepted related service, much of the background information in a report may be eliminated. Streamlined assessment reports are essential for districts where the therapist may be providing direct service to 20 or more students. The basic outline of the SEMTAP, however, can remain the same: documentation review, interviews, observation, music therapy assessment and written report with recommendations.

●

Assessment Case Study #1

J was a 10-year-old student diagnosed with autism. He was referred for a music therapy assessment by his IEP committee after a request from his parents. The assessing music therapist provided the team with a checklist outline of the SEMTAP and interviewed the student's mother and classroom teacher. The mother stated that she had requested a music therapy assessment because she had read that music therapy was an effective intervention for children with autism. The classroom teacher stated that although she utilized music each day in the classroom, she had not noticed that J responded differently to music than he did to other interventions.

Targeting objectives. Information gained in the interviews, as well as a review of J's IEP, resulted in the therapist's targeting the following objectives for J:

1. Count at least 5 objects with 1:1 correspondence.
2. Match color word to color.
3. Sequence 3 events in pictorial form.
4. Form sentence "I want " with communication system.
5. Follow 2 step directions with 1 verbal cue.

Non-musical observation.   Next, the therapist scheduled an observation in the classroom after talking with the classroom teacher about a time when she could observe J working on the objectives listed above. When the therapist arrived at the appointed time, the teacher commented that J might be "sluggish" because he had a headache, and she described how he had used his picture exchange communication system (PECS) to form the sentence "I want medicine." The therapist immediately rescheduled the observation. When she arrived for the second time, a substitute teacher was present and after a few minutes, the therapist determined that the substitute was not a familiar person to J and was not prepared to demonstrate his work on the targeted objectives. A third observation was scheduled and completed the following week.

During the observation period, J demonstrated the ability to count three objects independently (after a verbal cue) and four to five objects with one to two verbal prompts from the teacher. He accurately matched color words to colors for red and blue with moderate cues for attention, and matched "yellow" to yellow objects in 1 of 3 trials. After the teacher demonstrated the sequencing of three pictures, J completed three sequences with moderate cues for the steps ("What picture comes next?") and minimal cues for attention.

Throughout the observation period, the teacher provided opportunities for J to indicate choices using his PECS notebook. He did so twice in four opportunities presented. When instructions came in two steps (i.e., "Take the yellow ball and put it in the tub marked 'yellow'"), J completed them with one verbal cue in 70% of trials.

During the observation, the teacher stated that J had particular trouble following directions when using scissors. The therapist asked her to demonstrate this and observed that once J had the scissors in his hand, he cut indiscriminately without demonstrating any attention to the instructions of the teacher.

Music therapy assessment session. The music therapist planned an assessment session based on the targeted objectives from J's IEP and the observations she had made in the classroom. The strategies she chose were as follows:

1.   Greeting song;
2.   The Matching Game (a song adapted to cue J to match colored objects to color words);
3.   Six Little Fish (a one-to-one correspondence counting song);
4.   The Cutting Song (composed specifically for this assessment session, the song provides verbal, melodic, and rhythmic cues to stop and listen while cutting);
5.   What Instrument? (a song that cues the student to choose instruments using an "I want" sentence);
6.   Take Me Out to the Ballgame (a picture book for the song and cards showing two 3-step sequences from a baseball game); and
7.   Closing/Goodbye song.

Results and report. J was cooperative and pleasant throughout the music therapy assessment session; he went with the therapist without protest and did not attempt to leave the assessment area during the session. However, J did not demonstrate any distinctive responses to music therapy strategies or stimuli. This lack of response manifested itself in several ways. First, J did not show any change in his physical posture or movement when the therapist played her guitar and sang in an upbeat, rhythmic fashion; neither did he respond to a quiet, flowing presentation. Second, J did not respond to interruptions in the music as a nonverbal cue for refocusing his attention; if he looked away from the music therapist or music therapy materials, a sudden silence did not provide a cue for him to look back.

Most importantly, J did not demonstrate improved accuracy or consistency on the targeted IEP objectives. He matched one color to the printed word in four trials. He required the same type of verbal cues to count to four, five, and six as he had in the classroom. The musical presentation of counting did not improve his recitation. J used his PECS notebook appropriately during the instrument song, but did not demonstrate any increase in initiation or speed, and he required the same number and type of verbal cues to create his sentence requests. Because the cutting song was new to J, the therapist demonstrated it, showing

J how to pause along with the pauses in the music. Once she handed the scissors to J, however, he demonstrated the same unfocused cutting that he had in the classroom. The music therapist changed tempo, volume and pitch of the song, and occasionally stopped suddenly. There were no changes in J's cutting motion. J did not make eye contact with the songbook for "Take Me Out to the Ballgame." He completed one of two sequences correctly, but did not do so when the instructions were sung; he completed the tasks only when the therapist provided verbal cues and physical prompts.

In the summary report for this assessment, the music therapist stated:

> J was cooperative and compliant throughout the music therapy session. He followed verbal instructions and responded to physical prompts with accuracy. He did not, however, demonstrate any significant responses to music as a structure for IEP-related tasks. There were no visible indications that J responded pleasurably to music in his environment, and he did not show any improvement in attention, responsiveness or accuracy when music was the basis for a task.

The therapist presented the report at a meeting of J's IEP team, having delivered copies of the report to several members of the team (including the parents) ahead of time. She did not recommend music therapy services, stating that the assessment indicated that music therapy was not necessary for J to benefit from his special education program. J's mother stated that, although she was disappointed that he would not receive services, she felt J had been "treated with respect," that she understood how the decision was made, and that she would not pursue this related service at the present time.

•

Assessment Case Study #2

B was a 9-year-old student diagnosed with mental retardation and autism. She was referred for a music therapy assessment by her IEP committee after repeated requests from her parents and threats of legal action. The assessing music therapist provided the team with a checklist outline of the SEMTAP and interviewed the student's mother and classroom teacher. The mother attempted to relate the history of her disagreements with the school district and asked the music therapist to view a 6-month-old videotape of the student playing in her room while listening to music. The music therapist explained that these things could not be considered in the eligibility assessment process.

In her interview, the classroom teacher stated that if she was having difficulty directing B to tasks, music was an effective tool and that B's best participation occurred during the morning "circle" time in which music was used frequently. She stated that it might be difficult to conduct a "non-musical" observation of B because music was used so often in the classroom.

Targeting objectives. Information gained in the interviews, as well as a review of B's IEP, resulted in the therapist's targeting the following objectives for B:

    I.   Attend to tasks with "good looking" eyes engaged 2 out of 3 times.

2.   Respond to two-part verbal request from adult (pair with sign then fade to verbal only).

3.   Pair sign with a functional work activity and a Mayer-Johnson picture.

4.   Vocalize using single words or approximations to match/replace nonverbal communication while attending.

Non-musical observation. Throughout the 90-minute observation time, B was cued using three methods: spoken instructions, sung instructions, and picture symbols. Overall, B responded to sung instructions more quickly than spoken ones approximately 50% of the time.

After completing her routine for arriving at school, B chose to work at the computer, and was given a program based on the song "If You're Happy and You Know It." She used an adapted keypad with large picture symbols; the keypad activated the computer program that included a digitized voice singing the song. Lyrics changed according to the pictures selected. B demonstrated enjoyment through smiles and clapping, and pushed the keypad without cues; however, she did not demonstrate the ability to follow a specific command related to the pictures (i.e., "Find the picture of the feet").

During the circle time that followed, B responded to moderate verbal cues and minimal physical cues in using her arms to approximate the signs the teacher demonstrated. Circle time activities included working on the calendar, identifying the day's weather, and dressing a large cutout of a bear for the day (appropriate to the season). B required maximal cuing to make choices, and she made good eye contact with the pictures used for the choices 25% of the time—with her better performance coming after sung instructions. During these activities, B frequently scooted her chair backwards, away from the teacher, requiring the teacher to move her back into the circle.

B required maximum spoken and sung cues to make a transition to her work station. The teacher worked 1:1 with her during this time with tasks that included (a) finding small candies under cups, (b) pulling apart plastic beads from one bin and placing them in a second bin, and (c) taking rings off a pole. B required maximum verbal (including sung) cuing for good eye contact with objects and completion of tasks.

Music therapy assessment session. Following is a list of strategies the therapist selected for the music therapy assessment:

1.   Greeting song (establishing vocal range; encouraging vocalization);

2.   How are you? (choosing a picture symbol; placing appropriately);

3.   "Goodnight Room" (using manipulatives, making choices);

4.   Instrument playing (following verbal, visual, and musical cues);

5.   "That Bear" (visually attending, using a switch, encouraging vocalization);

6.   "Fill the Basket" and "Ravioli" (making picture choices, following instructions);

7.   Body parts song (identifying body parts, following instructions);

8.   Work station song (maintaining focus on task).

The music therapy assessment session with B lasted 45 minutes.

B demonstrated significantly different responses during the music therapy session than those seen during the observation. Her eye contact with the therapist and with the manipulatives and instruments used was significantly more consistent than she had demonstrated during the observation period. Her accuracy in making choices was markedly better. She made significantly more vocalizations, and many more of them were accurate approximations of the lyrics. She was immediately responsive to contingent music: for making choices, for following one- and two-part instructions, and for moving between areas of the classroom. Finally, her ability to remain cooperative with a previously unknown person for almost 45 minutes of musical strategies was significant, given that she usually moves between activities in the classroom every 10 to 15 minutes.

The therapist presented the report at a meeting of B's IEP team, having delivered copies of the report to several members of the team (including the parents) ahead of time. She recommended music therapy services, stating that the assessment indicated that music therapy was necessary for B to benefit from her special education program. After the IEP meeting, the special education administrator for the district asked to meet with the therapist. During this meeting, in which the therapist took the administrator step-by-step through the SEMTAP report, the administrator stated, "I never understood the difference between the music the teacher uses in the classroom and music therapy. Now I do." A music therapist was hired by the school district to serve B and to provide consultant and assessment services to other classrooms in the district.

•

The Use of the SEMTAP for Independent Assessments

Over the past three years, the authors have had the opportunity to provide independent music therapy assessments for 22 students in 10 districts that, in most cases, had little or no experience with music therapy. The SEMTAP was used for each of these assessments. The students had a variety of disabilities and recommendations were varied. In only one case, however, did a district continue to refuse to provide service after the SEMTAP recommended it; and in only one case did the parents continue to fight for music therapy services after a recommendation against it by the assessing music therapist. In eight of these assessments, statements made by the district or by parents indicated conflict and/or animosity between the two. In some of these same situations, however, district representatives stated that the SEMTAP had educated them about the role of music therapy in special education. In three situations in which music therapy service was denied, parents expressed regret or sadness about the decision but did not pursue it further.

•

Conclusion

Increased publicity about the power of music and the efficacy of music therapy intervention likely will result in increased requests for music therapy services in public school special education. Music therapists must be prepared to guide parents and school districts in a step-by-step assessment process that respects the individual needs of each student while conforming to federal and state law. Our goal should not be to defend our profession through conflict and legal challenges, but rather to provide the education and professional standards that will make parent/district animosity and court cases rare.

A single, standardized test is not necessary to meet the standards of special education assessment. On the contrary, such an instrument may take the "individual" out of the Individualized Education Program. A standardized process, however, such as the SEMTAP can provide consistent, lucid recommendations in a format that educates parents and professionals about the unique role of music therapy as a related service in special education.

●

References

Alley, J. M. (1977). Education for the severely handicapped: The role of music therapy. Journal of Music Therapy, 14, 50–59.

Bateman, B. D. (1998). Better IEPs: How to develop legally correct and educationally useful programs. Longmont, CO: Sopris West.

Boxill, E. H. (1985). Music therapy for the developmentally disabled. Rockville, MD: Aspen Press.

Bruscia, K. E. (1987). Improvisational models of music therapy. Springfield, IL: Charles C. Thomas.

Gfeller, K., & Baumann, A. A. (1988). Assessment procedures for music therapy with hearing impaired children: Language development. Journal of Music Therapy, 25(4), 192–205.

Grant, R. E. (1995). Music therapy assessment for developmentally disabled clients. In T. Wigram, B. Saperston, & R. West (Eds.), The art and science of music therapy: A handbook. Switzerland: Harwood Academic.

Individuals with Disabilities Education Act Amendments (1997, 20 U.S.C. 1400).

Individuals with Disabilities Education Improvement Act of 2004, Final regulations, Federal Register 71(156) (2006).

Johnson, F. L. (1996). Models of service delivery. In B. Wilson (Ed.), Models of music therapy interventions in school settings: From institution to inclusion. Silver Spring, MD: National Association for Music Therapy.

Martin, R. (1991). Special education law in America: The rights of the student and the responsibilities of those who serve. Arlington, TX: Future Horizons.

Rider, M. (1981). The assessment of cognitive functioning level through musical perception. Journal of Music Therapy, 18, 110–119.

Chapter 6

Goals and Treatment Objectives, Settings, and Service Delivery Models for the School Age Years
Ruthlee Figlure Adler, MT-BC

Music reaches students who may be unreachable through other means. Students who may not respond to traditional teaching methods may have perfect pitch, "dance to the beat," or understand through melodic tones. Music helps us all to move and develop, but its rhythm resonates especially well for those with special needs in school settings.

•

Considerations

Age

Chronological Age

The school-age population typically encompasses children between the chronological ages of 5 and 18 years. In the special education system, services may begin as early as age 3 and continue until age 21. Many districts classify 3- to 5-year-olds as being part of a separate Early Childhood program, yet in other districts, students may enter kindergarten before their 5th birthdays. Elementary school usually refers to the grades of kindergarten through 5th grade, middle school years are usually grades 6–8, and high school encompasses grades 9–12. Some school districts, however, may determine different age parameters. This chapter will mainly focus on the school ages from kindergarten and beyond (note that kindergarteners also are included in chapters in this monograph that pertain to early childhood).

Developmental Age

Music therapists in the public sector often work with those students who are receiving special education support services. In many cases, their chronological ages may differ from their developmental ages. Therefore, the school grade for special education students often does not correspond with that of their peers who do not have special needs. Goals and objectives must be written to meet individual needs. However, sometimes group needs are addressed. Music activities and experiences need to be age appropriate. Furthermore, music therapists working in an education setting should be aware of national and state standards for arts education when working with a music therapy referral in an educational setting.

The National Standards for Arts Education

The *National Standards for Arts Education* (Consortium of National Arts Education, 1994) state what every young American, grades K–12, should be able to do and know in dance, music, theatre, and the visual arts. Written into federal law with the passage of *Goals 2000: Educate America Act*, their intent is to ensure that the arts are named as integral core subject areas in every student's academic education, regardless of ability. They are organized in three levels—grades K–4, 5–8, and 9–12—and include specific essential competencies guided by Content (knowledge) and Achievement (skills) Standards. However, they do not delineate how each competency is to be achieved. It is the responsibility of states, local school districts, and individual teachers to determine the curriculum and specific instructional activities necessary for students to attain these standards.

Content Standards

In the area of Music, there are nine broad Content Standards:
1.   Singing, alone or with others, a varied repertoire of music;
2.   Performing on instruments, alone and with others, a varied repertoire of music;
3.   Improvising melodies, variations, and accompaniments;
4.   Composing and arranging music within specified guidelines;
5.   Reading and notating music;
6.   Listening to, analyzing, and describing music;
7.   Evaluating music and music performances;
8.   Understanding relationships between music, the other arts, and disciplines outside the arts;
9.   Understanding music in relation to history and culture.

Achievement Standards

Achievement Standards are delineated under each Music Content Standard. In grades 9–12, standards are further divided into "Proficient" and "Advanced" levels. Every course in music, including performance courses, should provide instruction in creating, performing, listening to, and analyzing music, in addition to focusing on its specific subject matter (Consortium of National Arts Education, 1994).

State or Local Regulations

States, local school districts, and even individual schools may have specific rules and regulations that may influence and thus guide the way music therapists may be employed in an educational setting. It is imperative for the music therapist to stay abreast of policies and procedures that may affect job considerations.

Goals and Objectives

Most students who participate in music therapy will have a current Individualized Education Plan (IEP). As part of a student's IEP, these music therapy services will require ongoing evaluation and documentation for continuance, effectiveness, and mastery. In addition, the formal documents may require comparing the student's progress both with and without musical supports in the classroom or other specified setting.

Different school districts utilize varying formats documenting their IEPs. Some use computer programs that allow for a choice of pre-written goals and objectives. Music therapists may repeat the terminology used by their predecessors or other instructors in stating goals and objectives. It is important to realize that music therapy skills may need to be generalized to other settings to be considered effective.

Some IEP goals are dictated by the federal government and/or individual states (such as the *National Standards* mentioned earlier), as well as the goals mandated by the individual educational setting (e.g., public school district). Many states have standards in both music and academic areas (such as reading or math) that may be addressed via music therapy. When writing goals to include these standards, the music therapist needs to consider music therapy objectives, the student's IEP, developmental and chronological age, and tailored individualized needs.

Traditional Goals

Traditional goals encompass functional skills that are broad-based and provide targets for improvement. Major targeted goal areas may be classified as: Motor Development, Communication, Sensory Integration, Pre Cognitive and Cognitive Development (Academic), and Social/Emotional Interaction (Adler, 1988). The names of these domains may vary depending upon state or district terminology. Furthermore, states and school districts may require that additional domains be targeted (e.g., Functional, Daily Living, Vocational, Language and Literacy).

The examples of broad skill areas and specific related skills that follow may be applicable to more than one broad category. They are only listed in one area to avoid repetition.

Specific Targeted Objectives

Using the previously mentioned traditional goal areas, the music therapist may design or target clearly defined, measurable short-term objectives. Coleman and Brunk (2003) suggest using the acronym SMART when developing objectives. Each should be **S**pecific, **M**easurable, **A**ttainable, **R**ealistic, and must define a **T**ime frame for their achievement.

Music therapy services in the school setting are provided in time allotments that may be based on federal and local school district standards. For example, a student may be allocated "a total number of _____ sessions for a marking period, semester, or the entire school year," or "a _____ minute session, one time per week." The specified amount of time takes session length and frequency into account, with assessments allowing for "reasonable" progress. Regular written interval progress notes also may be requested. Sometimes music

Coleman and Brunk (2003) suggest using the acronym SMART when developing objectives. Each should be Specific, Measurable, Attainable, Realistic, and must define a Time frame for their achievement.

therapy may be combined with other services in a session using a team approach to goal achievement.

Motor Development

Motor Development is the growth of small and large motor skills necessary for one to function in his or her environment. Related Motor Skills may include:

- *Balance*: automatically shifting one's center of gravity while maintaining body positions. Balance is important in sustaining posture for seated tasks (e.g., writing and reading) as well as locomotor tasks, such as walking, running, hopping and dancing.

- *Bilateral Motor Coordination*: using both sides of the body together to execute a motor action. This includes jumping with both feet or clapping hands (symmetrical tasks), as well as playing a musical instrument with each hand doing something different, e.g., one hand holding or grasping a resonator bell while the other plays it with a mallet (asymmetrical task).

- *Eye–Hand Coordination*: the ability of the eyes to function as the guidance system in successfully performing gross and fine motor tasks. Examples could include signing, playing instruments, and manipulating objects.

- *Fine Motor*: tasks requiring precise, fine finger movements. Examples could include playing a keyboard or piano, strumming a guitar or autoharp with a pick or one's finger.

- *Gross Motor*: performing or imitating basic movement/motions using upper and lower extremities. Examples include moving spontaneously or reaching for an instrument or object.

- *Motor Planning*: being able to carry out and plan motor acts that are new or not habitual. Examples could include playing an instrument, imitating walks and dances. Music and words may act as reinforcements in this area, as well as assist with breaking the task into component parts.

- *Rhythm*: a consistently recurring movement with the same accent or beat. It can be the ability to follow the rhythm set by an instrument or handclapping, as well as the inner rhythm with which we move or walk.

Sample Motor Development Goals/Objectives

- *The student will purposefully grasp an instrument for _____ seconds/minutes . . .*
- *The student will imitate fine/gross motor movements . . .*
- *The student will perform a sequence of _____ movements . . .*
- *The student will reach to touch an instrument presented at midline . . .*

Communication

Communication is an individual's ability to share information, thoughts, and ideas with someone else. Related Communication Skills may include:

- *Auditory Discrimination*: the ability to distinguish one sound from another. It involves recognition of how high or low a sound is (pitch), how loud or quiet (dynamics or intensity), how long it lasts (rhythm), and the beat (meter). Auditory discrimination is a prerequisite to reading and making sound symbol associations.
- *Auditory Memory*: remembering what is heard, such as song lyrics, the sound of an instrument, a musical selection, or a vocal sound. The ability to follow directions is a significant factor associated with good auditory memory.
- *Auditory/Visual Reception*: the ability to give meaning to what is heard based upon previous experiences.
- *Following Directions*: the ability to carry out and retain (either from being shown or told) a sequence of things to do in the correct order. This can include performing a dance routine or playing a piece on an instrument. Following Directions includes all the communication components (e.g., discrimination, reception, interpretation, and the ability to then process and carry out a response).
- *Non-Verbal Expression*: the ability to respond to or imitate verbal directions, inner feelings or music through gestures, facial expression, signing, playing instruments, movement, or by using picture symbols, props, art, or drama. Without using speech, the student is encouraged to listen to the rhythm, mood, and tempo of the music in order to understand the concepts or feelings created and then respond.
- *Sound Localization*: being able to identify the source of sound. This enables the student to focus attention while being aware of the constant environmental stimuli that are ever present.
- *Verbal Expression*: responding or imitating orally to a visual, sensory, or auditory stimulus by initiating or repeating words, sentences, or phrases. Musically, students choose songs or instruments, answer questions, and fill in the blanks or phrases when original or specific answers are requested.
- *Vocal Expression/Singing*: the ability to respond or imitate orally by using speech sounds, humming, or singing.

Sample Communication Goals/Objectives

- *The student will produce vocal sounds . . .*
- *The student will imitate vocalizations . . .*
- *The student will create song lyrics . . .*
- *The student will sing _____ songs from memory . . .*

Sensory Integration

Sensory *Processing* is the ability to take in information from all our senses and sort it out appropriately so that we can accurately interpret our environment (Gambrel & Allgood,

2000). It includes visual, tactile, auditory, vestibular, and proprioceptive processing (Ayers, 1979). Sensory *Integration* is the process of receiving information about the world around us with all our senses and from inside our bodies. Through integrating and organizing all these senses—auditory, kinesthetic, visual, olfactory, taste, gravity, and movement—we are able to interact comfortably and efficiently at work or play, as well as in caring for ourselves and others. Music is able to invoke all our senses.

Related Sensory Integration Skills may include:

- *Auditory Perception*: the process that enables an individual to understand what is heard and respond to changes. Starting or stopping on cue, adjusting body movements and rhythm to the music, and distinguishing between sound and no sound are examples of Auditory Perception.

- *Body Awareness/Image*: realization or knowledge of one's body (e.g., identifying body parts and how to use them, and knowing that the body has two sides). Music provides a safe setting for movement exploration through rhythm, melody, and lyrics while stimulating the senses.

- *Imitation*: the ability to mimic, copy, or follow a behavior, reproducing a motor or verbal action. In music, the student may imitate singing, as well as small and large body movements.

- *Relaxation*: the act of resting, loosening muscles and lessening tension. Music provides the framework for relaxing one's muscles and mind. Art and drama also may be used in conjunction with music to achieve this same purpose.

- *Tactile/Kinesthetic Perception*: an awareness of information coming from one's skin. Playing instruments, clapping, and moving stimulate these senses. The student responds in dance or movement through the tactile/ kinesthetic system to music heard through the auditory system.

- *Visual Perception*: the process that enables an individual to understand, attend to and recall what is seen. Visual perception can be reinforced in music with picture symbols (pic syms), signing, hand signals, pictures, facial expression, color-coding, and body movement.

Sample Sensory Integration Goals/Objectives

- *The student will respond to auditory and tactile stimulation . . .*
- *The student will enhance visual tracking skills (used in reading) by following the printed note line across the page while playing the melody on an instrument . . .*
- *The student will play instruments appropriately . . .*

Cognitive and Cognitive Development (Academics)

Pre Cognitive and Cognitive Development involve generalizing information obtained from gross and fine motor skills, communication, and the senses into other situations. Music may provide effective additional practice via a multi-sensory hands-on approach. Music may also introduce concepts and offer opportunities for repetition and the creation of original ideas.

Related Cognitive Skills may include:

- *Colors*: a totally visual concept. In music, colors can be used to provide visual cues for playing instruments, reading scores, or starting, stopping, sequencing, and learning songs. Auditorily, music reinforces learning to name and discriminate colors.

- *Creativity*: the art of doing something that has not been thought of or experienced previously. Creative movement, as well as using instruments and other artistic media to express inner thoughts and feelings, may be inspired by music.

- *Directionality*: the ability to use and internalize concepts and prepositions relating to one's position (e.g., left/right, up/down, forward/backward, near/far, in front/behind). Scale pitches, the contour of a melody, and movement activities musically reinforce these concepts.

- *Figure/Ground Perception*: the ability to focus auditorily/visually on relevant stimuli while screening out irrelevant sounds and sights. These attending behaviors may be developed through playing musical instruments, singing a round, and performing specific actions.

- *Form and Space Perception*: the ability to understand and distinguish the relationship of objects in space, to oneself, and each other. The ability to distinguish musical instruments and notes, as well as matching, recognizing, and sorting shapes is form perception. Spatial perception includes understanding size, distance, and position to organize ourselves in our environment and move from one place to another.

- *Numbers/Letters*: Music and rhythm instruments may be used for developing number concepts and one-to-one correspondence, and understanding directions (e.g., first, second, and third) (Adler, 1988). Numbers and letters also may serve as cues for playing instruments, reading music, and developing a sense of rhythm. Furthermore, songs may teach and reinforce the actual learning of numbers and letters.

- *Opposites*: concepts that help us relate and understand environmental happenings. Musical opposites include quiet/loud, fast/slow, up/down, and high/low.

- *Sequencing*: the ability to recall the order of words or verses in a song, details in a story, daily routines, and a series of events. Sequencing is an essential skill for playing an instrument, performing movements or dances, and following directions.

Social Interaction

Social Interaction is learning to play and work together, internalizing judgments and values of society and culture, and knowing how to approach others.

Related Social Interaction Skills include:

- *Awareness of Self*: knowing oneself as a unique and separate person. Music provides opportunities to sing about oneself, perform with movement and on instruments, thus enhancing one's feelings of self worth.

- *Awareness of Others*: becoming more conscious of other people. Music provides opportunities to observe the behavior of other group members, to hold hands, pass and share instruments, and participate in activities with others.

- *Expression of Feelings*: being able to make known—verbally and nonverbally—one's reactions to a situation. Music may provide an outlet for expression through movement, drawing to music, singing, drama experiences using gestures, and facial expressions.

- *Group Participation*: to take part with others. Playing instruments, singing, moving or dancing, and other musical experiences provide opportunities for all ages to participate together in group settings.

- *Peer Interaction*: learning to appropriately respond and approach others in the same age group or classroom. Music sets a framework for peer interaction (e.g., waiting a turn, sharing instruments, singing and talking to one another, watching and listening).

- *Self-Help Skills*: daily living activities that enable one to function independently in society. Signing, playing instruments, and musical finger plays enhance necessary fine motor skills. Songs may include lyrics that refer to actions, time of day, and other basic daily skills. (Adler, 1988)

Refer to Chapter 13 of this monograph for more information about developing goals and objectives that utilize technology, adaptations, and augmentative tools. For more information on specific treatment objectives, see *Multimodal Psychiatric Music Therapy* by Michael and Julia Cassity (1994). Their music therapy interventions can be easily adapted for writing special treatment objectives with the school age population.

●

Types of Service Delivery Models in the School-Age Educational Setting

Music therapists working in school-age educational settings may deliver services via a specific model or a combination of models. Three models common to educational settings are Direct Services, In-Service Education, and Consulation.

Direct Service

Direct music therapy services may be delivered in several ways. The following are optional types of direct service found in schools:

- Conducting music therapy sessions with individuals or classes;
- Working with or assisting an assigned music educator for a self- contained classroom ;
- Providing a child with necessary skills for future integration into a classroom setting ;
- Accompanying a student with special needs to regular music education class to assess skills and provide assistance for further instruction.

In-Service Education

At times, music therapy services may include or be limited to educating others about the strategies of using music with students:

- Consulting with or teaching educators strategies or techniques for successful inclusion (e.g., adapting instruments and equipment, simplifying musical arrangements);
- Developing augmentative devices and showing teachers how to incorporate music therapy strategies into their regular classroom instruction;
- Demonstrating effective ways for music to be embedded into the regular academic curriculum.

Consultation

In a consultative model, music therapists may be responsible for:

- Assisting staff in the implementation, design, and development of appropriate music programs for teachers or therapists of students with special needs;
- Demonstrating appropriate programs for music educators of students receiving special education services.

Settings

Music therapists work with clients in many settings and situations. We may see students individually, in small or large groups, in self-contained classrooms, in inclusion settings, and in integrated groupings. In addition to the settings described here in more detail, music therapists at times may be called upon to deliver extant educational services in hospital, residential, or community placements, or in private practice.

One-on-One Sessions

Clinical music therapists may see clients individually, in a "pull-out services" model instead of in the classroom setting. In other situations, students may receive one-on-one music therapy in addition to regular classroom music. Private sessions may be held in a music therapy studio, with recommended time duration of 45–60 minutes once a week, or two 30-minute sessions. Delivering music therapy services in this manner offers the advantages of working at each individual's pace and helping the student progress at a faster rate. Generally, the private practice sessions are in conjunction with or build upon the IEP and educational team goals for each client. Additional music therapy goals and objectives may be added to reinforce other areas of skill development. Families and health care providers are part of the process and are encouraged to incorporate music goals into family daily lives and the community at large. Private practice clients may continue to receive music therapy service far beyond their school age years.

Small and Large Groups

Music therapists frequently are called upon to conduct small and large group music therapy sessions. In this role, it is advantageous for the music therapist to create compatible groups comprised of students who have similar strengths and needs, complementary goals and objectives, and can benefit by learning and sharing while working with others. Increased self-esteem comes from being in a group setting with appropriate behavior role models, hopefully leading to increased receptivity to participate in new social situations.

Inclusion

The placement, when deemed appropriate, of a student with an IEP into activities and classes with his or her typically developing peers is called *inclusion*. It is viewed on a continuum from partial to full inclusion. In the former, special education students may be mainstreamed into a general classroom for participation in music, art, physical education, lunch, recess, assemblies, or other special events. For the remainder of their school day, they receive instruction in their self-contained educational classrooms where their individual needs are addressed. In full inclusion settings, special education students are placed in typical education classrooms for the entire school day. An inclusion specialist may team teach the class or make supervised adaptations. In other cases, students may have their own individual educational aides (paraprofessionals) who also assist with program adaptation and implementation.

The placement, when deemed appropriate, of a student with an IEP into activities and classes with his or her typically developing peers is called inclusion. It is viewed on a continuum from partial to full inclusion.

The music therapist needs to consider the individual student's inclusion program when determining goals and objectives. The music therapist plays an integral part as a member of the interdisciplinary team, working with the student's parents as well as the staff and therapists. The role of the music therapist also may include providing input regarding cultural opportunities within the community that might be appropriate for the students.

Integrated Group Music Experiences

Examples of Integrated Group Music Experiences include, but are not limited to: choral groups, instrumental groups and ensembles (e.g., high school band), as well as expressive arts groups (e.g., musical productions). Frequently, these groups have opportunities to perform within their educational settings, as well as in the larger community.

Creating and sharing age-appropriate music with general education peers is extremely important for all students, regardless of ability. Music therapists can facilitate this process by:

- Providing student (or staff) mentors—a role model or assistant who accompanies the student during practice, performances, as well as during free time whenever possible (this person could be a music therapy intern or volunteer working in the classroom).
- Modifying music notation—
  - using letter names for notes versus reading traditional music notation.
  - enlarging and/or highlighting lyrics for those with visual impairments.
  - teaching key phrases—allowing for repetition that helps the student internalize language and basic concepts.
  - simplifying arrangements—striving for quality not quantity.
- Including opportunities for listening and practicing with recorded music (e.g., providing audio practice tapes or CDs to be used in the classroom, during free time, and at home).
- Exposing students to concerts and performances in the community.
- Creating original musical productions incorporating the creative ideas and energy of the students.
- Combining music therapy groups with music groups from a neighboring school or setting (working cooperatively with the music personnel in advance to create a compatible, successful program for all participants).

Tools to Facilitate Goals and Objectives and Enhance Learning

> ### A Bag of Tools
>
> *"Isn't it strange*
> *That princes and kings,*
> *And clowns that caper*
> *In sawdust rings,*
> *And common people*
> *Like you and me*
> *Are builders for eternity?*
>
> *Each is given a bag of tools*
> *A shapeless mass,*
> *A book of rules;*
> *And each must make*
> *Ere life is flown*
> *A stumbling block*
> *Or a stepping stone."*
>
> Poem by R. Lee Sharpe

As effective clinical practices music therapist, regardless of the population or setting in which you are employed, you will need your own "Bag of Tools" ready and available. The following is a representative sample for the school-age educational setting.

Musical Instruments That Offer Multiple Learning Opportunities
- *Traditional rhythm instruments* such as drums, sticks, tambourines, eggs, wood blocks, maracas, shakers, musical spoons, cymbals, castanets, ocean drum.
- *Melody instruments* such as bells, autoharp, Omnichord, Qchord, chimalong, Orff instruments (xylophones, metallophones, glockenspiels), tone chimes, resonator bells, precorders, recorders, horns, keyboard, guitar.
- *Ethnic multicultural instruments* such as agogo bells, bongos, djembe, afuche, claves, conga, guiro, kalimba, kokoriko, buffalo drum, tubano, slit log drums, rainstick, steel drum.

Motivators and Props for Specific Goal Areas
- *Movement motivators* such as scarves, streamers, jump ropes, kites, hula-hoops, bean bags, balls.
- *Communication motivators* such as puppets, masks, mirrors, hats, costumes, white gloves to use with black lights, bubbles, whistles, bottles, kazoos, harmonicas, jugs, augmentative tools.
- *Sensory integration motivators* such as lotion, texture cards, seashells, kaleidoscope, feathers, wash cloths, glasses or bottles with water, boxes with rubber bands, containers filled with popcorn or beans, musical combs;

things that have interesting sound effects such as clickers, bird sounds, recorded sounds.

- *Cognition motivators* such as color, number, shape, letter and word cards, picture symbols, visuals, fruit and vegetable shakers.
- *Social intervention motivators* such as parachute, boomwhackers, paddle drums with balls or shuttle cocks, gathering drum.

Other items, though not actual "tools," are helpful to have on hand. Consider accumulating rubber bands, tissues, clothespins, Velcro, masking tape, colored markers and charts, safety pins, rubber gloves, sterile wipes, paper towels, and room deodorizer.

•

A Music Therapy Case Study

Jenny and Sam (all names have been changed to protect students' privacy privileges) were two 13-year-old students with autism, who had participated in one-on-one sessions in private practice, as well as in integrated groups at school. They were enrolled in a self-contained classroom and did not interact with other students except during music therapy activities such as choral groups and plays. Sam, an excellent reader, initially received only "roles" that were completely separate from the other group members, such as reading a poem or a few solo lines. Jenny loved to sing, but was very quiet, almost whispering, when she was with others in any peer setting.

Through coordinated efforts among the music therapist, special education teachers, and paraprofessionals (who accompanied the students to all group rehearsals), both Jenny and Sam eventually were able to actively participate in choral concerts and the end-of-the-year middle school musical. Each memorized lines, sang lyrics, and became active members in both settings.

Their music therapy goals and objectives included socially working as members of a group, following directions, creating music together, and performing as part of an ensemble. In addition, they were given the opportunity to appropriately express and define their emotions and feelings to their peers and staff members while further developing their speech and language skills.

Both Jenny and Sam have supportive parents and siblings who helped promote the transfer and generalization of these skills into their home environments and beyond. Jenny was able to perform a piano duet and sing a solo at a group music event and is now singing in a strong voice with her church choir in the community.

•

Coda

While terminology and style may vary by individual and setting, all music therapists will be guided by the needs and thereby the pre-determined goals and objectives of the students. Bear in mind that every student is unique. It is the music therapist's responsibility to provide the services each student needs to grow, learn, and be successful. Always look at the whole person and the opportunity music provides in enhancing development in all skill areas, from gross and fine motor to communication, sensory integration, cognition, and social interaction.

Traditional goals and specific targeted objectives, as well as arts and state standards, must be considered when designing treatment plans. Always do what is in the best interest of the student. Remember that the key to what music therapy services the student requires is the effect his or her disability has on the educational environment. Whether the placement is in an individual, small or large group, inclusion, or integrated setting, be prepared to share your musical expertise and the unique role of music therapy in these settings via direct service, in-service training, or consultation.

Use your creativity to constantly find exciting new ways to educate your school-aged students. For successful music experiences with exceptional students, special accommodations and modifications are frequently required. By providing diverse opportunities for creativity and discovery, we can design and implement goals and objectives that will affect profound changes and growth in our students. We, as professionals, will learn from them and grow, too, as we experience and create music together.

●

References

Adler, R. (1988). Target on music: Activities to enhance learning through music. Rockville, MD: Ivymount School.

Ayers, J. A. (1979). Sensory integration and the child. Los Angeles: Western Psychological Services.

Cassity, M. D., & Cassity, J. E. (1994). Multimodal psychiatric music therapy for adolescents and children: A clinical manual. St. Louis, MO: MMB Music.

Coleman, K., & Brunk, B. (2003). SEMTAP Special Education Music Therapy Assessment Process Handbook. Grapevine, TX: Prelude Music Therapy.

Consortium of National Arts Education. (1994). National Standards for Arts Education Dance–Music–Theatre–Visual Arts. Reston, VA: MENC.

Gambrel, M., & Allgood, N. (2000, November). Music therapy and sensory integration for children and autism. Paper presented at the national conference of the American Music Therapy Association, St. Louis, MO.

Goals 2000: Education America Act. (n.d.). Retrieved June 20, 2006, from http://www.ed.gov/legislation/GOALS2000/TheAct/index.html

Chapter 7

Goals and Treatment Objectives, Settings, and Service Delivery Models in Early Childhood and Early Intervention Settings

Amelia Greenwald Furman, MM, RMT; Marcia E. Humpal, MEd, MT-BC

In 1975, landmark federal legislation assured a free appropriate education to all children. In 1986, P.L. 99-457 extended the provisions of this law, thus providing services for young children with disabilities between the ages of 3–5. Amendments, additional educational programs, and recommended policies were developed in the years following these initial mandates. Now state as well as federal regulations direct how services may be provided to children from birth (see Chapter 3). A vital part of delivering effective clinical practice services to young children is determining appropriate goals and objectives that will guide their programs. This chapter will focus on ways that music therapists approach formulating goals when working in early childhood and early intervention educational settings.

●

Settings

The actual education of young children considered at-risk or having special needs may take place in a variety of locations. Public, private and parochial schools, as well as multi-district programs, may provide services. For the purpose of this chapter, the term *educational setting* will be used, recognizing that early childhood services may be delivered in an array of places (e.g., traditional schools, Head Start sites, the home, or wherever a program is located).

Regularly Scheduled Classes in an Early Childhood Center or School

Within a school setting, many types of early childhood classes may be present. Some examples of these are:

- *Inclusion*: The majority of children are developing typically; a few have IFSP or IEP driven programs.
- *Reverse inclusion* (sometimes called reverse mainstreaming): The majority of children have special needs; a few are peer models.

- *Integrated*: Children spend most of their time in self-contained special education classes but may share certain classes (such as music) with students from another classroom.
- *Self-contained*: All students are receiving special education services.

In addition, music therapists may work with children on an *individual* basis in an educational setting.

Regularly scheduled classes or sessions may be determined by the child's age (such as Infant, Toddler, Preschool, or Kindergarten) or by type of specialized program offered by the center (e.g., a class for children with Autism Spectrum Disorder or who are deaf/hard of hearing, or a course for parents and children). Furthermore, some classes may be noncategorical or cross-categorical in nature. Music therapy may not look the same in each class. Some classes may be somewhat structured, while others may be quite improvisational and child-directed. To insure consistency and meet the needs of the students, music therapists need to know how each class is routinely conducted as well as techniques that may be unique to specific programs. It is imperative to learn as much as possible about specialized methodologies or educational trends that are offered in the setting. For students with Autism Spectrum Disorder (ASD), there are numerous programs such as Picture Exchange Communication System (PECS), Treatment and Education of Autistic and Communication Handicapped Children (TEACCH), and Greenspan Floor Time. All of these programs have extensive training connected with them. For students in a Deaf/Hard of Hearing program, there may be cued speech or different types of sign language.

Music therapists are ancillary staff members and need to function as part of a team. Music therapy is the therapy that can reinforce all other therapies, but we must be aware of goals and strategies that are being implemented in all aspects of the child's programming in order to remain consistent and effective.

Family-based Settings

Part C of IDEA discusses services to infants and toddlers, birth through 2 years of age. For those children and their families, the Individualized Family Service Plan (IFSP) documents and guides the early intervention process. It contains information about the services necessary to facilitate a child's development and enhance the family's capacity to facilitate the child's development. The IFSP process is designed to have family members and service providers work as a team to plan, implement, and evaluate services tailored to the family's unique concerns, priorities, and resources.

Music therapists may serve as consultants to families of children birth through age 2, offering music strategies to the family or to other team members. They may provide direct service in educational centers, in the community, or on an individual basis.

Music therapy is the therapy that can reinforce all other therapies, but we must be aware of goals and strategies that are being implemented in all aspects of the child's programming in order to remain consistent and effective.

·

Guidelines and Standards

Developmentally Appropriate Practice

The National Association for the Education of Young Children (NAEYC) has a long history of research development and dissemination of information pertaining to young children. NAEYC's mission is to promote high-quality, developmentally appropriate programs for all children and their families. Their principles of practice are based on goals that address children's present needs as well as the attainment of skills that will guide them into adulthood. NAEYC strives to nurture personal characteristics that will help children develop into adults who contribute to a peaceful, prosperous, and democratic society. Developmentally Appropriate Practice (D.A.P.) recognizes that acquiring knowledge of human development and learning, individual characteristics and experiences, and social as well as cultural contexts is a dynamic process—for adults who work with young children as well as for the children themselves (Copple & Bredekamp, 1997).

Standley and Hughes (1996) documented that objectives and activity components in music therapy sessions for early intervention may effectively adhere to developmentally appropriate curriculum guidelines. Results indicated that children were able to sustain attention at a very high level during music activities. Furthermore, music therapy sessions simultaneously engaged children in social, motor, and cognitive tasks, utilizing strategies that were both developmentally and age appropriate.

See Chapter 12 for a more extensive discussion of D.A.P. and how this philosophy shapes the delivery of music therapy services to young children.

Early Learning Standards

Many factors impact what goals and objectives may be selected for a preschool student, and also how music therapists will construct and develop their goals and objectives. Music therapists should understand and adhere to standards and language that are in line with those of the rest of the interdisciplinary team.

Good Start/Grow Smart, a federal interagency early childhood program, encourages the development of state Early Learning Standards that align with existing state K–12 education standards. To find standards that pertain to your state, check your state department of education website and look under pre-kindergarten standards. These standards are in place for ages 3–5; a number of states also have developed, or are in the process of developing, infant and toddler standards. The guidelines specify what students should know when entering kindergarten. As these guidelines change and preschool screening forms are revised, the goals and objectives developed to assure that early childhood special education (ECSE) students will be successful in kindergarten will need to be revised accordingly.

These Early Learning standards are similar to traditional targeted domains, but they are described using language that is specific to early childhood education. In the past, early childhood goal areas typically were listed as communication, cognitive/academic, motor (fine and gross), and social or self-help/functional. After reviewing educational standards that align with those in grades K–12, several states now list prekindergarten areas as personal/ social, language and literacy, mathematical thinking, creative expression (the arts), and physical development. Furthermore, many preschool settings may include play goals for each child. These domain descriptors may vary state by state and even between agencies.

Literacy/prereading as well as math curricula sets now are available for preschool programs. These are created and marketed by the same companies that provide K–12 curricula. In following the educational trends in the upper grades, some preschool programs have a circle or group time dedicated to working on math and literacy skills. In some districts, Early Childhood Education, Early Childhood Family Education (ECFE), and Early Childhood Special Education (ECSE) departments have discussed separating the traditional cognitive/ academic goals into math and preliteracy goals for students at age 3. Studies by Standley and Hughes (1997) and Register (2001) indicate that music therapy may significantly enhance the attainment of print concepts and prewriting objectives.

Prekindergarten Music Standards

Music therapists who work with young children should also be aware of the *Prekindergarten Music Standards* developed by the MENC: The National Association for Music Education. These standards provide a framework for planning music experiences for all children age 2–4, regardless of where programs are located (MENC, 1995).

When *Goals 2000: Educate America Act* was passed in 1994, the arts were listed as a core subject in which students must demonstrate competence. An MENC task force developed music content and achievement standards spanning prekindergarten to grade 12. The standards for prekindergarten define what children should know and be able to demonstrate by the time they enter kindergarten. These achievement standards are:

1. Singing and Playing Instruments:
    *   Children use their voices expressively as they speak, chant, and sing.
    *   Children sing a variety of simple songs in various keys, meters, and genres, alone and with a group, becoming increasingly accurate in rhythm and pitch.
    *   Children experiment with a variety of instruments and other sound sources.
    *   Children play simple melodies and accompaniments on instruments.
2. Creating Music:
    *   Children improvise songs to accompany their play activities.
    *   Children improvise instrumental accompaniments to songs, recorded selections, stories, and poems.
    *   Children create short pieces of music using voices, instruments, and other sound sources.
    *   Children invent and use original graphic or symbolic systems to represent vocal and instrumental sounds and musical ideas.

3.   Responding to Music:
  •   Children identify the sources of a wide variety of sounds.
  •   Children respond through movement to music of various tempos, meters, dynamics, modes, genres, and styles to express what they hear and feel in works of music.
  •   Children participate freely in music activities.
4.   Understanding Music:
  •   Children use their own vocabulary and standard music vocabulary to describe voices, instruments, music notation, and music of various genres, styles, and periods from diverse cultures.
  •   Children sing, play instruments, move, or verbalize to demonstrate awareness of the elements of music and changes in their usage.
  •   Children demonstrate an awareness of music as a part of daily life.

[From National Standards for Arts Education. Copyright ©1994 by Music Educators National Conference (MENC). Used by permission. The complete National Arts Standards and additional materials relating to the Standards are available from MENC: The National Association for Music Education, 1806 Robert Fulton Drive, Reston, VA 20191.]

•

Service Delivery Models

Music therapy services in early intervention settings usually are delivered either as a specific service called for on the child's IEP or IFSP, or as part of programmatic services.

Music Therapy Services Driven by the IEP and IFSP

If music therapy is determined to be appropriate by the team, specific goals, objectives, or outcomes relating to music therapy will be written for the child's IEP or IFSP. Children may receive direct music therapy services in a 1:1 setting. However, if building skills in a group situation is indicated, the group itself is structured to meet these individual children's needs (refer to examples of specific music therapy goals and objectives later in this chapter).

Public Law mandates that each IEP or IFSP contain the following elements for each service: assessments or evaluation determining the need for service, information about present level of function, as well as goals specific to that area. The child's needs as well as where these needs will be met influence what goals and objectives will be developed for the child.

When developing appropriate goals, objectives, and outcomes for young children, it is important to consider the differences between the IEP and the IFSP (see Figure 20):

DIFFERENCES BETWEEN THE IEP AND IFSP	
IEP	IFSP
Emphasis is on product.	Emphasis is on the process.
Assessment is of the child only.	Family's strengths, needs and priorities are considered.
Develops goals (and perhaps objectives).	Develops goals/outcomes and services/actions.
The child's goals are derived primarily from assessments conducted by professionals.	Goals/outcomes are derived primarily from the family's concerns and are written in the language presented by the family.
Performance goals are written for the child.	Goals/outcomes are written for the child and the family.

Figure 20. Differences Between the IEP and IFSP. Source: Cuyahoga County Board of Mental Retardation and Developmental Disabilities [CCBMR/DD], 1992.

Programmatic Music Therapy Service Delivery

Programmatic services are those services offered as part of the scheduled day for all children in the program, a course that is offered in the community, or as an adjunct to programs offered by other specialists in a clinic or music school program (Furman, 2002; Hughes, Rice, DeBedout, & Hightower, 2002; Humpal, 2002). While the music therapist may be addressing global goals of specific children, his or her main responsibility may be to provide group music therapy that is programmatic in nature. Keeping in mind each child's needs, the music therapist plans and implements sessions as well as engineers the music environment in a way that supports established educational standards, themes, and curricula being emphasized throughout the child's entire educational environment.

The music (and how the therapist uses it) addresses these goals through various aspects of *singing* (or using the voice), *playing* (with instruments or props such as scarves or other objects that aid in expression), *moving*, and *listening*. Though he or she often presents the music experiences to a group, the music therapist is guided by the responses of the individual children.

Delivering music therapy services through a programmatic approach presents many challenges. Often, the ability levels of the children are extremely diverse and several different goals need to be addressed. Time is extremely limited. Planning for this type of service delivery requires a working knowledge of pre-K music standards as well as curricula and methodology being used in the particular agency, facility, and classroom. It is important to recognize that federal regulations are interpreted and specified at the state level, and then each district develops policies and forms. Each building and team has a culture or style that further impacts how services are provided, and goals and objectives are written.

Educational settings that have music therapists on staff may require that each class in the facility receive music therapy in a regularly scheduled classroom session. The music therapy class time may be used to meet contractual agreements for teacher preparation or break times. Furthermore, in order to meet requirements of some state boards of education, music therapists hired into a salaried position in a school district may need a teaching license. When investigating a position in an educational setting, be sure to inquire about certification or licensure requirements.

The realities of trying to maintain an integrated team approach have become more difficult in recent times. Budget cuts requiring reduction of staff, staff changes due to seniority, larger case loads, and the demands of third party billing for occupational therapy,

One of the great benefits of programmatic music therapy services is that the music therapist can design environments and opportunities for building groups skills.

physical therapy, and speech services all effect the amount of time staff may have for collaborating in the classroom. In addition, lack of space in buildings as well as mandates requiring more and more paperwork limit opportunities for informal teaming.

One of the great benefits of programmatic music therapy services is that the music therapist can design environments and opportunities for building group skills. Children with special needs may often receive services in 1:1 settings. When given the opportunity for group music therapy experiences, these children can develop skills for succeeding in future inclusion and school experiences or settings in the community (such as family education programs, church or park programs). For example, if the music therapist also has a pre-kindergarten group of typical students, the ECSE students can gradually begin to be included, thus making the transition to a larger group. Having the opportunity to encourage flexibility and pre-train skills helps the children feel successful. Their peers see them as capable and competent. The learning sequence is then complete.

C. was interested in being with other children, but easily became over stimulated in group settings. Once aroused, he had difficulty with self-regulation. The team decided that an appropriate goal for C. would be to calmly take part in group activities.

The music therapist structured her objectives and sessions with C. to gradually help him accept larger groups and more stimulating environments.

Initially, 4 to 6 students worked on playing and stopping with recorded and live music. Next, a stretchy cord (theraband tied in a circle) was used while the children were seated and listening to folk dance music with slow and fast sections (e.g., "The Shoemaker" or "Mexican Hat Dance"). The cord helped all students move to different tempos as appropriate. Greg and Steve songs, such as "A Walking," were used to facilitate moving in different ways to assorted tempos.

When C. was able to participate without difficulty, the group size was increased and typically developing peers were added to provide additional models. C. developed a repertoire of songs and activities that required self-regulation to transition between active and quiet sections within the same activity. Music therapy helped him master objectives that led to the attainment of his goal.

Some districts list programmatic music therapy as a service on the IFSP or the IEP; some do not. Nevertheless, programmatic music therapy is an integral part of services for the child. Music therapy that is delivered via this integrated therapeutic model is a valuable and viable approach to meeting students' needs (Chester, Holmberg, Lawrence, & Thurmond, 1999; Furman, 2002; Kern, 2004).

•

Goals and Objectives on the IEP

Goals are broadly written to focus on the skills and behaviors the student needs to learn. They should relate to the present level of performance and should be reasonably accomplished within a 12-month time frame. Objectives, sometimes called benchmarks, usually note the targeted behavior, criteria level (e.g., 4/5, 80%), evaluation schedule (e.g., weekly, monthly), and person responsible. The number of objectives written for each child may vary. IDEA 2004 requires that minimal goals be written on the IEP (see Chapter 3), and short term objective benchmarks are no longer required. However, some educational settings require two or more objectives that demonstrate a step-wise approach to attaining the stated goal. Style of writing also may be dictated by district policy. The following discussion is divided into the following ways in which music therapy can be incorporated into the IEP: as Integrated Goals/Objectives across disciplines for Programmatic Music Therapy, as Programmatic Goals on an IEP, and as Specific Music Therapy Goals/Objectives on the IEP. Examples represent various styles of writing, possible domain and goal areas (several optional domain descriptors are noted), as well as potential objectives or outcomes. How to write an activity sequence of instructional programs if required by the district also is described.

Integrated Goals and Objectives Across Disciplines for Programmatic Music Therapy

After the entire team devises the best treatment model, goals and objectives may be written across disciplines so that generalization may occur as part of the teaching process. The music therapist may be part of a child's global goal that has been written by the classroom teacher or another specialist. When an integrated programmatic approach is followed, music therapy may be noted either as a strategy or as a specific service under goals and objectives on the IEP.

Personal/Social/Communication/Language and Literacy
Goal: To increase group participation skills, including remaining with the group, physical participation and expressive language.

Objective: (Child) will listen to directions and participate appropriately with physical and verbal responses for up to 15 minutes with minimal adult cues in 2 out of 3 opportunities during groups as measured weekly by classroom teacher, speech clinician, and music therapist.

Objective: (Child) will accept new activities and materials during sessions while maintaining participation and attention with no more than 3 prompts during the activity; measured weekly by classroom teacher, speech clinician, and music therapist.

Personal/Social/Emotional

Goal: To increase socially appropriate interactions with adults and peers and decrease aggressions toward self and others.

Objective: Given proper wait time, (Child) will appropriately communicate his wants and needs (e.g., "I need a break," or "I need help," or "I'm all done") with no aggressions (i.e., hitting, throwing) with no more than 2 prompts and with 75% accuracy as measured weekly by the classroom teacher, speech clinician, and music therapist.

Objective: (Child) will sustain attention to an activity/stimulus for a minimum of 5 minutes with no more than 2 prompts and with 75% accuracy as measured weekly by the classroom teacher, speech clinician, and music therapist.

Objective: (Child) will independently initiate 75% of functional phrases without verbal, visual, or melodic/rhythmic cueing as measured weekly by the classroom teacher, speech clinician, and music therapist.

Mathematical Thinking/Cognitive/Academic/Pre-academic

Goal: To increase awareness of 1·1 correspondence and the concepts of "more than" and "less than."

Objective: (Child) will correctly match objects, instruments, or pictures in 4 of 5 opportunities for 3 consecutive sessions as measured by the classroom teacher or music therapist.

Objective: (Child) will add an object, instrument, or prop in a group activity, song, or free play setting to demonstrate "one more" in 4 of 5 opportunities for 3 consecutive sessions as measured by the classroom teacher or music therapist.

Objective: (Child) will remove an object, instrument, or prop in a group activity, song, or free play setting to demonstrate "one less" in 4 of 5 opportunities for 3 consecutive sessions as measured by the classroom teacher or music therapist.

Programmatic Goals on an IEP

Though not specifically mentioned, music therapy may be a vehicle or strategy for helping the child achieve programmatic goals. Other staff may monitor the child's progress as observed in music therapy sessions, or the music therapist may report to the teacher and/or the family.

Communication/Language and Literacy/Cognitive/Pre-Academic

Goal: (Child) will increase his ability to understand language from following routine directions and identifying objects in a familiar environment to appropriately responding to a variety of directions, identifying a variety of words and pictures, and understanding a question in an adult-directed activity.

Objective: During a structured activity, (Child) will respond to a simple direction (e.g., stop, come here) for 4 out of 5 opportunities on 3 different days as measured by school staff.

Objective: During a structured activity, (Child) will identify a requested item from a choice of 3 (e.g., get the _____) for 4 out of 5 opportunities on 3 different days as measured by school staff.

Objective: When his name is called by an adult or peer, (Child) will respond by stopping, looking, turning, etc. for 4 out of 5 opportunities on 3 different days as measured by school staff.

Specific Music Therapy Goals and Objectives on the IEP

Music therapists may write specific IEP goals and objectives for children. Depending on the policies of the state or particular school, these may be somewhat technical or more "reader friendly."

Personal/Social/Communication/Language and Literacy/Creative Expression/Musical Play

Goal: To increase group participation skills including eye contact, imitation, and receptive language, utilizing music therapy techniques.

Objective: During 1:1 music therapy, (Child) will maintain eye contact and/or focus on activity 50% of the time. To be increased with each periodic review date.

Objective: (Child) will increase participation by grasping and playing instruments, vocalizing, or imitating motions during 25% of the session time. To be increased with each periodic review.

Communication/Language and Literacy

Goal: To increase social language skills.

Objective: When presented with a song supported by words and pictures, (Child) will sing the song with a 50% increase in words for 3 consecutive sessions as measured by the music therapist.

Objective: Given instruction and practice, (Child) will use a song and instruments in structured turn taking activities with adults and peers for 2 of 3 sessions.

Communication/Language and Literacy/Creative Expression/Musical Play

Goal: (Child) will increase her expressive language skills through the use of singing and visual supports.

Objective: (Child) will decrease her rate of speech with external rhythmic cueing in 3 of 4 opportunities with 75% accuracy as measured weekly by the music therapist.

Objective: With the use of visual supports, (Child) will follow along with a color-coded sentence strip and sing independently with 75% accuracy as measured by the music therapist.

Objective: In response to singing the sentence, (Child) will answer 2 "wh" questions with visual supports in 3 out of 4 opportunities with 75% accuracy as measured weekly by the music therapist.

Personal/Social/Creative Expression/ Musical Play

Goal: (Child) will use appropriate social and play skills through the use of musical games and songs.

Objective: During group music therapy sessions, (Child) will initiate interactions with adults or peers (e.g., request to trade/share an instrument, find a partner) with no more than 1 verbal/visual prompt with 75% accuracy as measured weekly by the music therapist.

Objective: During a music therapy activity when given wait time, (Child) will increase his appropriate independent response to a specific request in 3 out of 4 given opportunities with no more than 2 verbal/visual prompts with 75% accuracy as measured weekly by the music therapist.

Communication/Language and Literacy

Goal: (Child) will increase his listening and language skills from inconsistent to consistent usage.

Objective: Given decreasing visual and verbal cues, (Child) will demonstrate awareness of the presence/absence of sound and then changing sounds, first with live music and then recorded as measured by the music therapist in monthly data collection.

Objective: During vocal play, (Child) will imitate a variety of sounds, pitches, and target sounds as measured by music therapist in monthly data collections.

Objective: (Child) will consistently use 10 words/sounds as part of finger plays and songs as measured by music therapist weekly for 4/4 sessions.

Objective: (Child) will listen to directions with visual cues and participate appropriately with physical and verbal responses for 20 minutes with no more than 4 redirections for 4 consecutive sessions as measured by the music therapist.

Sensory/Creative Expression/Musical Play

Goal: (Child) will increase her toleration for a variety of sounds, textures, instruments, and objects.

Objective: (Child) will accept new instruments, activities, and materials during music sessions while maintaining participation, with no more than 4 redirections for 4 consecutive sessions as measured by the music therapist.

Objective: (Child) will remain in the music play area for 10 minutes for both recorded and live music activities over 3 consecutive days.

Motor/Physical Development

Goal: To improve fine motor skills of pincer grip and finger independence.

Objective: (Child) will reach out and grasp a felt auto-harp pick using thumb and index fingers opposing and independently strum through an entire song of his choosing for 4 consecutive sessions as measured by the music therapist (adult will push the chord buttons).

Objective: Given a model, (Child) will imitate 3 note patterns on a keyboard using his index fingers, alternating right and left hands 4/5 patterns for 3 consecutive sessions as measured by the music therapist.

Motor/Physical Development

Goal: To increase upper body functional motor skills.

Objective: (Child) will imitate adult actions with instruments 3 times with 3 different instruments on 3 consecutive sessions as measured by the music therapist.

Objective: (Child) will demonstrate functional grasp and use of both hands with no more than 2 prompts while playing a musical instrument (e.g., sticks, mallets, and drum) with no more than 2 prompts during the song/activity for 3 consecutive sessions as measured by the music therapist.

Cognitive/Academic/Pre-academic/Communication/Language and Literacy

Goal: (Child) will improve ability to functionally use color, instrument and animal naming skills and improve concept labeling.

Objective: Given a choice of instruments and/or puppets, (Child) will correctly use at least 2 descriptors to make a selection (e.g., "I want the big, pink maraca") 3 of 4 opportunities for 3 consecutive sessions as measured by the music therapist.

Objective: Using picture cues, (Child) will select and then sing verses to songs using the correct descriptors 3 of 4 opportunities for 3 consecutive sessions as measured by the music therapist (e.g., "Down on Grandpa's farm there is a little white dog.").

Music/Musical Play/Communication/Language and Literacy/Creative Expression

Goal: (Child) will use her voice expressively to speak, chant, and sing (aligns with Pre-K Music Standards).

Objective: After direct instruction to learn songs and poems, (Child) will imitate, perform with the teacher, and finally, independently sing at least 3 songs and poems that use different combinations of speaking voices and singing (e.g., "Peanut Butter and Jelly").

Writing Activity Sequences or Instructional Programs

School districts may require staff to include plans or strategies for facilitating goals and objectives.

Goal: (Child) will expand his understanding of social interactions from limited attention getting skills, and turn taking and imitation of peers across settings, to increased understanding of appropriate attention getting (including eye contact before making a request/waiting for an answer), as well as increased peer imitation and turn taking.

Objective: During a structured activity (e.g., music, gym, games), (Child) will independently imitate a peer's actions or words (e.g., "follow the leader") for 3+ minutes a group per day, on 5 consecutive days as measured by staff.

Activity Sequence:

- Start with imitating the music therapist doing motions with background music. This initial activity builds the child's repertoire of motions from which to choose.

- Use Orff chant: *This is what I can do, everybody do it too, this is what I can do, now I pass it on to* _____ . Choose a friend to be the leader.

- Teach the folk song "Punchinello." The music provides the cues to imitate and change leaders.

Goal: (Child) will expand her play skills in a musical setting.

Objective: During musical play, (Child) will stay in the area of the musical activity for 5 minutes 3 times per session.

Strategies:

1.   Provide music session in specific area.

2.   Provide specific songs and materials for group musical activities within specific area.

3.   When child comes to the activity, imitate child's responses or actions.

4.   Expand on child's response.

5.   Lengthen activities as child begins to remain in area.

Error Strategies:

1.   Stop music, change stimulus/song/style.

2.   Go to child's area of play and introduce new materials.

3.   Lead/encourage child to return to area of music activity.

4.   Continue as above.

●

Goals for Children Birth Through Age 2

On the IFSP, the emphasis for determining goals for children's programming is always family-centered, regardless of where children are served. Goals for this process may be referred to as "outcomes." The IFSP:

- Addressees the needs of the family as well as the child, including medical and social needs;

- Includes outcomes targeted for the family, as opposed to focusing only on the eligible child;

- Includes service delivery in natural environments, including home or community settings such as childcare or library programs (this creates opportunities for learning in everyday activities and settings, rather than only in structured environments);

- Incorporates all agencies or programs working with the family on the IFSP team (the goal is to integrate all services into one plan); and
- Names a service coordinator to help the family during the development, implementation, and evaluation of the IFSP. (Bruder, 2000)

The IFSP consists of parent language and terminology, emphasizing a planning process between the family and professionals that considers informal and formal resources that may help families meet their goals for their child and themselves.

The content of the IFSP includes a statement of the major outcomes expected to be achieved for the child and family, the criteria, procedures and timelines used to determine progress toward achieving the outcomes, and whether modifications or revisions of the outcomes or services are necessary. In addition, the specific early intervention services necessary to meet the unique needs of the child and the family to achieve the outcomes are noted (Humpal, 2002).

Although each IFSP is different, the following are representative goals in which music therapy services and strategies could be included:

1. Child will generalize learned skills in a group setting.
2. Child will increase use of communication in a group setting.
3. Child will participate in a group setting with typical peers.
4. Child will increase and/or develop play skills.
5. Family will model and learn effective interventions.

Part of an IFSP that includes a stated outcome and the services of a music therapist as a member of the team might be written like this:

Outcome: (Child) will accept changes in her routine without crying.

Strategies:

1. Music therapist will develop transition songs with the family and introduce them to (Child).
2. Speech-language pathologist will take pictures for a picture schedule that will tell (Child) what will be happening next.
3. Early intervention specialist will work with (Child) and family to teach the process for carrying out these strategies.

●

Conclusion

Where services are delivered, the type of program, the model of service delivery, established standards and guidelines, and, of course, the children themselves and their specific needs all influence what goals, objectives, and outcomes are selected by music therapists when working in early childhood or early intervention educational settings. Music therapists must be dynamic learners, keeping abreast of current regulations, trends, methods, and effective clinical practice approaches to working with young children and determining the direction treatment will take. Goals, objectives, and outcomes shape effective music therapy service delivery and give a defined purpose and a mission to our work with young children.

●

References

Bruder, M. B. (2000). The Individual Family Service Plan. Arlington, VA: The Council for Exceptional Children. (ERIC Clearinghouse on Disabilities and Gifted Education Reproduction Service No. ECE 605)

Chester, K., Holmberg T., Lawrence, M., & Thurmond, L. (1999). A program-based consultative music therapy model for public schools. Music Therapy Perspectives, 17, 82–91.

Copple, C., & Bredekamp, S. (1997). Developmentally Appropriate Practice in early childhood programs (Rev. ed.). Washington, DC: National Association for the Education of Young Children (NAEYC).

Cuyahoga County Board of Mental Retardation and Developmental Disabilities (CCBMR/DD). (1992). Individual Family Service Plan manual. Cleveland, OH: Author.

Furman, A. G. (2002). Music therapy for learners in a community early education public school. In B. Wilson (Ed.), Models of music therapy interventions in school settings (pp. 369–388). Silver Spring: MD: American Music Therapy Association.

Goals 2000: Education America Act. (n.d.). Retrieved June 20, 2006, from http://www.ed.gov/legislation/GOALS2000/TheAct/index.html

Hughes, J., Rice, B., DeBedout, J., & Hightower, L. (2002). Music therapy for learners in comprehensive public school systems: Three district-wide models. B. Wilson (Ed.), Models of music therapy interventions in school settings (pp. 319–368). Silver Spring: MD: American Music Therapy Association.

Humpal, M. (2002). Music therapy for learners in an early childhood community interagency setting. In B. Wilson (Ed.), Models of music therapy interventions in school settings (pp. 389–428). Silver Spring: MD: American Music Therapy Association.

Kern, P. (2004). Making friends in music: Including children with autism in an interactive play setting. Music Therapy Today, 5(4). Retrieved from http://musictherapyworld.net

Music Educators National Conference (MENC). (1994). National Standards for Arts Education. Reston, VA: Author.

Music Educators National Conference (MENC). (1995). Prekindergarten Music Education Standards. Reston, VA: Author.

Register, D. (2001). The effects of an early intervention music curriculum on prereading/writing. Journal of Music Therapy, 38(3), 239–248.

Standley, J., & Hughes, J. (1996). Documenting developmentally appropriate objectives and benefits of a music therapy program for early intervention: A behavioral analysis. Music Therapy Perspectives, 14(2), 87–94.

Standley, J., & Hughes, J. (1997). Evaluation of an early intervention music curriculum for enhancing prereading/writing skills. Music Therapy Perspectives, 15(2), 79–86.

Chapter 8

Step by Step: A Hierarchical Approach to Group Music Therapy Intervention in Preschool Settings
Ronna S. Kaplan, MA, MT-BC

In recent years, music therapy has become more widely accepted as a mode of intervention in preschool settings for children with special needs. The literature supports the position that children with special needs, as well as their typically developing peers, may make many gains, particularly in behavioral/psychosocial skills (Gunsberg, 1988, 1991; Hughes, Robbins, MacKenzie, & Robb, 1990; Humpal, 1991; Kern, 2002; Robb, 2003; Standley & Hughes, 1996; Steele & Jorgenson, 1971), language/communication skills (Buday, 1995; Hoskins, 1988), and cognitive/academic skills (Register, 2001; Standley & Hughes, 1997; Wolfe & Horne, 1993), through participating in preschool music therapy programs.

•

Hierarchical Approach Rationale

Not only has it been demonstrated that music may play an important role in a preschool child's development, but several other sources also provide support for the establishment of a hierarchical approach to group music therapy intervention. Prominent social science theorists and educators have developed sequential, hierarchical models in many areas. Piaget proposed four main stages of intellectual growth in his *Theory of Cognitive Development*, while Erikson's *Eight Ages of Man* focused on an individual's psychosocial development. Kohlberg listed six levels within his *Stages of Moral Reasoning*, and Maslow outlined five levels in his *Hierarchy of Needs* (Gleitman, Fridlund, & Reisberg, 1999). Greenspan and Wieder (1998) enumerated and detailed six milestones constituting six early phases of development, from self-regulation and interest in the world, through intimacy, two-way and complex communication, to emotional ideas and thinking. In addition, researchers in early childhood, such as Linder and Parten, have described levels of children's social play (Linder, 1994).

Music therapists, too, have developed models that include hierarchies of skills. Briggs's (1991) "Model of Understanding Musical Development" defined and described four phases that blend musical and psychological development. Purvis and Samet (1976) wrote a curriculum guide utilizing a developmental therapy model that incorporates four stages, from "responding to the environment with pleasure" to "investing in group processes."

Presti, Cooper, Kallay, Summersgill, and Witt modeled *The Music Therapy Levels System* (Steele, 1985) after Harring's "Stages of Learning": acquisition, proficiency, maintenance, generalization, and adaptation. They arranged behaviors in a hierarchical order according to degree of difficulty or demands placed on students, while reinforcers were arranged in a hierarchical order from least to most preferred. One method the authors presented included arranging objectives in a sequence from each behavior class, or goal area, at each level, "with the expectation for each behavior raised at each successive stage."

Hanser (1999) gave many examples of "response hierarchies and objectives" in such areas as receptive and expressive communication, contributions within a music therapy session, and generalization. For a teacher-training workshop in 1996, the author of this chapter presented hierarchies for song-writing responses, independent music reading responses, and choir chimes playing. These lists were published in the *Proceedings of the Institute on Music Therapy with Young Children* (Davis, 2000) in a "building blocks" model, progressing from simple to complex, for a variety of musical tasks and responses.

●

A Hierarchical Approach to Group Music Therapy Intervention

Background

This chapter outlines a hierarchical approach to music therapy in preschool classrooms. The approach was designed and developed by the author during her tenure as a community music school music therapist contracted by three different preschool programs serving children with special needs and their typically developing peers. The reader may refer to the author's article on this subject in *Early Childhood Connections* (Davis, 2001).

Unlike traditional educational approaches, music therapy often is not curriculum-driven. While service delivery sometimes may utilize a programmatic approach, music therapy sessions and interventions are historically designed to fit the individual strengths and needs of the children. The music therapist determines goals and specific therapeutic objectives and designs and engineers the music structure to create natural opportunities in which to address these objectives. The music structure is also developed with the interests and ages of the children in mind.

Singing and chanting, playing instruments, moving, composing or creating, and listening are all part of the preschool music therapy experience, which uses guided group play. Within each session, children are given many opportunities to make choices, such as what instruments to play, whom to choose for a partner, and which words to put into song lyrics. One or more gross motor activities are programmed per session, particularly for the youngest children.

Design and Levels

The hierarchical approach outline presents the preschool team with an overview of how music therapy services may be organized to best serve the needs of young students

Singing and chanting, playing instruments, moving, composing or creating, and listening are all part of the preschool music therapy experience, which uses guided group play.

with special needs, particularly in settings where the children are retained in the classroom or building for more than one year. The outline is not all inclusive; however, it describes one program model upon which to build an effective music therapy service. The hierarchical format presents "building blocks" or steps through which children can learn, practice, and expand their repertoire of skills. This method of organizing presenting needs/skills, goals, objectives, and outcomes provides consistency and continuity of programming for children maintained in the program for several years. This approach, similar to that mentioned in the *Music Therapy Levels System* manual (Steele, 1985), builds upon and reinforces skills acquired at previous levels. While continuing to address unrealized needs, the hierarchical approach offers many spiraling sequences of opportunities for continued growth and more complex development.

It should be noted that the three levels described in this article may not always be this clearly delineated. A child's various skills may fall within more than one level, and children may be functioning at different levels in different areas. They may progress from one level to the next at different rates, depending on many factors, such as cognitive level of functioning, extent of developmental delay, motor involvement, and environmental influences. The following paradigm illustrates the basic goals that extend across all levels, while adding more complex goals within higher levels. The first four goals constitute the lowest step or level, and a new goal is then added at each succeeding level.

LEVELS OF FUNCTIONING AND RELATED GOALS: A HIERARCHICAL APPROACH						
					Level III	*Goal 6:* increase cognitive/ vocabulary skills
				Level II	*Goal 5:* increase visual attending skills	
Level I	*Goal 1:* increase social/ behavioral interaction skills	*Goal 2:* increase expressive communication skills	*Goal 3:* increase verbal social interaction with peers	*Goal 4:* increase receptive communication/ attending skills		
Figure 21. Levels of Functioning and Related Goals: A Hierarchical Approach.						

The presenting needs of the children as assessed by their teachers and the music therapist are the basis for the therapist's selection of goal areas and specific objectives within the goal areas. The objectives selected are suggested by classroom teachers and/or adapted from the Individualized Education Programs (IEPs) and designed to fit the music therapy setting. Sample music therapy experiences and structures, selected target objectives, and methods for evaluating progress toward the objectives for each level are suggested. This chapter focuses on two strands, increasing social/behavioral interaction skills and increasing expressive verbal communication in general and then with peers. Each strand is addressed in the outline to illustrate how the music experiences are developed and continued from one year to the next.

Level I

Children at Level I are *new to the preschool setting*. Very often this is their first school or group experience. They may evidence some strengths but also possibly one or more of the basic needs and/or weaknesses listed on the chart in the Appendix to this chapter.

Commonly addressed objectives in the social/behavioral realm at Level I include:

- increasing play skills;
- broadening repertoire of activities;
- improving basic motor participation;
- decreasing interfering behaviors such as leaving the area or hands not to self;
- increasing ability and/or willingness to wait for one's turn; and
- increasing verbally prompted motor social interaction with peers (passing or trading with a peer, sharing an object with one or more peers, or holding hands in a circle/ movement game).

Children at Level I who exhibit "low language skills" are encouraged to:

- increase spontaneous or imitative verbalizations or vocalizations;
- increase sign language;
- use simple pragmatics of language, such as making choices, requesting or responding.

Children at this level can begin to increase verbal social interaction with others by:

- greeting peers and adults during "Hello" and "Goodbye" songs in the sessions.

Increasing receptive communication/attending skills at this level is accomplished by:

- gaining compliance in following simple one-step directions with prompting in the music therapy setting.

Two sample Level I music experiences and corresponding structures that have been utilized successfully with many young children in preschool music therapy groups are shown in the accompanying chart found in the Appendix of this chapter.

Level II

Children at Level II have experienced at least part or all of one year of preschool. They are *returning* to either the same teacher/classroom or a different one within the same school. These children ideally may have gained some skills and achieved a degree of success in their first preschool year. They may demonstrate one or more of the strengths listed in the chart (see Appendix) but might still require modeling or cueing to interact with a peer, either on a motor or verbal level.

Examples of social/ behavioral music therapy objectives at Level II include:

- increasing spontaneous rather than prompted independent motor interaction with peers (passing/trading, holding hands, or sharing with a partner);
- increasing waiting for one's turn cooperatively; and

- making transitions from play to music therapy with no prompting.

More advanced objectives possible at Level II in expressive communication include:
- increasing children's mean phrase length or use of sentences.

Higher level tasks for verbal social interaction with peers at this level involve:
- increasing the frequency of spontaneous speaking to a peer;
- greeting a peer;
- asking someone else to play;
- verbally responding to a request from a peer;
- verbally leading the group (giving directions for how or when to play or move);
- making comments or asking questions related to the music or discussion topic;
- decreasing instances of verbal interruptions.

Receptive communication/attending skills at Level II are approached through:
- increasing children's willingness and/or ability to follow one-step directions without prompting, including directions with prepositions, such as "in," "on," "under," "in back," and so on.

The goal of increasing visual attending skills is often added at this level, with target objectives such as:
- following the adult or child leader to play or move; or
- visually attending to index cards with one color or picture each to play a song by "matching to sample."

Charted are two sample music experiences and structures for Level II goals and objectives (see Appendix).

Level III

Finally, the reader may consider children who may be returning to preschool and are now placed in a *prekindergarten* setting. They are often in their second or third year of preschool. Their increased independence and variety of strengths and continued areas of need can be noted in the chart (see Appendix).

Advanced social/ behavioral target objectives at Level III may include:
- waiting cooperatively for a longer time before receiving one's turn in an activity.

A Level III target objective for expressive communication skills might be:
- answering "wh" ("what," "where," "who," "when," etc.) questions regarding music experiences.

A more advanced skill to encourage verbal social interaction with peers at Level III would be:

- speaking to a peer and taking successive turns reciprocally in a conversation about a designated topic.

Further work on receptive communication/attending skills at this level may be achieved by:

- increasing children's willingness and/or ability to follow two- or three-step directions; or
- encouraging them to repeat information they have heard other students or the music therapist say.

Objectives at Level III to further enhance visual attending skills are:

- increasing or sustaining eye contact with the music therapist, other speaker, or the task in the music therapy setting; or
- playing a one-line song by matching colors/symbols from a song sheet to colors/symbols on the instrument with pointing prompts only.

It is often appropriate to address cognitive/vocabulary skills in the music therapy plan with children functioning at Level III. Suggested target objectives in this area include:

- increasing vocabulary related to classroom themes;
- naming primary colors or common shapes;
- matching and/or recognizing letters or numerals;
- recognizing one's printed name; and
- counting objects or playing the correct number of beats requested.

As with the two previous levels, two sample music experiences and their corresponding structures are described in chart form in the Appendix of this chapter.

Being in Step with Teachers and Other Therapists

The importance of being a "team player" in the school setting cannot be overemphasized. This process will be described in greater detail in Chapter 9. In addition, the reader may again refer to this author's *Early Childhood Connections* article (Davis, 2001). However, the following information in this area is offered for the reader's consideration.

Teachers or other therapists may request that the music therapist lead, introduce, and teach music or movement experiences during large group circle time, free play, or gross motor time, in addition to conducting group music therapy sessions. The teacher or therapist can then repeat the activities with coaching or feedback from the music therapist. Upon request, music and materials may be provided to assist classroom personnel in building their repertoire of music experiences.

During small group music therapy sessions, children who have mastered music therapy target objectives are systematically instructed to generalize these skills in other areas of the classroom (Davis, 1990). To establish whether skills gained in music therapy are being generalized, the music therapist observes children's responses in music or nonmusic experiences within various other classroom settings, such as circle time, gross motor, table time, snack time, and free play. Based on these observations, the music therapist then reinforces the performance of children who demonstrate generalization of a targeted skill, or reminds children who are not generalizing the skill that they may use what they have practiced in small group music therapy sessions at other times during the school day.

Conducting music therapy in the preschool classrooms has several benefits, including allowing the music therapist to gain access to classroom equipment and supplies, and permitting other professionals to observe the children readily in music therapy. Team members are invited at any time to attend music therapy groups, where they may encourage or assist with participation and serve as role models. They are able to reinforce each other's efforts in a united approach that increases uniformity and consistency in responding to the children and may help the children move from one step to another in a more timely fashion.

●

Summary

This chapter has outlined a hierarchical approach to group music therapy intervention with preschool children with special needs and their typically developing peers. Music therapy structures and experiences created within a hierarchical format build upon and reinforce goals and objectives accomplished at previous levels. Success at each level of the preschool hierarchy becomes a building block or step toward the next level. The music therapy program, integrated closely with the total preschool experience, contributes significantly toward laying a strong foundation for each child's future.

●

References

Briggs, C. (1991). A model for understanding musical development. Music Therapy, 10(1), 1–21.

Buday, E. M. (1995). The effects of signed and spoken words taught with music on sign and speech imitation by children with autism. Journal of Music Therapy, 32(3),189–202.

Davis, R. (1990). A model for the integration of music therapy within preschool classrooms for children with physical disabilities or language delays. Music Therapy Perspectives, 8, 82–84.

Davis, R. (2000). First steps in preschool: A hierarchical approach for group music therapy intervention. In R. Davis & M. Humpal (Eds.), Proceedings of the Institute on Music Therapy With Young Children (pp. 45–59). Silver Spring, MD: American Music Therapy Association.

Davis, R. (2001). Taking first steps in preschool together: A hierarchical approach to group music therapy intervention. Early Childhood Connections, 7(2), 33–43.

Farnan, L., & Johnson, F. (1988). Music is for everyone. New Berlin, WI: Jenson Publications.

Gleitman, H., Fridlund, A., & Reisberg, D. (1999) Psychology (5th ed.). New York: W. W. Norton.

Greenspan, S., & Wieder, S. (1998). The child with special needs. Reading, MA: Addison-Wesley.

Gunsberg, A. (1988). Improvised musical play: A strategy for fostering social play between developmentally delayed and nondelayed preschool children. Journal of Music Therapy, 24(4), 178–191.

Gunsberg, A. (1991). A method for conducting improvised musical play with children both with and without developmental delay in preschool classrooms. Music Therapy Perspectives, 9, 46–51.

Hanser, S. (1999). The new music therapist's handbook. Boston: Berklee Press.

Hoskins, C. (1988). Use of music to increase verbal response and improve expressive language abilities of preschool language delayed children. Journal of Music Therapy, 25(2), 73–84.

Hughes, J., Robbins, B., MacKenzie, B., & Robb, S. (1990). Integrating exceptional and nonexceptional young children through music play. A pilot program. Music Therapy Perspectives, 8, 52–56.

Humpal, M. (1991). The effects of an integrated early childhood music program on social interaction among children with handicaps and their typical peers. Journal of Music Therapy, 28(3), 161–177.

Music therapy structures and experiences created within a hierarchical format build upon and reinforce goals and objectives accomplished at previous levels. Success at each level of the preschool hierarchy becomes a building block or step toward the next level.

Kern, P. (2002, November). Hey you! Integrating children with autism on childcare playgrounds. *Paper presented at the National Conference of the American Music Therapy Association, Atlanta, GA.*

Linder, T. (1994). The role of play in early childhood special education. In P. Safford (Ed.), Yearbook in early childhood education, volume 5: Early childhood special education *(pp. 72–95).* New York: Teachers College Press.

Purvis, J., & Samet, S. (Eds.). (1976). Music in developmental therapy. *Baltimore: University Park Press.*

Register, D. (2001). The effects of an early intervention music curriculum on prereading/writing. Journal of Music Therapy, *38(3), 239–248.*

Robb, S. L. (2003). Music interventions and group participation skills preschoolers with visual impairments: Raising questions about music, arousal, and attention. Journal of Music Therapy, 40(4), 266–282.

Standley, J., & Hughes, J. (1996). Documenting developmentally appropriate objectives and benefits of a music therapy program for early intervention: A behavioral analysis. Music Therapy Perspectives, 14, 87–94.

Standley, J., & Hughes, J. (1997). An early intervention music curriculum for enhancing prereading/writing skills. Music Therapy Perspectives, 15(2), 79–86.

Steele, A. L. (Ed.). (1985). The Music Therapy Levels System: A manual of principles and applications. *Cleveland, OH: The Cleveland Music School Settlement.*

Steele, L., & Jorgenson, H. (1971). Music therapy: An effective solution to problems in related disciplines. Contingent socio-music listening periods in a preschool setting. Journal of Music Therapy, 8, 131–145.

Wolfe, D., & Horne, C. (1993). Use of melodies as structural prompts for learning and retention of sequential verbal information by preschool students. Journal of Music Therapy, 30(2), 100–118.

Appendix

Student Needs by Developmental Level With Corresponding Objectives, Activities, and Evaluation Formats			
Presenting Needs/Skills	*Typical Goals/Objectives*	*Music Activity/Structure*	*Data Collection/ Evaluation*
New Students—Level I • Often first preschool experience • Frequently out of seat/area • Possible low language • Low interaction with peers • May be self-centered or self-absorbed • Inconsistent or low participation in group • Difficulty with taking turns or waiting for turns • May display attention-seeking behaviors • May talk out of turn • May be self-abusive or aggressive to others • May display separation anxiety—missing mom, dad, or other caregiver may inhibit participation	New Students—Level I *Goal 1: To increase social/ behavioral interaction skills* *Objective: ___ will expand repertoire of instruments played willingly and/or independently from a baseline to a mean of 25% or more above baseline for 3 consecutive sessions.*	• "Play in the Band" (Purvis & Samet, 1976) • Child verbally or nonverbally chooses from array of instruments. • All children play at once, either walking, marching, standing, or sitting. • Music therapist sings. • Teacher and aide assist. • Child may trade with other children and repeat. • Music therapist may change song. • Music therapist may offer preferred instrument as reinforcer for playing less preferred instrument.	*Use scale of 0–3, with 3 = participated independently, 2 = with any type of prompts, 1 = with physical assistance, and 0 = resisted or refused. Add scores from each activity and take mean for session.* *Another method is to list total instruments presented and total with which child played, giving a percentage of responses/opportunities.*

Figure 22. Student Needs by Developmental Level

Presenting Needs/Skills	Typical Goals/Objectives	Music Activity/Structure	Data Collection/Evaluation
Student Needs by Developmental Level With Corresponding Objectives, Activities, and Evaluation Formats			
New Students—Level I • Often first preschool experience • Frequently out of seat/area • Possible low language • Low interaction with peers • May be self-centered or self-absorbed • Inconsistent or low participation in group • Difficulty with taking turns or waiting for turns • May display attention-seeking behaviors • May talk out of turn • May be self-abusive or aggressive to others • May display separation anxiety—missing mom, dad, or other caregiver may inhibit participation	New Students—Level I *Goal 2: To increase expressive communication skills* *Objective: _____ will increase willingness and/or ability to imitate the music therapist's model with voice from baseline (% of opportunities/ session) to a mean of 25% or more above baseline for 3 consecutive sessions.*	• "Clap, Clap, Clap Your Hands"—traditional • Music therapist sings song, encouraging all to do actions. • Music therapist gives each child a turn with microphone to imitate in chorus—start with "la, la, la," then add other sounds that music therapist, speech therapist, teacher, etc., would like children to imitate ("ba," "ma," "ee," "oo," etc.). • Repeat for desired number of movements and sounds.	Music therapist notes total number of sounds presented and total which child imitated, giving a percentage of responses/ opportunities. Music therapist notes which sounds were imitated.

Figure 23. Student Needs by Developmental Level

Student Needs by Developmental Level With Corresponding Objectives, Activities, and Evaluation Formats

Presenting Needs/Skills	Typical Goals/Objectives	Music Activity/Structure	Data Collection/Evaluation
Returning Students—Level II • Basic group participation • Improved language • Ability and/or willingness to wait longer for turns • Ability and/or willingness to follow group structure or routines • May need modeling or cueing to interact with a peer, either on a motor or verbal level	Returning Students—Level II **Goal 1: To increase social/behavioral interaction** **Objective: _____ will increase spontaneous independent motor social interaction with peers (passing, trading, holding hands in a circle or partner dance, sharing an instrument) from baseline (% of opportunities/session) to a mean of 25% or more above baseline for 3 consecutive sessions.**	• "We Are Playing" (adapted lyrics to "Are You Sleeping"): *We are playing (2x)* *Playing the chimes (2x)* *We are playing together (2x)* *Now we stop now we pass.* • Music therapist distributes one choir chime to each group member, using either notes of C major chord, or notes of pentatonic scale, depending on number of children in group. • Music therapist instructs children to play until the words say to stop and then pass to person next to him/her. • Music therapist assists each child as necessary to pass at end of verse • Levels of intervention: *Question—"Who gets that chime?"* *Direction-"Everybody pass" or "(Name), pass to (Name)."* *Pointing—to child who is to receive chime.* • Repeat until chimes have been all the way around group or until another designated stopping time. • Music therapist may lead similar activity with other instruments and songs.	*Use scale of 0-3, with 3 = participated independently, 2 = with any type of prompts, 1 = with physical assistance, and 0 = resisted or refused. Add scores from each activity and take mean for session.* *Another method is to score with a check or "S" for spontaneous or with question only, "V" for verbal cue (direction) needed, "P" for pointing cue, and "A" for physical assistance needed. Count total checks or "S" marks given out of total opportunities and convert to percentage.*

Figure 24. Student Needs by Developmental Level

Student Needs by Developmental Level With Corresponding Objectives, Activities, and Evaluation Formats

Presenting Needs/Skills	Typical Goals/Objectives	Music Activity/Structure	Data Collection/Evaluation
Returning Students—Level II • Basic group participation • Improved language • Ability and/or willingness to wait longer for turns • Ability and/or willingness to follow group structure or routines • May need modeling or cueing to interact with a peer, either on a motor or verbal level	Returning Students—Level II **Goal 3: To increase verbal social interaction with peers** *Objective: _____ will increase frequency of spontaneous speaking to a peer from baseline to a mean of 25% or more above baseline for 3 consecutive sessions.*	• "Look Who's Come to Music Today" (Farnan & Johnson, 1988) • Music therapist chooses child to play guitar first, offering selection of regular or adapted picks. • Other children may ask if they can play along too. • If someone asks spontaneously and child responds "yes," then begin song. • If another child starts playing without asking, music therapist models asking "Can I play with you?" • If child then asks, allow for response from first child. • If no response, music therapist points out that "_____ wants to play with you. Can he?" If no, encourage. "No, thank you." • Begin song with those children who were granted permission to share. • After each child's name is sung, have each group member say "hi" to that child. • If no spontaneous greeting, music therapist prompts first with gesture and then verbally if necessary. • Repeat until each child has had turn to play song.	*Use scale of 0-3, with 3 = participated independently, 2 = with any type of prompts, 1 = with physical assistance, and 0 = resisted or refused. Add scores from each activity and take mean for session.* *Another method is to score with a check or "S" for spontaneous, "V" for verbal cue needed, "P" for pointing cue, and "X" for no response. Count total checks or "S" marks given out of total opportunities and convert to percentage.*

Figure 25. Student Needs by Developmental Level

Student Needs by Developmental Level With Corresponding Objectives, Activities, and Evaluation Formats

Presenting Needs/Skills	Typical Goals/Objectives	Music Activity/Structure	Data Collection/Evaluation
Pre-Kindergarten Students—Level III • Often display independent interaction with peers • Often second or third year of preschool • Language may continue to improve. • May display ability to delay gratification, e.g., in waiting for a turn, even longer than previously • May need to develop kindergarten readiness skills (related to colors, letters, shapes, numbers, etc.) • May need to develop ability to follow more complex types of directions or sequences of directions.	Pre-kindergarten students—Level III **Goal 1: To increase social/ behavioral interaction skills** **Objective: _____ will increase waiting for turn (step 1—to be fourth, step 2—to be fifth) cooperatively with hands to self to play, sing, or move from baseline (% of opportunities/ session) to a mean 25% or more higher than baseline for 3 consecutive sessions.**	"Mailman, Mailman" (Bitcon) • Music therapist prepares cards with each child's name on them and places in "mailbag." • Music therapist chooses child to play tone bell ostinato (High C, G, A, G) and child to be "mailman," then instructs others to wait for their turns. • Music therapist begins singing song and having child play bells while other stands or walks in area. • At end of song, music therapist instructs "mailman" to take out a letter and "read" it and deliver it to that person. • If "mailman" does this task independently, song continues with person receiving mail as the new mailman and former mailman as new bell player. • If "mailman" does not read independently, music therapist assists with initial sound or entire word. • Repeat until all children have had turns to play and be "mailman." • If child waited cooperatively, music therapist offers choice of preferred song in next activity.	Music therapist scores a "check" or "S" for spontaneous waiting, "V" for a verbal cue needed, "A" for physical assistance needed. Count total checks or "S" marks given out of total opportunities and convert to percentage of waiting out of total opportunities.

Figure 26. Student Needs by Developmental Level

Student Needs by Developmental Level With Corresponding Objectives, Activities, and Evaluation Formats

Presenting Needs/Skills	Typical Goals/Objectives	Music Activity/Structure	Data Collection/Evaluation

Pre-kindergarten Students—Level III
• Often display independent interaction with peers
• Often second or third year of preschool
• Language may continue to improve.
• May display ability to delay gratification, e.g., in waiting for a turn, even longer than previously
• May need to develop kindergarten readiness skills (related to colors, letters, shapes, numbers, etc.)
• May need to develop ability to follow more complex types of directions or sequences of directions
	Pre-kindergarten students—Level III
	
	Goal 3: To increase verbal social interaction with peers
	
	Objective: _____ will increase spontaneously speaking to a peer about a designated topic or activity from baseline to a mean 25% or more above baseline for 3 consecutive sessions.
		• "Roving Reporter Song" (to tune of "Chiquita Banana" song):
		  My name is _____ and I'm hear to say
		  Some of my favorite things today.
		  My favorite TV show is _____
		  My favorite food is _____
		  And my favorite color is _____.
		• Music therapist plays and sings song first with her own answers.
		• Music therapist then shows pictures of person eating, watching TV, and various colors.
		• Music therapist instructs children to choose a partner and ask partner what his/her favorite TV show, food, and color are.
		• If children respond, music therapist or other adult writes in blanks on song sheet
		• If no response, music therapist may give choices and then repeat above.
		• Music therapist gives each pair a turn to play Q-chord, with one pressing chord buttons and other strumming, while the music therapist sings their new versions of the songs.
		• Repeat until all pairs have had turns for their songs to be played and sung.
			Music therapist records the number of turns taken in conversation or number of comments made on topic.

Figure 27. Student Needs by Developmental Level

Chapter 9

Collaboration: Being a Team Player
Nicole Allgood, MSEd, MT-BC

To meet the needs of children in an educational setting, music therapists often are called upon to serve in a variety of roles. Music therapists must be able to work as part of a team that may include parents, paraprofessionals, teachers, and related service professionals. Through effective collaboration, music therapists can develop partnerships that will increase the level of benefit to the students being served. This chapter will offer a definition of and frameworks for collaboration as well as foundational knowledge for working with related service professionals, music educators, paraprofessionals, and parents.

•

Background Information

History of Collaborative Practices in Music Therapy

A history of collaborative practices is represented in the music therapy literature for models of co-treatment, system support, and one-to-one consultation. Steele and Jorgenson (1971) discussed the importance of working with professionals from other disciplines and claimed that music therapists cannot feel content just functioning on their own. The authors presented case examples of cooperative work with an educator and a speech therapist. Collaborative models were expanded to focus on developing larger supportive programs (Steele, Vaughan, & Dolan, 1976). The School Support Program was designed to collaborate with a larger system. One to one collaboration was defined in the role of a consultant. The consultant worked individually with an educator to discuss student progress and gather needed resources for the student (Steele, 1977).

According to Alley (1977), music therapists are uniquely prepared to serve as part of the educational team. Alley stated that music therapy is distinctive because of its broad scope of practice. The methods and interventions used in music therapy can be applied to a variety of different age and disability levels. In the educational setting, the music therapist may be seen as "service-gap filler, a problem solver, a curriculum support service" (Alley, 1977, p. 54).

Register (2002) surveyed music therapists to learn about collaborative and consultative practices. Participants worked in a variety of health care and educational settings. Participants indicated that they engaged in collaborative and consultative practices with a variety of parties including: parents/caregivers, occupational therapists, speech therapists, educators, physical therapists, clients and other music therapists.

Standards for Collaboration

Current professional documents demonstrate the ongoing importance for music therapists to function as a member of a team. The American Music Therapy Association (AMTA) maintains professional documents including the *Standards of Clinical Practice*, *Code of Ethics*, and *Professional Competencies*. A review of these documents yields several key points related to providing treatment within a collaborative model. Figure 28 highlights relevant excerpts from the professional documents.

EXCERPTS FROM PROFESSIONAL DOCUMENTS	
Document	Related Excerpts
AMTA Standards of Clinical Practice (AMTA, 2004, pp. 18–22)	• *4.3 The Music Therapist maintains close communication with other individuals involved with the client.* • *7.3 The Music Therapist will contribute to the education of others regarding the use and benefits of music therapy.*
AMTA Code of Ethics (AMTA, 2004, pp. 23–26)	• *3.9 The MT will use every available resource to serve the client best.* • *4.0 Relationships with Colleagues* • *4.1 The MT acts with integrity in regard to colleagues in music therapy and other professions and will cooperate with them whenever appropriate.* • *4.3 The MT will attempt to establish harmonious relations with members from other professions and professional organizations and will not damage the professional reputation or practice of others* • *4.4 The MT will share with other members of the treatment team information concerning evaluative and therapeutic goals and procedures used.*
AMTA Professional Competencies (AMTA, 2004, pp. 27–29)	• *22 Interdisciplinary Collaboration* • *22.1 Demonstrate a basic understanding of the roles and develop working relationships with other disciplines in the client's treatment program.* • *22.2 Define the role of music therapy in the client's total treatment program.* • *22.3 Collaborate with team members in designing and implementing interdisciplinary treatment programs.*

Figure 28. Excerpts from Professional Documents

Language in the professional documents clearly indicates an expectation of professional practices that foster collaboration with other service providers and team members. Music therapists are charged with the responsibility of reaching out to members of other professions for the benefit of the students being served and the field.

Collaboration: Definition and Strategies for the School Setting

Music therapists must function as a part of a team in school settings. Teamwork relies on collaboration. Collaboration is defined as a "voluntary endeavor, in which there is a common goal, shared responsibility for decisions, accountability for outcomes, and a belief that all participants involved have something valuable to contribute" (Combs, 2002, p. 33). Effective collaboration is a process that requires dedication and hard work. Imel and Zengler (2002) defined key characteristics of successful teams: regular communication, customer (student)-centered focus, shared leadership, structure, and respect for team members. In order to effectively collaborate with other members of the team, music therapists should consider the roles of different group members, potential goal areas to be addressed for students, and the contributions that the music therapist herself or himself can make. This requires a careful assessment of the setting, the needs of the student(s), and the skills of the music therapist.

Collaborative programming resonates with current trends in education. Many schools are shifting their leadership and organizational models to focus on more collegial, collaborative programs. This trend has been heralded by those who write about Professional Learning Communities (PLC). A PLC is a dynamic community that focuses on learning, collaboration, and accountability (DuFour, 2004). Teamwork is at the core of a PLC. Members of the team engage in "collaborative conversations . . . to make public what has traditionally been private—goals, strategies, materials, pacing, questions, concerns, and results" (DuFour, 2004, p. 10). The PLC model encourages shared responsibility for student learning and development. According to Hord (1998), there are five key components to a PLC: (1) supportive and shared leadership, (2) collective learning and application of learning, (3) shared values and vision, (4) supportive conditions, and (5) shared personal practice. In a PLC, a music therapist would serve on a team of school professionals and parents who have a shared vision for the student. All of the various components of the program must work together.

●

Collaborative Partnerships

Collaborating With Related Services

Students with special needs in school settings typically are served by a team that includes the special education staff and related service providers. To promote the generalization of skills across different environments, the music therapist should develop a foundational understanding of the role of different members of the team. By developing a sense of common language and vision for the student, the music therapist can function effectively as a member of the collaborative team. Collaborative opportunities also can strengthen the value of music therapy services for the students. Figure 29 lists a sample of some special education service providers and their roles on the team.

SPECIAL EDUCATION SERVICE PROVIDERS	
Special Education Service Providers	Typical Role on the Team
IEP Case Manager	This may be a teacher or other staff member who is assigned to the student to make sure that the IEP is being implemented. The case manager monitors the student's educational program including goals and related services.
Occupational Therapist (OT)	Occupational therapists work on fine motor, gross motor, and activities of daily living. The OT also may address issues of sensory integration.
Physical Therapist (PT)	Physical therapists work more with gross motor types of skills. A PT would be helpful with movement adaptations.
Behavioral Consultant	These staff observe behavior situations and then assists the team to develop strategies to help increase appropriate behaviors.
Speech Language Pathologists	These therapists deal with receptive and expressive language and communication.
Assistive Technology Staff	These team members work with communication devices and various computer software or technology that support the child's educational program.
School Social Worker	The school social worker may work on emotional and social issues with the family. The social worker may also work closely with the family.
Resource Teacher/Special Education Teacher	Members of the teaching staff provide academic programming for students. Teachers develop academic adaptations for individual and/or small group instruction.
Paraprofessionals/Instructional Aides	These staff members may work 1:1 with a specific student or provide assistance for instructional support under the supervision of a certified teacher.
Adapted Physical Education Instructors	Adapted physical education teachers provide an alternative physical education experience for students with special needs.

Figure 29. Special Education Service Providers (Allgood, Carnahan, Fahsbender, Grossardt, & Storm, 2003)

Developing Team Goals

Some special education teams make a decision to develop team-based goals rather than individual therapeutic or academic goals. The team takes a holistic look at the needs of the student. Goals are written in all pertinent areas of need including academics, functional skill development, and other domains (see other chapters within Section III for a more in-depth discussion). The student's goals are written in more general language. The music therapist works within the team to select appropriate goal areas to specifically address in music therapy. Those who decide to write team goals must establish clear procedures for reporting the student's progress towards goals and structures for re-evaluating not only the student's goals but also the team process.

Implementing Team Goals

Effective implementation of team goals demands strong collaboration. Team members must be able to communicate how various parts of the program complement each other. The team must be able to work as a unit to re-evaluate the student's goals. Team goals benefit the student because members of the team can problem solve and bring creative ideas to the group.

Collaborating With Music Educators

Since the passage of Public Law 94-142, more children with disabilities are receiving music education as part of the educational experience. Least Restrictive Environment demands that students with disabilities are educated with typically developing peers to the greatest extent possible. Adamek (2001) described that many music educators feel unprepared to work with children with special needs. Collaboration and consultation between music educators and music therapists can provide important connections that will improve service delivery and educational opportunities for children with disabilities.

Music therapists should work with music educators to clearly define their roles. The field of music education offers "a body of knowledge for the development of normalized and valued music experience which are important to the growth of all children," while music therapy "maximizes the enjoyment and teaching potential of music within the paradigm of sound special education techniques to enhance the learning process and facilitate the growth of each child" (Alley, 1979, p. 114). The work of music therapists can complement the child's music education experience or help children to develop prerequisite skills for music education.

Music therapists can provide valuable consultation to music educators to maximize the music education experience for children with disabilities. Culton (2002) reported that music educators often have little or no input into placement decisions, lack information about individual students, and may have inadequate teacher preparation and training. Music therapists are well trained to evaluate skills and assess a student's needs. Furthermore, music therapists are trained to develop interventions specific to the student's needs. Music therapists can provide consultation on specific interventions and models as well as broader in-service training that address foundational knowledge about working with students with special needs.

Collaborating With Paraprofessionals

Paraprofessionals have a key role in the education of students with disabilities. They have been defined as "employees who, following appropriate academic education/instruction and/or on-the-job training, perform tasks as prescribed, directed, and supervised by fully qualified professionals" (National Joint Committee on Learning Disabilities, 1999, p. 25). Many music therapists will have the opportunity to interact with paraprofessionals in school settings, especially in group therapy settings. The paraprofessionals may provide assistance for transportation or transitions; facilitate participation in interventions, communication support, or interpretation; and direct care for students as needed. Because paraprofessionals frequently accompany students with special needs to nonacademic settings, they can provide valuable information about students' progress and performance as well as general emotional or physical states.

Paraprofessionals can be valuable partners in the delivery of music therapy services in school settings. They can serve as models for desired musical behaviors, provide appropriate prompts to stimulate a student's response, and assist with the evaluation of a student's performance on a given goal. The music therapist must take the time to communicate with the paraprofessional regarding the nature of the intervention and what specific behaviors

Collaboration and consultation between music educators and music therapists can provide important connections that will improve service delivery and educational opportunities for children with disabilities.

or outcomes are being targeted. Paraprofessionals may benefit from a separate in-service session or written information to learn more about the intention of the music therapy process and how music therapy fits into the students' educational programs. Paraprofessionals also may benefit from the opportunity to explore their own feelings and experiences as active music makers in order to best model for the students. Respect for the paraprofessional and communication are key components of the process.

Paraprofessionals often accompany students with special needs into inclusive general music education settings. Bernstorf (2001) stated that school districts have differing policies about the role of paraprofessionals in music education settings, but the paraprofessionals should be included in a meaningful way. Bernstorf highlighted the point that some paraprofessionals may feel uncomfortable in music settings because of their perception of their own musical abilities. She recommends specific ways of including paraprofessionals in the music education settings, including: (a) sharing appropriate information; (b) recognizing what supports the paraprofessional can provide; (c) integrating the paraprofessional into instructional delivery; (d) seeking ways to promote carry over and generalization of skills and behaviors across different settings; and (e) engaging the paraprofessional as an interpreter to communicate to the student, use devices, and interpret students' responses. The role of the paraprofessionals may vary according to the nature of the music setting (e.g., general music or performance). Paraprofessionals can provide a crucial piece that enables students with special needs to have access to arts education.

A music therapist who is providing consultative services for inclusion experiences can provide an important link for paraprofessionals. Music therapists typically understand the language of "both worlds" (i.e., special education and music education), so they are therefore ideal people to provide the needed one to one training for paraprofessionals who will be supporting students in inclusive settings. Music therapists can work with paraprofessionals to cue them to model desired responses (Hughes, Rice, DeBedout, & Hightower, 2002). Music therapists can describe musical concepts and assist paraprofessionals with developing strategies for on the spot modifications. Music therapists Hughes, Rice, DeBedout, and Hightower provided the following "do's and don't's" list for paraprofessionals:

Guidelines for Paraprofessionals in the Music Classroom

Things Paraprofessionals Do That Music Teachers Love:
- Model desired behaviors by participating in the singing, dancing, playing instruments, etc., as the children are expected to do.
- Sit or move about the room as the activity directs, in order to assist all students, not only those in ESE (Exceptional Student Education).
- Actively and enthusiastically participate in all activities.
- Allow students enough time to perform expected task or behavior before assisting. First give them the freedom to try.
- Redirect inappropriate behavior.
- Correct students "up close and personal."
- Assist the music teacher in any way possible by being another pair of hands and eyes.

Music therapists typically understand the language of "both worlds" (i.e., special education and music education) so they are therefore ideal people to provide the needed one to one training for paraprofessionals who will be supporting students in inclusive settings.

- Tell the music teacher about any unusual problems before class begins.
- Ask questions in order to clarify instructions or procedures.
- Give suggestions on how materials or parts may be adapted for individual students.
- Serve as a communication link between ESE teacher and music teacher.
- Sign everything in the class for students with hearing impairments.
- Physically help students experience an activity by assisting them when needed.
- Outside of music class, make/adapt materials so all children can fully participate.
- Teach prompting/assisting skills to peers. Model the interaction, then allow classmates to interact within personal time frames.

Things Paraprofessionals Do That Drive Music Teachers "Out of Tune"
- Are not on task (reading the paper, grading papers, eating lunch, etc.).
- Look bored, disinterested, irritated, or sleepy.
- Talk to others or the music teacher during class.
- Discuss a student in front of the student.
- Shout instructions or corrections to students during class.
- Use discipline which conflicts with that of the music teacher's.
- Expect "more or better" behavior from the student who is mainstreamed.
- Use rude, condescending, or irritated voices when addressing students.

(Hughes et al., 2002, p. 340)

Collaborating With Families

Collaboration with families of students with disabilities is not only a way to strengthen therapeutic service delivery, but it is also supported by law. The Individuals with Disabilities Education Act, IDEA, PL 105-17, calls for "more and better collaboration across service delivery systems, specifically involving parents and providers" (Sperry, Whaley, Shaw, & Brame, 1999, p. 17). The intent of the law is to promote family and professional collaboration for determining goals and service delivery systems. The law reflects the paradigm shift in beliefs regarding parental involvement in education. Promoting a strong parent/professional relationship strengthens therapeutic services because parents are a source of knowledge about the child, are affected by the disability, and can promote generalization of skills. Parents also may become a more active part of the educational process and therefore more accountable for the growth of the student (Register, 2002).

To better understand the role of parents in the treatment/education of children with disabilities, theorists look toward Bronfenbrenner's Ecological Model (Turnbull, Blue-Banning, Turbiville, & Park, 1999). Bronfenbrenner regards the child as an authentic member of the family's and community's ecological environments. The ecological model offers a framework for understanding the interdependence of the various systems in which the child lives: immediate household, community, and overriding cultural beliefs and values (Shea & Bauer, 1992). Therefore, to best serve the needs of the individual child, it is advantageous to work within the framework of the ecological context.

Communication is essential in order to develop collaborative relationships with parents. Taylor (2000) highlighted some recommendations for building effective communication with parents. School professionals must first establish rapport with parents by recognizing and respecting the parents' role with the child. Active listening should be used in order to better understand parents' perceptions. Active listening includes attentive listening, attempting to reflect how the parent feels, and restating the parents' comments. Music therapists should be empathic and try to understand situations from the parents' perspective.

Music therapists can seek out collaborative relationships with parents through a variety of means: workshops, video tapes of sessions, phone calls, input on goals, and providing home based interventions for families to use. Music therapists should take the time to educate parents regarding the nature of music therapy. Education can occur through workshops, participation in school open houses and parent/teacher conferences, and sharing of written literature. Parent workshops can include introductory information about music therapy services as well as experiential exercises. Experiential exercises can provide parents with insight into the nature of music therapy interventions and how those interventions may help their child develop certain skills.

Parents also can experience the risk taking that is necessary in order to participate in music therapy interventions. School music therapists can educate parents through the vehicles of traditional parent outreach programs such as curriculum nights, open houses, and parent/teacher conferences. Each of these types of programs presents an opportunity for the music therapist to meet parents and share information. If schedules do not allow for presentations, a music therapist could prepare a display table or share written information with parents. For example, during parent/teacher conferences, a music therapist might present parents with a M.U.S.I.C. note. The note could spotlight a few updates about their child's music therapy experience.

Music Therapy Note
Most improvement David is greatly expanding the length of his musical engagement. He has participated in instrumental exploration for periods of up to 10 minutes.
Unusual occurrence We are pleased to report no "unusual" events. David is consistently willing to try any activities presented to him.
Special happenings David is expanding his joint attention and cooperative play with his peer. Last week he explored the ocean drum with his peer for over 7 minutes. David and his peer encouraged each other to stay involved.
Interesting info David appears to enjoy instruments such as the ocean drum and small percussion instruments such as the cabasa. Given the opportunity, he will use PECS to request instruments or turns to play.
Coming attractions We will continue to explore the sound environment and keep looking for expansion of attention and musical relationships.
Prepared by the Music Therapy team for the Parent Teacher Conference

Figure 30. Music Therapy Note. (Giant Steps Illinois, Inc., 2004)

Other written literature such as therapist made fact sheets or fact sheets created by the American Music Therapy Association can be distributed. Information sharing is an important way to build foundations for collaboration.

Collaborating With Other Music Therapists

The music therapy community is rich with its own internal resources. Within this community exists a variety of opportunities for collaborative learning and inquiry. Music therapists often work isolated from other music therapists. Collaboration with other music therapists outside the workplace can provide networking, peer supervision and support, and professional development. Music therapists can collaborate to create therapeutic materials and programming, clinically based research, and professional presentations. Collaboration between music therapists is fostered through on-line listservs, news groups, and professional conferences.

●

Conclusion

Collaboration is a process of developing partnerships that help fulfill a common goal. Being a member of the team involves learning about the components of the team and working to develop a sense of shared purpose. The profession of music therapy defines that its members should team with other professionals in order to best serve their clients. Music therapists are important members of the team in educational settings. Through collaboration, music therapists can enrich therapeutic services, promote generalization of skills, and advance their own learning. Being a team player will strengthen music therapists and the services that they deliver.

●

References

Adamek, M. (2001). Meeting special needs in music class. Music Educators Journal, 87, 23–26.

Alley, J. (1977). Education for the severely handicapped: The role of music therapy. Journal of Music Therapy, 14, 50–59.

Alley, J. (1979). Music in the IEP: Therapy/education. Journal of Music Therapy, 16, 102–110.

Allgood, N., Carnahan, M., Fahsbender, L., Grossardt, J., & Storm, V. (2003). In harmony: Music for all learners. Unpublished project funded by the Special Projects Grant of the Great Lakes Region of the American Music Therapy Association.

American Music Therapy Association (AMTA). (2004). AMTA member sourcebook. Silver Spring, MD: Author.

Bernstorf, E. (2001). Paraprofessionals in music settings. Music Educators Journal, 87, 36–40.

Combs, C. (2002). Experience in collaboration: McDenver and McDonald's. Journal of Physical Education, Recreation & Dance, 73, 33–35.

Culton, C. (2002). Inservice training: A major key to successful integration of special needs children into music education classes. In B. Wilson (Ed.), Models of music therapy interventions in school settings (pp. 109–140). Silver Spring, MD: American Music Therapy Association.

DuFour, R. (2004). What is a "professional learning community"? Educational Leadership, 61, 6–11.

Giant Steps Illinois, Inc. (2004). M.U.S.I.C. Note: Parent/Teacher Conference Communication. Burr Ridge, IL.

Hord, S. M. (1998). Professional learning communities: What are they and why are they important? Issues . . . about Change, 6, 11–15.

Hughes, J., Rice, B., DeBedout, J., & Hightower, L. (2002). Music therapy for learners in comprehensive public school system: three district-wide models. In B. Wilson (Ed.), Models of music therapy interventions in school settings (2nd ed., pp. 319–364). Silver Spring, MD: American Music Therapy Association.

Imel, S., & Zengler, C. (2002). *For the common good: Learning through interagency collaboration.* New Directions for Adult and Continuing Education, *95,* 41–49.

National Joint Committee on Learning Disabilities (NCJCLD). (1999). *Learning disabilities: Use of paraprofessionals.* Learning Disabilities Quarterly, *22,* 23–30.

Register, D. (2002). *Collaboration and consultation: A survey of Board Certified Music Therapists.* Journal of Music Therapy, *39,* 305–321.

Shea, T., & Bauer, A. (1992). Parents and teachers of children with exceptionalities: A handbook for collaboration. *Boston: Allyn and Bacon.*

Sperry, L., Whaley, K., Shaw, E., & Brame, K. (1999). *Services for young children with autism spectrum disorders: Voices of parents and providers.* Infants and Young Children, *11(4),* 17–33.

Steele, A. (1977). *Directive teaching and the music therapist as consultant.* Journal of Music Therapy, *14,* 17–26.

Steele, A., & Jorgenson, H. (1971). *Music therapy: An effective solution to problems in related disciplines.* Journal of Music Therapy, *8,* 131–145.

Steele, A., Vaughan, M., & Dolan, C. (1976). *The school support program: Music therapy for adjustment problems in elementary schools.* Journal of Music Therapy, *13,* 87–100.

Taylor, G. (2000). Parental involvement. *Springfield, IL: Charles C. Thomas.*

Turnbull, A., Blue-Banning, M., Turbiville, V., & Park, J. (1999). *From parent education to partnership education: A call for a transformed focus.* Topics in Early Childhood Special Education, *19,* 164–172.

Chapter 10

Methods, Techniques, and Effective Clinical Practice in School Age Settings
Jean M. Nemeth, MA, MT-BC

Since the implementation of Public Law 94-142 in the mid-1970s, the American education system has undergone dramatic changes. This landmark legislation marked the onset of the infusion of children with more pervasive special needs into the core of the public education system and led to many changes in the way education is administered to all students (Adamek, 2002). Educators today must work within a system rife with changes that reflect implementation of federal mandates as well as local statutes and policies, the influence of the latest theories and research, increasing budgetary constraints, and the problems inherent in the practical application of all of these competing parameters. Despite the confusion that has resulted from nebulous language in the current reauthorization of IDEA, parents and educators have increasingly recognized the efficacy of including music therapy as a related program or IEP service.

Music therapy intervention in educational settings can take on a variety of forms. An in-depth discussion can be found in *Models of Music Therapy Intervention in School Settings* (Wilson, 2002). School-based music therapy programs are delineated for learners with severe disabilities, autism, learning disabilities, deaf and hard-of-hearing, and early education and early childhood. In addition, district-wide models are described, reflecting how music therapy operates as a related service in the school setting from early intervention through high school in both a consult and direct service role. Furthermore, this resource explains placement options for those with more pervasive disabilities, settings and programs developed to address specific needs, considerations indigenous to specific populations, as well as how music therapy services are best imbedded within these contexts.

An ever-increasing volume of research literature exists pertaining to the effective use of music-based programming and music therapy techniques to elicit positive change in students with special needs in both segregated and integrated educational settings (American Music Therapy Association, 2000). Jones and Cardinal (1998) discuss the growing evidence that suggests "service may be better delivered within an integrated setting" (p. 36) and that music therapists believe that inclusion provides a social and academic advantage to both special and general education students. Adamek (2001) suggests that the concepts of partial participation, normalization, interdependence, and individuality are inherent in successful integrated programs. There is increasing discussion as to how collaboration among music therapists, special educators, and music educators increases the success and effective inclusion of children with varying disabilities in the music class (Colwell, 1995; Music Educators National Conference, 1997; VanWeelden, 2001). Patterson (2003) describes how music educators can assist in obtaining music therapy services for children they feel will benefit. Hammel (2004) points out that after 30 years we are "still learning how to include special learners in our classrooms" (p. 33) and that research demonstrates the effectiveness of music to support positive change. This entire discourse has implications for those designing and implementing music therapy programs for special learners in schools.

●

On the Road Again

When working as a music therapist in an educational setting, the operative term is *itinerant*. The number of students who are deemed to require music therapy within a single school system may be too small to warrant a full-time music therapist. As a result, work is often contracted on a case-by-case or program-by-program basis. The music therapist may operate as a private practitioner, contracting services with one or more towns. However, some clinicians, especially those employed in larger metropolitan areas, may be hired into part- or full-time salaried positions.

Logistics

Employment in a school setting involves working across a range of grade levels, separate buildings, and diverse schedule formats. This creates a number of logistical problems that must be considered when planning an overall music therapy program. Creating a workable schedule is no small feat. Within a school system, each level—preschool, elementary, middle, and high school—generally operates under a separate time frame. Moreover, each building may individually set its own internal schedule. The times when individual students or classrooms are unavailable (e.g., lunch, recess, gym/art/music classes, dedicated reading time) differs across buildings and grade levels as well. Multiply this by varying amounts of therapy time allocated to individual students or programs by the IEP, the juxtaposition of various related services in a student's schedule, and the incorporation of more than one town's scheduling frameworks into the mix, and the complexity of the situation begins to emerge.

Scheduling

The music therapist must approach scheduling with great care, first gathering all the pertinent information and then meticulously attempting to accommodate the wide variety of needs. It is often necessary to persuade staff members to accept less than their ideal choice of scheduled time. When scheduling, show flexibility and concern for the needs of fellow special education staff as well as recognition that there may be days when one's personal lunch or prep time is sorely limited. Focus also must be given to "caring" for the music therapist as well; there is a limit to the number of sessions that can feasibly be presented by one person in a day!

A Flexible Chameleon

When moving from setting to setting—often several times within a day—the itinerant music therapist is faced not only with an ever-changing schedule and diverse caseload, but also with the intricacies of melding in and out of various program formats, physical environments, grade levels, and teaching modes. Inherently, the music therapist must interface with a wide variety of personalities, teaching styles, program models, and school "cultures." This brings into focus another very important component of this type of work, namely the ability to be a "chameleon." It is imperative when working within this multi-faceted framework that the music therapist remain highly flexible. Adaptability is often the key component in whether a music therapy program will be successful in the rigid, yet ever-fluctuating environment of a school system.

Keep in perspective that a music therapist is the outsider entering an already established schedule and routine. The ability to work within the format is essential, not only in regard to accessing students, but in order to garner support for what music therapy can add to a student's educational experience. The task goes beyond being able to identify student needs and preferences. Observance, acknowledgment of, and at least partial adherence to how the classroom is run will be most helpful, not only in building the necessary relationship and camaraderie with staff, but to assure student comfort as well. Establishing this working base will lead to greater acceptance of the role music therapy can play in the educational process.

●

Into the Trenches

The actual structure and components contained in a school-based music therapy session are highly variable and relate directly to both the service format and needs of the individual or group. One exciting aspect of this type of work is the wide scope of student disabilities and needs that is consistently part of the therapist's schedule. In this setting, a music therapist may work with ages extending from very young to near adult children with a wide range of functioning levels and specific diagnoses. This diversity provides a challenge to the clinician who must plan and administer the music therapy programming, especially in the group setting.

Session Location

The location and set-up of the music therapy sessions are among the first decisions that must be addressed. In consultation with staff and administration, identify where music therapy will take place. Often, creative use of such areas as an unoccupied cafeteria, auditorium, backstage, dead end hallway, or smaller therapy room is necessary. Having equipment that is portable is essential.

Physical Set-up of the Session

In the group setting, a **circle format** usually works well. All the students have a clear view of both the therapist and potential peer models. Direct visual line also fosters less opportunity for students to lose focus or engage in inappropriate behavior patterns. Moreover, this open setting allows the therapist the freedom to move in whatever direction necessary to provide closer modeling or support to individual students and engenders group cohesiveness not as easily maintained in clustered seating. Passing and sharing activities work well in this formation, as does group ensemble play that requires students to watch conductor cues. The open circle format also provides a controlled space for gross motor movement activities. Clearly communicate the importance of this design to classroom teaching staff in order to gain their assistance in making minor adjustments to the environment as necessary.

With younger children, floor sitting on a carpet or individual rugs is both appropriate and convenient while providing very effective grounding. A circle of chairs is more age-appropriate and usually preferable with older children and teens. In groups containing students in wheelchairs, peers should also use chairs in an effort to keep seating levels more even and inclusive. Adult staff members who participate in the session should be encouraged to join the group seating as well.

Specialty Sessions

Music therapists may encounter the need for providing individual sessions to those students who require a higher level of support. These are generally the students who present with the more pervasive levels of disability or show greater difficulty with success in the group setting. Often, a one-to-one intensive intervention is necessary to elicit and foster appropriate responses with these children. However, in the educational setting, the goals always remain focused on ultimately improving performance **in the classroom**.

Collaborative Groups

The ability of the music therapist to form good working relationships with other team members may lead to opportunities to create work formats that include collaborative sessions. The music therapist may lead music activities that target specific articulation, expressive language, or receptive processing skills, thus enabling the speech therapist to work directly on student output in a functional context. Similarly, music-occupational therapy groups may include music activities that incorporate fine motor skills that may then be addressed by the occupational therapist. While students are engaged in reinforcing musical movement or instrument play activities, the physical therapist may target gross motor skills. Frequently, the music-based programming is able to elicit student responses that are not naturally exhibited in other therapy settings. While students are engaged in singing, moving, and playing instruments, need areas can be addressed by personnel with greatest expertise in a particular area.

The music therapist may lead music activities that target specific articulation, expressive language or receptive processing skills, thus enabling the speech therapist to work directly on student output in a functional context.

●

A Typical Session—If There *Is* One!

The structuring of session content and sequence is paramount to the delivery of effective music therapy services. Though the actual form of the session will vary from therapist to therapist and setting to setting, effective components can be identified that will create a learning environment conducive to skill development.

Greeting Activities

Each session should have a definitive beginning such as a greeting song. During this opening activity, students must attend to the therapist (e.g., make eye contact or maintain listening posture as dictated by ability) and participate actively by performing some form of greeting at the appropriate point in the song. This response varies according to student ability. It may range from a head turn or sustained eye contact to a reach, reach and grasp, assisted handshake, wave, vocalization, hi/hello approximation or full handshake and phrased greeting ("Hi, ___ !").

Many therapists create their own greeting song based on personal style and the needs of their students. It may consist of a simple, readily accessible structure of short, repetitive phrases such as:

> *Well, **Hello** to everybody (or a specific name), Hello, hello **today**, (repeat)*
> *It's so **nice to see you**, So **nice to be here** with you,*
> *Hello to everybody, Hello, hello, today.*

Lyrics that express both a greeting and the immediate time frame as well as positive sentiment about the meeting are usually very effective (as in boldface type above). A well composed song, though very simple, can work equally well with all ages if it lends itself to alterations from simple I, IV, V block chording to blues or rock or perhaps a slow, finger pick guitar style.

While focusing on individual greeting responses, involve the entire group throughout the duration of the activity. Perhaps have the group participate by sustaining bilateral knee tapping (patchen) as the therapist greets each member individually. The incorporation of this repetitive, rhythmic movement keeps the group engaged during individual greetings.

A consistent greeting activity format may prove successful across all age ranges. Learned at a young age, the students carry this song and sequence with them throughout their participation in music therapy. By mid-elementary level, most are able to independently perform the greeting song, without therapist support in many cases, and have progressed to where they complete peer greetings among themselves. Enjoyment of this activity, and the camaraderie it fosters, carries all the way through to the upper grade levels. The importance of an enjoyable, engaging greeting activity cannot be underestimated. It provides both a successful social interaction opportunity and a very effective preparation for what will follow in the session.

Movement to Music

The remainder of the session may be comprised of a series of rhythmic movement, instrument play, and vocal or singing activities, though the exact order of these components may vary across sessions. Employ a generally consistent structure. Following the individualized and sometimes protracted greeting activity, engage the group as a whole. The chosen activity must initially be simple enough to ensure success of all group members regardless of level. Often this takes the form of basic, repetitive movement to music. Clapping, tapping, rocking, and stomping are all high probability activities for most active children. There is generally a very short delay between the onset of the activity and engagement of the entire group. Those with greater physical limitation may approximate the response or be assisted as necessary by either the therapist or a nearby staff member. Getting the entire group "going" is imperative to carry forward the energy initiated in the greeting activity.

The specific movements used in these activities will vary according to both age and ability of the group. In general, following the developmental sequence of movement patterns is most effective. Simple bilateral knee tapping is a good place to start unless pervasive physical limitations are present (assistance is necessary in these instances—it is important for these students to feel rhythmic movement even if they are unable to independently produce it). This motion is usually accessible to most children and avoids the potential issues of bringing hands to or across midline that arise for some younger children or students with more limitations.

Subsequent alteration of the position of the repetitive taps (e.g., to head, to stomach, to legs) in imitation of a visual model is helpful both in sustaining attention and working through a series of motor coordination patterns:

- A useful technique: Structure movement changes in rondo format (ABACADA, etc.), returning to the initial knee tapping after each position change.
- The duration of each response should be dictated by the needs of group members.
- As group accuracy increases, response length can be abbreviated. Make sure that the increased tempo does not trigger response escalation.
- Return to steady knee tapping to control response escalation.
- Substitute different body part movements (clap hands, stomp feet, nod head, etc.) into the alternating sections.

Keeping the experience enjoyable is the key. Successful participation and skill enhancement should always remain the focus.

Bilateral coordination and steady beat (carryover skills from the preschool level for most students) should be solidly in place before more complicated responses are introduced:

- Various unilateral responses (e.g., tap with one hand on various body locations);
- Crossing midline, (e.g., left hand to right knee);
- Alternation (e.g., left tap, right tap);

- Spatial orientation (up/down/out/in);
- Left-right differentiation;
- Multi-step (2, 3, 4) movement pattern.

Variations of tempo, dynamics, and sound–silence (start/stop) are but a few of the components that can be incorporated into these activities. In the group setting, alternating subgroups emphasizes turn taking and attending skills. Performing each motion sequentially down the row of students fosters group awareness and impulse control. The skills that can be incorporated into rhythmic movement to music encompass a wide range and should reflect the needs of the specific groups or age levels.

Musical Accompaniment

In planning these activities, care needs to be given to the choice of musical accompaniment. If using recorded music, draw song selections from a wide variety of musical genres and styles. Consider how a particular selection matches the needs of the student or group in terms of tempo, complexity, volume, age appropriateness, and the potential effect the piece will have on successful response of the students involved:

- Forceful rock music would not be the best choice for students who have demonstrated discomfort with loud volume levels.
- Soft, flowing, gentle music may not be able to stimulate the necessary rhythmic feel to elicit a steady beat response.
- Multi-layered scoring may actually inhibit the response of students who shut down when over-stimulated.

Use knowledge and good judgment of both the particular students and the potential effects of the music in choosing accompaniment.

Within the music therapy profession, there is an ongoing discussion about the efficacy of using live versus recorded music. It may be best to opt for a combination of both. Using recorded music allows the therapist the physical freedom to provide visual models of desired movement responses. Since most music therapists working in educational settings do not have the luxury of working in tandem with another therapist or trained staff, using carefully chosen recorded music is often a necessity to free the therapist to use hands and voice in other ways (e.g., modeling, visual cues, verbal reinforcement, physical assistance). Many students are unable to respond accurately to verbal directives alone and require these visual or tactile cues to assist their participation. Recordings also provide a richness of scoring and instrumentation that would be quite difficult for a single player to replicate. The reality of therapist stamina limitations must also be taken into account. A schedule of up to ten sessions in a day often precludes the "live performance only" approach. Moreover, children benefit from exposure to the wider variety of musical experiences that a combination of live and recorded music provides.

Instrument Activities

As with movement sequences, the form that specific instrument activities will take relies heavily on the age, ability, and interest of an individual or group. The use of instruments in music therapy holds a twofold purpose: developing or refining specific skills and motivating the student(s) to respond. For the majority of students, the instrument play portions of music therapy sessions frequently are the most enticing. Many students who do not readily engage in either the greeting or movement activities will suddenly show high levels of interest and engagement when instruments are presented. Carrying instruments and equipment in a closed bag or suitcase and only revealing specific objects as they are needed can be a most useful technique. This method effectively holds students' interest while avoiding potential overload or impulse control issues that result when all the equipment is laid out beforehand.

Guitar-Based Activities

Due to portability or personal preference, guitar may be the chosen accompaniment instrument for many music therapists. In addition, sessions may contain a specific guitar-based activity that incorporates either movement, voice, or instrument play components. Guitar is a very popular instrument in our culture. As a result, many students are highly motivated to engage in guitar strumming and thus practice a wide variety of skills:

- Unilateral, bilateral, alternating hand/arm movement patterns while strumming a guitar placed directly in front of them.
- Counting and one-to-one correspondence skills.
- Turn-taking, pair play, alternating play and specific rhythmic responses.
- Social interaction skills addressed by having pairs of students play together.
- Learning concepts (e.g., numbers/math facts, letters/reading/spelling, colors, shapes, curriculum content areas)—students accompany their answers by strumming.
- Group counting—the guitar moves progressively around the circle; each student strums once as group counts. Variations are endless: each student individually saying the next number; counting by 2/5/10; moving in random sequence around the group to hold student focus; giving each student a different number amount to count/strum, etc.
- Cognitive responses: spelling, name and address, choice making, phrase recitation, categorization, color identification with corresponding strums.
- General curriculum: specific answers to questions on various curricular topics (e.g., science, social studies) self-accompanied by strumming.

Most students work very hard for the opportunity to answer a question by strumming it on this popular instrument. One-to-one correspondence (Play What You Say) is fostered in all these activities along with focus, motor coordination, and cognitive processing.

Rhythm Instruments

A typical session may include one or more instrument-based activities with the specific music and instrument selection varying from week to week. Instruments are employed to address social, communication, cognitive, and motor skills as appropriate for each level or group. Certain instruments (e.g., hand drums, tambourines, shaker eggs, maracas, chiquitas, wrist bells, sticks) may be considered staples and used on a frequent basis. Novel instruments (e.g., bongos, cabasa, cowbell, shekere, finger cymbals) may be introduced intermittently to address specific skills or motor patterns, provide added interest, and increase motivation. In addition, props such as groan tubes, koosh balls, beanbags, and picture cards may be employed for specific effects or to focus on skills.

Bilateral, Hand-held Instruments

Maracas, egg shakers, sticks, and jingle bells can be incorporated into many types of movement activities. Instrument play can add a motivating dimension to practice of motor coordination skills; the response may be expanded to include a grasp component. Unilateral, bilateral, cross midline, spatial orientation (shake the bells in front of/in back of/over/under/ next to yourself, etc.), directional reach (under your leg), and eye–hand coordination (e.g., tap your egg shaker on the bottom of your shoe) are enhanced by the addition of hand-held instruments. The colorful designs of these instruments also promote the practice of color recognition, color directives (e.g., red play now, blue play now), turn-taking skills, and sequencing (blue first, red second, green third).

Drums and Tambourines

Most students thoroughly enjoy playing drums. When introducing a large drum, ask students to tap it with an open hand. Present the drum in various positions to assess eye-hand and spatial coordination skills. The same sequence then incorporates fisted hand position followed by bilateral open/fisted hands, alternation, cross midline, and various reach and tap positions. Students are eager to experiment with drum playing and should also be given opportunities to play freely. In addition, drums may be used in a wide variety of ways to foster numerous other skills:

- Learn to play/stop on cue.
- Develop concepts of steady pulse, pacing, tempo, dynamics, etc.
- Practice number concepts (tap a specified number).
- Give answers to number problems.
- Accompany answers to all types of questions (play/say).
- Enhance social skills, group work, and turn taking.
- Use rhythmic tapping to:
  – Motivate speech responses.
  – Practice articulation and speech patterning skills.
  – Develop and enhance rhythmic awareness of musical or spoken phrases.
  – Develop accurate rhythmic or speech skills through repetitive phrase imitation. *Example*: Move the drum around the circle with students playing a repetitive phrase each time it occurs in a song.

Partner Activities

Various rhythm instruments can be employed to enhance a wide range of social skills. Sharing and turn taking are important skills within the context of the school setting. Working with a partner to play an instrument incorporates cooperation skills (e.g., take turns hitting the gong). Appropriate social exchanges can be embedded in activities in which students must ask a peer for a turn to play an instrument. "Pair Play" involves choosing a peer and playing together on a large instrument such as drum, guitar, or Omnichord (one pushes chord buttons, one strums).

"Play-then-Pass" is an activity that can be utilized in a variety of ways. In its simplest form, it involves one instrument that is passed around the circle, as cued, with each child taking a turn to play it. This type of activity provides practice with delay of gratification, waiting, appropriate social manners, attending, sharing, as well as give and take skills. The desire to play a novel or interesting instrument often provides higher motivation to comply with the social rules. Once the basic pass-play skills have been established, this activity can be altered in a number of ways to accommodate the needs and skills of the group:

- The number of passing instruments can be increased (2 to 3 to 4, etc.).

- Two (or more) instruments can be passed in opposite directions, necessitating intermittent exchanges of instruments.

- Instruments can be passed according to direction cues (pass left, pass right, pass across) thus altering the passing sequence.

- A popular variation: Take a group of small instruments (e.g., egg shakers) or objects (e.g., small stuffed animals) and attempt to pass all of them around the circle before a recorded song ends. This activity often involves both passing and taking during each turn.

- Using musical or lyric cues for passing is popular with older students (e.g., pass every time a word or phrase is heard in the song; pass each time the music gets loud).

Props

Occasionally, unique objects can be effectively introduced to support development of specific skills:

- Koosh balls work well as a "gentle" means of practicing eye hand coordination and throwing skills. Most students find them more interesting to pass than beanbags or blocks. They work well in activities that involve body awareness or spatial orientation (rub the koosh on your arm; shake it under your leg; pass it to the person next to you). Toss koosh balls into a therapist-held tambourine on a musical or word cue (children revel in the "crash" as it hits!).

- Picture cards are most useful to provide a visual cue or assist with categorization activities.

- Groan tubes (plastic tube with an internal stopper that moves from one end to other when the tube is turned over, producing a groaning sound) almost always elicit immediate delight from students, regardless of age. These tubes are useful for producing sound effects or musical accents. They also foster arm rotation (hold tube in center and rotate hand inward/outward to move stopper) or opposing hand-arm movements (hold tube on ends with two hands and simultaneously move one arm up and other down to rotate the tube and move stopper).

Singing Activities

Music activities lend themselves well to the refinement of expressive language skills. The production of singing sounds and vocalizations inherently provides practice of phonation, articulation, and the physical coordination necessary for speech production. Sustained vocalizing strengthens and develops muscular control and stamina. Students should be consistently encouraged to use whatever singing abilities they possess, from a simple vocalized hello to multi-verse songs. Vocalizing and singing skills should be initiated in the early childhood years. Thus, by the time the students move onward to elementary school and beyond, a comfort level is present that usually circumvents most issues regarding "willingness" to sing.

Accept whatever level of response a child is able to give. Criticism should never be employed; instead, encourage and gently shape the response. We live in a culture that does not "naturally" sing. For the most part, children are surrounded by music that is proffered only by a cadre of "professionals." The music therapist needs to remain sensitive to these issues. Singing is fun and should be kept that way. As with any other skill, the more children sing, the more proficient and comfortable they become.

Start with a greeting activity. Over time, a vocalized, spoken, or sung response tends to emerge for most students. By elementary school level, many students also can sing at least a portion of the greeting song. This activity promotes both increased verbal proficiency and all the skills inherent in appropriate social interaction (eye contact, focus, appropriate social distance, intimate social exchange, etc.). Cognitive components can be incorporated when this activity is turned into a game:

- Ask a student to say hello to someone who is wearing "red" (involves color discrimination, visual location, and processing skills).
- Incorporate a variety of directives—"say hello to a girl," "someone from your homeroom," "a person on your soccer team," or "the person whose shirt has letters on it."

Singing and Chanting

Musical chanting and call and response games provide an excellent medium for expressive language practice. Syllables and sounds represent an accessible beginning point. While it is usually easy to engage young children with animal sound songs, care should be taken as to the age appropriateness of these activities as students move upwards through the grade levels. However, syllable singing is an excellent means of practicing phonation, articulation, and speech clarity, skills that are often more difficult for children with special needs. Here the therapist needs to get "creative." By choosing the right songs, these activities can be not only highly useful in fostering speech skills but engaging and enjoyable for the students as well:

- Numerous contemporary songs contain syllable singing in the lyrics.
- Scat singing, performed in call and response (C and R) style, is an excellent vehicle to use with older students.
- Folk songs often contain syllables in the lyrics, as do many traditional songs and carols.

These songs are easily adapted to include whatever sounds a particular group needs to practice by simply changing a consonant or vowel.

Call and Response Chanting or Repetitive Phrases

Traditional songs often incorporate call and response chanting or repetitive phrases that are most useful for practice of speech patterning and phrases. After only brief exposure, many students quickly catch on to "their part." Students often show far less frustration with repetitive practice of a speech skill when engaged in singing. Emphasize rhythmic patterning as well. Have students tap or strum their responses on an instrument. A wide range of spirituals and traditional song material contains repetitive chants or C and R formatting.

Speech Patterning and Expressive Language Skills

Answering questions by playing the response on an instrument is highly reinforcing to most children. This component can be incorporated into most all discussion topics. It motivates children to participate while focusing their attention on the discussion (especially when the "rule" is to not repeat what anyone else has said). It also combines work on eliciting responses with speech patterning as well ("Play What You Say").

Use students' names to form rhythm patterns:

- Pass a hand drum around; each person plays and says his or her name.
- Chain names together to form various patterns; play on an instrument (e.g., log drum).
- Alter the order in which children play their names to change the pattern.
- Ask students to "sing" their names to add a melodic dimension.
- Allow older students to set the order (e.g., change seats or stand in a row) to provide opportunities for individual control and creative response.

Using names lends a familiarity that creates a medium for success and comfort with the activity. The activity can then be expanded into any category of interest to the group (e.g., favorite foods, sports, toys, games). Using the Omnichord or Q Chord works well for these activities. They are easily passed, most enticing, and simple to play.

Assistive Communication

For some students, speech will not be their primary mode of expressive communication. They may rely on manual communication in the form of either sign language or an assistive communication device. The music therapist must consult with either the speech therapist or classroom teacher to determine what method is being emphasized (see Chapter 13).

As a general rule, the therapist should consistently combine verbal directives and discussion with gesture and basic signs whenever the group contains a child who has limited language or is nonverbal. This visual component aids clarity not only for the particular student but for all group members as well. Learning signs as a group can enhance the musical experience of a song. Other visual aids, such as pictures, Picture Exchange Communication System, and communication boards, may be employed whenever appropriate.

Closing Activities

The incorporation of some type of closing activity provides the necessary ending structure to the session. Depending upon time or other schedule constraints, these activities may take on different forms, ranging from a simple collective goodbye to the group to an actual activity that incorporates a specific learning or social skill:

- A student may be required to make eye contact and say goodbye to all his peers.
- A good-bye may be passed from student to student around the circle.
- Each student may play the answer to a question or recall one thing that happened that day.

Whatever the content, the closing activity provides a definitive end to the music therapy session and signals the transition that will next occur.

●

Building Skills

Emphasis on cognitive processing is inherent in all presented activities. Spatial concepts, bodily awareness, recall and memory, as well as general thinking skills are intertwined in all activities that involve student responses. Sessions also can be designed to address specific thinking and memory skills as appropriate to the needs of a particular group. Incorporating current classroom curricular content whenever appropriate empowers students to take charge and tell you what they know. In addition, motor skills are enhanced in rhythmic movement and instrument play activities. Gross motor skills may be addressed through structured circle games and folk dances, while fine motor skills are evident when grasping and playing different instruments, participating in finger play games, or using manipulatives as part of a music therapy protocol. Social/emotional and behavioral aspects can be addressed across all activity types. By the very nature of the music therapy group, social interaction and appropriate social behaviors are modeled and practiced. Emotional expression can be developed through melodic percussion improvisation, song-writing, or even song or instrument choice. Music can become the motivation or reward for appropriate classroom behavior, and appropriate social behavior can be taught through social stories set to music.

Communication Skills

Music therapy provided in the social group context is by nature heavily language- and communication-based. Despite a significant musical emphasis, often the majority of the session is directed verbally. Success in the school setting is highly dependent upon a student's ability to operate in a language-rich environment. Thus, it is crucial that music therapy programming stresses development of expressive language and singing, as well as adequate receptive skills.

Receptive Language Skills

Singing, chanting, and playing of answers may focus on expressive skills. However, receptive language skill practice is inherent in all session content. Often students with special needs have more problems with language processing than with language expression. Many of these students show pervasive difficulty comprehending complex language. For them, the beauty of music therapy lies in its multi-dimensional qualities. Music-based programming provides aural stimulation as well as visual display (e.g., therapist's models and gestures, instruments' visual presence, or peer models). Actively making music provides rhythmic structuring, repetitive content, and kinesthetic input. As a result, students are inherently given far more cues to draw from than at other times in their day.

The ability to function within the classroom social group setting necessitates the development of discrimination skills and the ability to "read" social cues. For students with processing difficulties, this is no easy task. Often a student loses focus, fidgets constantly, is predominantly off-task, or shows very poor impulse control. Attention issues interfere or poor grasp of language impedes proper responding. Music-based programming is often effective for all of these presenting behaviors. Novel or interesting instruments tend to grab and hold attention. The rhythmic impulse of lively music can act both as stimulation or an external control agent, and the multi-sensory medium provides more opportunity for grasping the meaning of the accompanying words. Keep the following parameters in mind when planning for these types of students:

- Properly designed music activities prove enjoyable for most students, resulting in higher levels of engagement and opportunity for learning.
- In the social group setting, music therapy is very much a language-based approach with components that naturally enhance the experience.

Direction Following

Following instructions may take on a myriad of forms in the music therapy setting. At the simplest level, students may be expected to follow the social rules of the group setting (e.g., stay seated, keep quiet, look at me). More specifically, directions may be used to elicit specific responses (e.g., take the drum) or to guide how a process will work (e.g., red taps first, blue taps second). Receptively, students must be able to respond to these instructions in order to be successful with the activities. During movement activities, the therapist can accompany visual models with verbal descriptions. In this way, the verbal label of the response is paired with what the student is seeing and doing. Given the repetitive nature of these movements, these labels can be successfully reinforced several times during an activity.

Numerous songs or recorded selections include specific directives within the lyrics. Initially, the therapist can reinforce the words but later fade the prompt so that the students must listen and respond to the song itself. Using lyric-embedded directives is often effective for students with receptive difficulties. The way words are inflected in music usually places emphasis on the important content words. Thus, the musical and rhythmic emphasis accentuates what the student needs to "hear" most.

Likewise, during instrument play, words are often paired with actions. Instrument play itself takes on several dimensions during music therapy sessions. At times, emphasis is placed on the actual playing and the motor coordination or technique involved in producing sound. However, instruments also may act as props for other activities. For example:

- A drum can be a vehicle for spatial orientation skill practice when a child is asked to tap a koosh ball on the drum, shake it under or over the drum, put it in the drum, rub it on the drum, etc.
- Guitar play can be used to stress motor coordination directives when students are asked to strum with their left hand alone, right hand alone, left then right, etc.

The possibilities are endless. The therapist must first determine the skill focus and then seek to design the most enticing way of fostering these receptive skills.

Music Ensemble

As students develop greater competency with music and learning skills, a music ensemble should become an integral part of music therapy sessions. Beginning with a very simple call and response format, the therapist can seek to develop not only accurate imitation responses, but also the ability to work together in a group to accurately reflect the modeled response. Rudimentary musical concepts may be stressed, namely the ability to match sound/silence, tempo, dynamics, rhythm, and motor patterns. Call and response (C and R) activities can be presented in a variety of formats, such as movement, instrument play, and vocalized chanting or singing. The goal across these different types of activities is always the same: *to develop the receptive skills and processing necessary to discern the nuance involved (e.g., loud vs. soft; start/stop of the music) and the coordination to perform the appropriate response.*

The logical place to begin is with sound and silence. Regardless of age, most all students show great enjoyment of movement or instrument play activities that contain the element of sudden, unexpected stops and starts. This can be expanded by combining these musical pauses with added elements of tempo acceleration or deceleration, or gradually changing dynamic levels to make musical activities more challenging and engaging.

Once therapist/student C and R patterning is well established, group-to-group alternation can be introduced. This format lends itself to many possibilities for singing, moving, and instrument play. Most simple four-phrase songs are easily amenable to dividing the group in two and having one half sing a line and the other repeat it. Perform movement activities in the same manner. Alternate the lead and imitation roles to add another dimension. Instrument play variations are limited only by the therapist's or group's imagination. Often the most successful experiences come from the spontaneous ideas of the students themselves. Cognitive components are inherently embedded in these instrument play activities. For example, patterns can be alternated according to color, shape, size, or category (drums vs. maracas, boys vs. girls). Introduce the skill of following the conductor's cues for entrances and cut-offs.

Begin to incorporate these skills into activities in which groups of instruments are assigned to play the rhythms of repetitive song lyrics or chants. At first, the entire group may practice the rhythms using movement (e.g., clapping, moving). Then add instruments. The group learns to play the rhythms each time the word or phrase occurs in the song. Next, teach two groups to alternate responses in recorded selections that contain C and R lyrics. As group skill increases, introduce more difficult rhythms and sequence patterns.

By middle to upper grade levels, many groups are able to engage in more intricate ensemble groupings, assigning different groups to accompany different parts of a familiar song. Culminating activities may include the ability to work in true orchestral fashion, and different "sections" of instruments entering or exiting as "conducted" by the therapist or a peer leader. These techniques work well across many genres of recorded music. The musical style can be chosen according to age level or preference, as well as to broaden the musical exposure of the group. Design the ensemble according to the varying needs and skill levels of all group members to ensure success. When appropriate, group members can also undertake the design and conductor roles. At the highest level, these conducting activities can become spontaneously improvised, which will result in actual creation of music within the established framework.

A wide variety of skills and competence levels must be attained for groups of students to perform in ensemble format. These types of activities simultaneously draw upon attention and focus, cognitive processing, motor performance, receptive and expressive communication, and social proficiency. Involving students in the active process of creating musical expression often proves both highly motivating and successful with all types of students. If these activities have been properly designed, individual students will be able to participate at their own level while gaining the benefit of the group experience.

●

Techniques for Mainstream and Inclusion Settings

As a result of the legislation that prohibits exclusionary practices in the public education system, many children with special needs are now serviced directly within the regular education classroom. Music therapy, like many other support services, has begun to move into the general education classroom as well. Integrated educational services take one of two general forms: mainstream or inclusion. Mainstreamed students are based in a special education classroom but spend portions of their day in a regular education setting. Inclusion students, on the other hand, spend all or most of their day in the regular education classroom with most supports provided there. A music therapy program can be effectively provided directly in the regular classroom within either of these scenarios.

The student is not "pulled out" of the regular classroom setting to receive music therapy services. This minimizes classroom disruption, and the student does not miss work that would be presented while he or she is out of the room. The format for this type of music therapy supports one of the major tenets of inclusion: avoid singling out a child as different. Fortunately, music therapy works extremely well in this format. The full class setting provides a larger number of peer models whose responses more closely resemble those desired of the

These types of activities simultaneously draw upon attention and focus, cognitive processing, motor performance, receptive and expressive communication, and social competence.

child with special needs. Moreover, children are often more interested in watching their peers. Helpful peers may spontaneously assist the child in making appropriate responses. If the children with special needs are familiar with the music therapy format, they may really be able to "shine." Furthermore, being a participating part of a group music session enables the child to feel he or she is a true part of the class. This is not always the case during academic subjects. Additionally, the strategies and skills contained in music therapy sessions benefit everyone, not only the designated child.

A circle formation on the floor is an easy and quick way to set up the group. Classes in the lower grades often have an open carpeted area that is usually very amenable to a music therapy circle. In other cases, it may be necessary to be a bit creative. Classroom teachers usually become very helpful once they understand the importance of a bit of "reorganizing."

Nonetheless, challenges do exist. The disparity between the skill levels of typical children and those with special needs is often greater in mainstream or inclusion classrooms than in self-contained classrooms. At times, the child with special needs is viewed as less able or is treated differently by his or her peers. Some peers may take on a protective, "mothering" role that interferes with independent responding. Many more personalities and social dynamics are present in the larger class grouping. The programming must be appropriate for all the class members to be successful.

Designing Appropriate Group Music Activities

Properly designed music activities can be most effective in overcoming the challenges presented by this larger, more diverse group setting. The multi-dimensional aspect of music involvement can work to "level the playing field". Design activities that play to the strengths of the designated child. Begin with musical experiences that will highlight the child with special needs as a successful member of the group:

- Employ a greeting activity already familiar to this child.
- With a nonverbal or very shy child, begin with a waved greeting for everyone.
- Allow the child to hold the tambourine as each peer taps and says "hello."
- Ask the child to show his peers how to properly strum a Q Chord or Omnichord.

Tune into the group dynamics. It is crucial to immediately establish an engaging environment that "hooks" the class. Being cognizant of what musical behaviors are likely evident across chronological ages can assist the music therapist in designing effective music activities.

Structuring the Mainstreaming or Inclusion Session

Initial sessions should contain activities that the students find appealing and that involve the group in a success-oriented, "fun-filled" process. Setting this paradigm early establishes therapist credibility and a relationship with the students that can be drawn upon later when less compelling material must be introduced.

- Model knee tapping during the greeting sequence and engage the entire class immediately. This provides group cohesiveness during the extended process of individually greeting this larger size group.
- Learn the students' names quickly to establish group control and rapport. A game format may be helpful.

> *Greeting game: First, ask the students to name a person sitting next to the therapist in the circle. After greeting that child, have him or her introduce the next child and proceed around the group in the same manner. Accompany this sequence with a guitar song. After each group of 4–5 children, go back and " remember" by naming all the children up to that point. Enlist the group or individual children to assist this "memory." By the time the entire group is greeted, the therapist should know most of the names. Finish by attempting to go around the entire circle naming each child. The students delight in this activity, which usually forms a very quick and solid bond between the group and therapist.*

- Engage the entire group with imitative rhythmic movement, utilizing a lively, recorded selection in a style that typically interests that age level.
- Use a "follow the leader" format to present a series of repetitive movement patterns that allows the therapist to assess the skill level of the group (a rondo form anchors this activity well).

> *A highly motivating activity is to use a guitar-accompanied song such as "You Gotta Sing When the Spirit Says Sing." In a series of verses, different movement responses (clap, tap, stomp, etc.) are substituted. Instruct the students to follow the directions given in the song. Start each verse at a moderately slow tempo. Slowly increase the tempo until the response is very fast Stop playing suddenly and require the students to stop immediately when they hear the music stop. Begin again with another movement.*

- From the "mysterious" depths of the instrument bag, introduce novel yet easily played instruments, such as egg shakers, for group play.

> *Use a song such as Hap Palmer's "PAUSE" (found on Movin'). Pass out instrument pairs such as egg shakers, wrist bells, or maracas. Begin the tape and start playing without instruction; the group will spontaneously join in. This song contains intermittent "pauses" at regular and then more random intervals. Stop and look confused on the first pause—the group will generally follow. After a few stops, they will catch on and then try to guess where the next stop will be. Random intervals make this increasingly more difficult. Various movement patterns can be spontaneously incorporated through therapist model. Emphasize stopping immediately when the music stops.*

- Proceed to a single instrument activity (guitar strumming, passing a cabasa, taking turns on a large drum).

> *Using rhythmic, moderate tempo recorded music as accompaniment, hold a small tambourine in each hand. Move in front of a child and present the tambourines horizontally at waist level. Ask the child to tap one tambourine with each hand several times simultaneously. Then move the tambourines to a new position—upward, apart, downward— keeping them at even level. After the child taps several times in this position, move again. Proceed in this fashion, placing the tambourines at various positions. As appropriate, increase the difficulty by placing the tambourines at different height levels: hold in vertical positions that require hitting from the side; turn them over to be hit from the bottom; place one in vertical and one in horizontal position, one top up and one top down, etc. Decrease the number of taps in each position (the most difficult is one tap per position). Move around the circle giving members turns to play. This is a very motivating way to work on bilateral and eye-hand coordination, as well as to sustain focus.*

- Leave time at the end of the initial sessions to again recall student names during a closing activity.
- End with the Omnichord, Q Chord, or another novel and engaging instrument. Allow each student to play a goodbye.

Making Sessions Fun and Interesting

Fill initial sessions with high probability activities and interesting instruments to ensure that the class will be eager for a "return engagement." Initial sessions are designed to set the stage for working on skills and IEP-driven goals or objectives in the future. Employ a very similar format for several weeks with minor alterations in the instruments and music employed. Choose activities that are highly developmental in nature and designed to foster success of the entire group, including the designated student(s). After a few weeks, the session format may be altered to include various other types of movement, singing, instrument play, and ensemble work.

Be sure to establish early the rules for instrument use. Consistently enforce these placements across sessions until the response is automatic whenever instruments are not being played. These strategies control the sound level in a group setting.

- "Eggs Go in the Nest": Draw a connection between egg shakers and the "nest" created by a cross-leg sitting position. All small instruments are kept there until the group is ready.
- "The Stick Garage": Students "park" sticks or other pairs of larger instruments, one on each shoulder.

Engineering Ensemble Activities

The larger number of students in inclusion or mainstream classes provides strength for ensemble activities. Ensemble work lends itself well to the various skill and developmental levels present within the group. Peer models and more skilled class members can be used to anchor subgroups for singing or playing. The designated students work within the close-knit structure of these smaller groups, often cued by peers without therapist assistance. Parts can be assigned according to student strengths, or for group members to work on different skills as needed. For example, a drum group can be practicing steady beat, while a maraca group is working with syncopated rhythm patterns. Ensemble work focuses on creating a "whole" and encompasses various group and social skills important to success in the regular classroom setting.

The many demands placed upon older students' time often preclude full class programming. In these instances, it may be necessary to employ reverse mainstreaming, a format in which the designated child and a small number of classmates attend a music therapy session in some other location. This smaller group fosters closer and more positive relationships between the identified student and his or her peers. The students all benefit from the small group format and enjoy the active input in the decision-making process that is more feasible than in the large group. Most importantly, this format sets up spontaneous social situations and relationship building opportunities for the designated child that may be unavailable in the classroom.

Considerations at the Secondary Level

Encouraging Initiative

Though the actual session format may remain quite similar, at the secondary level, far more emphasis may be placed on taking ownership of the activities. By the time many students reach the middle and high school level, they may be able to independently begin and complete the greeting activity with little or no therapist support. Movement and instrument play activities may incorporate more frequent opportunities for group members to lead or make independent choices of how the motions or instruments are performed. For example:

- Encourage each member to take a turn leading a repetitive movement of his or her choosing. The leadership is passed around the circle. When a person is finished leading, he or she cues the next person to take over.
- Have student "conductors" lead either movement or instrument play ensembles.
- Allow group input regarding the choice of music or instruments to be used.
- Provide a list of planned activities and allow the group to choose the sequence.

Developmental and IEP-related goals and objectives continue to drive the programming of the sessions at the secondary level. However, the actual materials or music used can be quite varied.

Music Ensembles

A greater emphasis often is placed on music ensemble work at the upper grade levels. Ensemble work fosters many of the skills secondary students need to be successful in work environments or social settings. The ability to make positive social connections and contribute to a group experience is important for students who may soon be leaving the protected school environment. Additionally, self-esteem and confidence are engendered through participation in activities where students must work together to successfully produce a musical "product."

Age-Appropriate Music

The therapist should continue to utilize a wide variety of music styles and genres that are age appropriate for older students. This includes current popular music. Secondary students need to be exposed to the music of their chronologically aged peers. Interestingly, most students are able to discern when music is or is not "appropriate" for the school setting and are generally accepting of limits set in this area. However, many students are equally or more interested in familiar "oldies" or pop standards and readily engage in activities that incorporate these selections.

"DO WAH DITTY" Ensemble: Begin by teaching the title phrase using call and response (C and R) until group sings it accurately. Use therapist–students C and R to teach the "looks good" "looks fine" parts as well. Play the recording and have the group sing the sections as practiced. Divide the class into 3 groups. The center group is given sticks and assigned the "Do Wah Ditty" phrase. Practice this a cappella with sticks. The left group does the calls on maracas and the right group does the responses on wrist bells. Practice these C and R alternation parts several times a cappella until the group is fairly accurate. Play the parts with the recording. Use conductor cues to have groups 1 and 3 play alternately on the phrases of the break section (have the students raise and lower the instruments slowly once per phrase on the words "whoa, I knew I was falling in love" section). Perform the entire song, fading prompts when possible. This activity could take several sessions to fully develop; students may have suggestions for improving it. Experiment!

See Chapter 14 for a quick reference guide of strategies that address special needs of students in school music settings.

●

Conclusion

The specific design and content of music therapy sessions will necessarily vary according to the setting, therapist, and students involved. Assure that a fairly consistent structure is in place. Students will rely upon this structure for support as new or challenging skills are addressed. Actual session formats are the providence of each individual music therapist. The content of this chapter is offered as a jumping-off point as the clinician seeks just the right combination of ideas for success in a particular setting. The crucial aspect is the development of a trusting, safe, and satisfying environment, a setting where students want to be and feel able to respond and take risks. Creating an environment and building relationships that promote student growth are the true underpinnings of a successful music therapy program. The chapter Appendix provides a Summary of a Developmental Schedule for Music Behaviors to be used by the clinician when designing music applications for early childhood and school-aged settings.

References

Adamek, M. S. (2001). Meeting special needs in music class. Music Educators Journal, 84(4), 23–26.

Adamek, M. S. (2002). In the beginning: A review of early special education services and legislative/regulatory activity affecting the teaching and placement of special learners. In B. Wilson (Ed.), Models of music therapy interventions in school settings (pp. 15–24). Silver Spring, MD: American Music Therapy Association.

American Music Therapy Association. (2000). Effectiveness of music therapy procedures: Documentation of research and clinical practice (4th ed.). Silver Spring, MD: Author.

Colwell, C. M. (1995). Adapting music instruction for elementary students with special needs. Music Therapy Perspectives, 13(2), 97–103.

Graham, R. M., & Beer, A. S. (1980). Teaching music to the exceptional child: A handbook for mainstreaming. Englewood Cliffs, NJ: Prentice-Hall.

Hammel, A. M. (2004). Inclusion strategies that work. Music Educators Journal, 90(5), 33–37.

Jones, L. L., & Cardinal, D. N . (1998). Descriptive analysis of music therapists' perceptions of delivery services in inclusive settings: A challenge to the field. Journal of Music Therapy, 35(1), 34–38.

Patterson, A. (2003). Music teachers and music therapists: Helping children together. Music Educators Journal, 89(4), 35–38.

Music Educators National Conference. (1997). In step with inclusion. Teaching Music, 5(3), 56–57.

VanWeelden, K. (2001). Choral mainstreaming: Tips for success. Music Educators Journal, 88(3), 55–60.

Wilson, B. L. (Ed). (2002). Models of music therapy interventions in school settings. Silver Spring, MD: American Music Therapy Association.

Appendix

Summary of Developmental Schedule for Music Behaviors

Music Age (In Years)	Developmental Characteristics of Music Behaviors
1.0	Follows simple instructions; gurgles, coos to music; walks with two-hand support. Claps, not on beat.
1.5	Hums/sings—octave range. Performs body-part songs (pointing). 10 or more word vocabulary. Total body response to music stimuli.
2.0	Talks/sings in short phrases (not on pitch generally). Enjoys rhythmic movement to music (e.g., rock/tap feet). Can relate songs to common pictures. Walks to music (not on beat). Fascinated by sound sources.
2.5	May know parts of songs. Singing not on pitch or beat. Sings spontaneously. Use of small intervals (minor 3rd). Enjoys circle movement games. Runs, gallops, swings, sways (not on beat).
3.0	Can reproduce short songs—not on pitch. Can match pitch from adult. Moves in character of the music, not always on beat.
3.5	Sings a few nursery rhymes alone with most of essential pitch/rhythm. Executes finger plays. Maintains general tonal center.
4.0	Singing rapidly developing; some entire songs on pitch with rhythm. Sings in groups but also enjoys solo singing. Experiments with musical sounds. Recognizes familiar tunes by name. Likes Orff and rhythm instruments.

5.0	Small singing voice but with vocal characteristics. Sings several short songs with good pitch/rhythm/pulse. Likes dramatic songs. Can move rhythmically/in character of the music.
5.5	Singing voice small but developing. May sing alone/with recordings. Can learn simple songs on piano. Enjoys dancing—not always in step, particularly with slower tempos.
6.0	Generally good singing voice with practice. Better able to keep faster tempos in movement and instrument play.
6.5	Matches pitch well, imitates simple songs quickly. Plays instruments with preferred hand. Has some difficulty with two-hand coordination of mallets, triangles, etc. Can run on pulse if tempo matches child's natural pace.
7.0	Good singing voice. Imitates singing of adults and recordings. Group singing important. Marches steadily at various tempos. Moves in character of music (e.g., run/hop). Good two-hand coordination for playing instruments.
7.5	Can hold a voice part (round/descant). Can execute all movement repertoire including skipping. Performs Orff ensembles.
8.0	Sings longer, more complex songs. Ready for hand signals or solfeggio. Conducts all common meters. Increasingly proficient on rhythm instruments. Plays autoharp.
8.5	Strong singing voice with developed style and song preference. Performs fairly complicated dance steps and complex eye-hand skills. Shows interest in orchestral and recreational instruments.
9.0	Interested in "pop" tunes. Full range of singing ability. Definite music preferences. Understands meter, mode, modulation, dynamics. Ready to begin formal instrument study.
10.0	Some have interest in youth choirs. Others continue interest in pop music. Various skill levels with instruments. Intricate dance steps and sustained dancing/eurhythmics.
11.0	Male voices begin to drop. Female voices fuller. Can sing 2- to 3-part music. Developing technique on instruments; some can accompany selves on piano or guitar.

(Drawn from Graham, R. M. & Beer, A. S. (1980). Teaching music to the exceptional child: A handbook for mainstreaming. Englewood Cliffs. NJ: Prentice-Hall.)

Chapter 11

Strategies for Serving the Special Needs of Individuals in Public School Music Settings

Jane E. Hughes, MA, MT-BC; Brenda Robbins Rice, MME, MT-BC
Reprinted from Models of Music Therapy Interventions in School Settings,
Brian Wilson, MM, MT-BC (Ed.)

The strategies presented here address special needs of individuals in public school music settings. They were compiled by the authors from their own professional experiences with students, music therapy colleagues, music teachers, special educators, music therapy interns, practicum students, parents, and others working with students with special needs. The strategies have all proven to be effective in school music settings and specifically address the learning needs of students. This section can be used as a quick reference guide by music therapists working in school music settings.

●

Music Skills

Skill Area: Singing

Suggested Strategies

- Explore ways in which the voice moves up and down (e.g., compare the voice to an elevator)
- Produce sounds such as sirens, ghosts, owls.
- Use pictures, graphs, physical gestures and instruments to visually and/or aurally display movement of sound
- Use physical gestures (moving arms from high to low and vice versa)
- Provide good vocal models (peers, teachers, paraprofessionals)
- Echo sing phrases or individual tones within the appropriate vocal register
- Listen, think, and hum pitches before singing
- Use a minimum of accompaniment to focus on the vocal line
- Teach ostinatos, echo songs and rounds

- Discuss and demonstrate the differences between the speaking and singing voice
- Explore ways in which to use the voice (whisper, speak, scream, cry, laugh, hum, sing)
- Vocalize using vowel and consonant sounds
- Model deep breathing techniques
- Have the students take deep breaths in and out, laugh, yawn. Feel the muscular action and expansion of the rib cage
- Emphasize the relaxed jaw and open mouth position
- Whisper and speak words clearly
- Emphasize soft singing
- Have students hold an imaginary candle and slowly blow out the flame to improve breath control
- Sing phrases staccato, marcato, legato
- Use songs that elicit free vocalization on open syllables
- Allow the student time to respond vocally
- Use some songs with melodic and rhythmic repetition (e.g., repeated phrases, words or refrain after every verse)
- Find songs within the vocal range of the student having difficulty matching pitches
- Provide outside assistance to practice specific music skills such as solfege syllables and Curwen hand signs used in the Kodaly philosophy of teaching
- Have students put solfege syllables to favorite songs
- Provide several opportunities for students to hear the melody (sing it, outline the melody with your hand, use Curwen hand signs, play it on instruments)
- Incorporate sign language into song activities
- Practice matching pitches using kazoos, step bells, xylophone

Skill Area: Playing Instruments

Suggested Strategies

- Place instruments, visuals (charts, posters, flash cards) and yourself directly in front of the student's line of vision
- Use color coding or braille markings on instruments
- Have mallets in a variety of sizes available so that the student may find one that feels comfortable in his/her hand
- Remove wheelchair trays to enhance physical contact between students during instrument and action song activities
- Allow students with physical limitations to choose their manner of participation (they usually will tell you the successful way)

- Have a peer hold the instrument while the other student plays with his/her dominant hand
- Adapt instruments only after the student has demonstrated that he/she has difficulty manipulating it correctly
- Design rhythm activities that allow the student to respond in his/her own tempo or pattern
- Provide outside assistance to practice rhythm skills
- Echo clap rhythms
- Incorporate movement activities to develop a sense of basic beat and rhythm
- Practice using a variety of percussion instruments
- Use a variety of activities to develop rhythm skills (singing, clapping patterns, moving, playing the recorder and barred instruments, i.e., xylophones)
- Practice verbal and visual cues such as "ready," "begin," and "stop" during all activities
- Model correct playing techniques (peers, paraprofessionals, and teachers)
- Provide several opportunities for students to hear the rhythm patterns (clap it, sing it, play it on instruments)
- Provide outside assistance to practice playing barred instruments
- Use flash cards to teach the letter names on xylophones and other melodic instruments

Suggested Strategies for Recorder (A wooden or plastic woodwind instrument)

- Provide outside assistance to practice recorder skills
- Use a variety of creative games, notation exercises and familiar songs when practicing recorder
- Provide much repetition
- Use appealing visuals (posters, flash cards, large music staff)
- Use Suzuki precorders for beginning recorder players

Skill Area: Listening

Suggested Strategies

- Keep directions simple—give a series of directions one step at a time (e.g., 1. "Open book"; 2. "Turn to page 1")
- Use movement to reinforce listening to form
- Provide several opportunities for students to hear the melody and rhythm patterns (sing it, clap it, play it on instruments)
- Play a familiar song; have students identify the "mystery tune"
- Sing a portion of a song and stop on a specific word. Students identify that word
- Sing a song. Students listen and sing silently (mouth words)

- Teach rhythm echo activities
- Use call and response songs
- Provide several visuals illustrating form, melody, rhythm, harmony, timbre
- Use activities that are short and simple with much repetition
- Use a multisensory approach (provide movement, visual aids, auditory cues, singing, playing creating)
- Place student closer to the sound source
- Provide visual cues through facial expressions, signs, movements, lights flicking, etc.
- Check with students wearing hearing aids to determine the optimum levels needed for music
- Use a variety of appealing sound sources to capture attention and motivate participation and musical growth

Skill Area: Moving

Suggested Strategies
- Provide sufficient space for wheelchairs
- Design activities that emphasize the students' motor strengths
- Provide activities for the student to develop body skills to move about the classroom with ease and safety
- Allow the student an opportunity to experience movement at his/her own level (moving eyes, fingers, head, hands, etc.)
- Train peers to assist students
- Remove wheelchair trays to enhance physical contact between students during activities
- Develop ways for all students to participate in activities involving dancing and moving through space. Wagons, tricycles, scooterboards, and other devices could be used if wheelchairs are not feasible
- Say and do all movements when first teaching a dance (step right, tap, tap)
- Partners perform side-to-side or face-to-face rather than pushing the wheelchair. Use two peers if necessary—one to push and one to be the partner
- If necessary, design alternative strategies so that all students participate in the same movement activities and reinforce music learning
- Move creatively with scarves, streamers, paper, parachutes, masks, puppets and other motivators

Skill Area: Creating/Composing

Suggested Strategies
- Have students create their own rhythm patterns and accompaniments
- Encourage exploration and improvisation

- Provide a comfortable environment in which students are free to risk sharing new ideas
- Encourage and ensure peer respect
- Design activities where the students can develop their own creative movements
- Use dramatization in the classroom to act out favorite songs, listening selections or environmental events
- Create sound pieces
- Use appealing stories and poems and have students create sound effects
- Use props such as colorful scarves, paper hats and articles from nature

Skill Area: Reading/Writing

Suggested Strategies

- Pair reading notation with visual and auditory cues (pair sound with symbol)
- Sing songs that will assist the student in remembering and understanding note values
- Practice various rhythms by using the verbal music concepts of Kodaly and Orff or any other consistent manner of counting
- Practice the names of the lines and spaces by using an oversized music staff
- Play word association games
- Provide opportunities for repetition with fun ways to practice
- Provide outside assistance to practice reading and notation skills
- Break down the steps into the simplest form possible
- Use a variety of learning and response modes
- Demonstrate and model correct written response first
- Find alternative ways to evaluate the students
- Use repetition and visuals to teach musical language concepts
- Provide rote learning when reading is not possible
- Use clear and uncluttered charts
- ESE teacher provide magnified or braille materials if needed
- Adapt written worksheets if necessary
- Be aware that some students may need to be placed closer to written words and symbols to process the material

●
General Skills

Skill Area: Participating

Suggested Strategies
- Use a wide range of appealing activities to ensure success
- Have a peer or paraprofessional model appropriate responses
- Have a paraprofessional physically assist the student
- Use a variety of learning and response modes
- Vary classroom groupings (large groups, small groups)
- Place a "peer/buddy" next to the student to model correct responses
- Accept all efforts as praiseworthy
- Assign the student a "buddy" who can spend time with the student in other activities outside of the music class
- Provide individual praise within the group when the student participates
- Provide outside assistance to practice music skills
- Place student between two good role models

Skill Area: Staying On Task

Suggested Strategies
- Use positive reinforcement when the student is on task
- Teach small amounts of materials at a time and gradually increase the number and length of activities
- Provide outside assistance to practice music skills
- Use a multisensory approach (presenting information in many diverse ways)
- Present small tasks to accomplish and reinforce upon completion
- Seat student near teacher or paraprofessional
- Assign a student to be a "buddy/partner"
- Paraprofessional physically assist the student if necessary
- Teacher physically assist student if possible
- Place student in front of the room
- Give verbal cues to encourage the student to attend
- Upon completion of the music class, send a behavior sheet back to the ESE teacher
- ESE teacher reminds student just prior to the class what is expected of him/her in the music class
- ESE teacher provide positive reinforcement in the classroom for good progress at the conclusion of the music class
- Reinforce with verbal praise

- Give directions in multisensory ways (say it, point to it, write it)
- Provide a structured classroom environment
- Give directions more than once during an activity
- Reduce the number of distractions
- Look directly at the student when giving instructions
- Simplify tasks to the level of the student to ensure success
- Assign the student a "buddy" who can also spend time with the student in other fun activities outside of the music class
- Use appealing visual aids
- Provide a variety of fun and appealing activities (singing, moving, playing, creating)

Skill Area: Following Directions

Suggested Strategies

- Look directly at student when giving directions
- Limit the number of new ideas presented at one time
- Demonstrate while giving directions
- Have the student repeat step-by-step instructions as they are given to ensure understanding
- Simplify the tasks to ensure success
- Make your directions simple
- Model correct behaviors and responses
- Give directions in multisensory ways (say it, point to it, write it)
- Give directions more than once during an activity

Skill Area: Reducing Behavior Problems

Suggested Strategies

- Review the rules of appropriate social behavior in the music classroom prior to the class
- Model correct behaviors and responses
- Be firm and always positive
- Be consistent with student expectations, classroom rules, teaching routines and classroom environment
- Have paraprofessional sit next to student to provide assistance if necessary
- Instruct paraprofessional in nonverbal prompting techniques to prevent distractions or interruptions
- Place student next to a good peer role model
- Assign the student a "buddy" who can spend time with the student in other activities outside of the music class
- Recognize student success (social and musical)

- Provide much positive reinforcement for appropriate behavior
- Explain consequences for behaviors
- Use school-wide classroom warnings and time-out procedures
- Send the student back to the classroom only if he/she is very disruptive, making it difficult for other students to learn
- Place student in the front of the room
- Give directions more than once during an activity
- Discreetly use the same positive reinforcement program used in the ESE classroom to achieve the desired behavior in the music classroom
- Find the students' strengths and plan opportunities for success
- Through your own language model, encourage and ensure respect among peers

Skill Area: Improving Motivation

Suggested Strategies
- Place student next to a good role model and friend
- When doing small group work, assign a good role model and friend to that group
- Find the student's strengths and plan chances for small successes
- Provide much positive reinforcement when the student shows an interest
- Provide outside assistance to practice music skills
- Make the student feel comfortable when participating in class activities
- Provide a variety of fun and appealing activities
- Let the student know it is all right to make mistakes
- Relate music concepts to the student's interests and favorite music selections

Skill Area: Increasing Understanding

Suggested Strategies
- Present tasks slowly to allow for success, then gradually increase the level of music difficulty
- Model correct music responses
- Provide outside assistance to practice music skills
- Teach small amount of material at a time
- Place student closer to the teacher
- Provide a variety of activities
- Provide concrete examples
- Use dramatization to increase understanding by acting out song text and listening to musical selections
- Emphasize for the student specific music skills learned in all activities
- Provide much repetition in many fun ways
- Use several appealing visuals

- Provide immediate positive reinforcement
- Give directions clearly

Skill Area: Discussion/Oral Expression

Suggested Strategies

- Have discussions about the songs
- Accept all efforts as praiseworthy
- Provide praise when student shows interest in the discussion
- Ask questions that require short "yes/no" responses
- Find the student's interest to encourage a greater feeling of comfort
- Use call and response songs
- Use visual aids (posters, rhythm flash cards)

Chapter 12

Learning Through Play—
A Method for Reaching Young Children

Marcia E. Humpal, MEd, MT-BC; Rebecca Tweedle, MEd, MT-BC

It is often said, "Play is a child's work." Yet often play is trivialized and dismissed as meaningless activity. *Play* and *work* actually may be part of a continuum of how young children typically explore, act, and learn. Whereas play may be intrinsically motivated, spontaneous, and process-oriented, work often is viewed as being extrinsically motivated, forced, and goal-oriented (Frost & Klein, 1984). Throughout history, play has been viewed in several different ways. Play has been seen as a vehicle to use surplus energy, a way to avoid boredom and renew energy, as practice for adulthood, and even as recapitulation, that is, a way to relive periods in the evolutionary history of the human species (Hughes, 1999).

The mention of the word *play* no doubt conjures up a myriad of pictures in one's mind . . . experimenting, pretending, contemplating, demonstrating, analyzing, wondering, searching, examining, investigating, solving, interacting, running, dancing, cooperating, and enjoying. We all have vivid memories of play (and hopefully, we all continue to include play in our lives). Play is a powerful way for children to explore the world and learn about themselves. Therefore, it is only right that any discussion of young children and music therapy should include a discussion of play, for a child's world is filled with and fueled by play. While true play may be voluntary, spontaneous, and intrinsically motivated, with some children, it is often necessary to expose and teach the fundamentals of free play options.

This chapter seeks to examine and answer the following questions:

What is play?

How does the young child use music in play?

How can music therapists use music play with young children—those with special needs as well as those who are developing typically?

We will describe and discuss the theoretical underpinnings of a play-based approach to music therapy, how children develop musically, and, finally, effective clinical practices, methods, and techniques that are often successfully employed when working with young children.

The National Association for the Education of Young Children (NAEYC) defines Early Childhood as the stage of life between birth and 8 years. However, we have chosen to limit our discussion of Early Childhood to the ages from birth through 5. This monograph addresses service delivery that is educational in nature. Therefore, these delegated age groupings seem logical because of the natural division between preschool and full-day school age settings (note that kindergarten could feasibly be a part of either grouping).

Early Childhood may be further divided into two subgroups: birth to 2, and 3 to 5, aligning with the way federal legislation mandates service. Early intervention services are available for families and children from birth to age 2 who have or are at-risk for developmental delay. An Individualized Family Service Plan (IFSP) guides these services, while individuals from age 3 to 21 are served by an Individualized Education Program (IEP). Furthermore, states may vary in the way they define and deliver services to those children below school age (refer to Chapter 3 for an extensive discussion of these documents).

●

Play

There are many ways that play may be interpreted. What is play to one person may not be play to someone else. However, this chapter will be based on the developmentally appropriate practice philosophy of play-based learning (often referred to as D.A.P.). This philosophy believes that play is fundamental and that children learn skills in such areas as cooperation, problem solving, language, and mathematics, as well as develop curiosity, self-esteem, strength and coordination, self-direction, and values when we enrich their play (McCracken, 1997). Note that this statement does not say "when *they* play," but rather, "when *we enrich* their play." Some early childhood educators have questioned whether D.A.P. can apply to all young children and whether play is the most effective way to reach all children. Some argue for "engaged pedagogy" where the facilitator is constantly reexamining his or her teaching style as well as the child's learning style, acknowledging that a child's culture and ability level play a huge role in the way he or she learns (O'Brien, 2000). However, these divergent views of D.A.P. do not diminish the value of play for young children.

●

Theoretical Underpinnings of a Play-based Approach

How Children Learn—Theoretical Framework

Many theorists have made references to the role of play in child development. However, the philosophy of D.A.P. is based on the works of Piaget and Vygotsky. The following is an overview of Brett's (1997) descriptions of these views of play.

Piaget felt that play consolidates learning and allows for new learning to occur. Known as the father of Constructivism, Piaget represents a cognitive developmentalist point of view. He noted that children need concrete experiences and thus learn through active involvement and interaction with the environment. He theorized that children construct knowledge based on these interactions. Piaget's first two stages relate to early childhood. The sensorimotor stage, from birth to age 2, dwells on functional play and repetitive movements. The pre-operational stage, ages 2–7, finds children using symbolic play, pretend play, and constructive play.

Vygotsky noted that play offers a way to reconstruct reality. Vygotsky, also a cognitive developmentalist, is best remembered for two concepts. The first, the *Zone of Proximal Development*, describes the range of activities that a child can accomplish with the help of more advanced peers or adults. The second, *scaffolding*, refers to the guidance and assistance that allows children to take over responsibility for tasks within their zone of proximal development. This guidance and assistance may be referred to as *bumping up* the child. This technique will be discussed in more depth later in this chapter.

Levels of Play

Young children move through different *stages* of play. Many theorists have described various levels of play, but in general, play may be categorized along *cognitive* dimensions and also along *social* dimensions.

Piaget's sensorimotor stage is characterized by functional play (such as banging and babbling). In Piaget's pre-operational stage, play extends from being constructive (such as stacking tambourines into a tower), to becoming more symbolic (such as using props to act out a song, or using props such as scarves to dramatically represent the music or musical story), and even to playing games with rules (such as "Musical Chairs").

Parten (1932) described *levels* of social play. The first level is that of *unoccupied behavior*. Next is the level of *onlooker play*. The remaining levels and how they may relate to musical play follow:

- *Solitary play*: A child removes sticks from the instrument box and sits by himself and taps out a rhythm on the floor.
- *Parallel play*: Two or more children are sitting in the music area independently playing instruments of their choice.
- *Associative play*: Two children are playing rhythms on the same drum.
- *Cooperative play*: Two children are taking turns tapping out question and answer phrases on a drum.

Later, Linder (1990) expanded upon these categories and stages of play and wrote of a play-based approach to working in early intervention. Musical examples have been added (Humpal & Dimmick, 1996):

- *Exploratory*: discovering one's environment through many senses—*making noises with the mouth as it is pressed against a hand.*
- *Relational*: using objects in play for their intended purpose—*playing an instrument according to function.*
- *Constructive*: manipulating objects for the purpose of creating something—*stacking drums according to their size and pitch.*
- *Dramatic*: pretending to do something or be someone—*using props in a song.*

- *Games with Rules*: playing a game that has accepted rules and limits—*singing and playing "The Farmer in the Dell."*
- *Rough and Tumble*: moving and playing in a boisterous and physical manner (note that this category includes a sensorimotor component, thought by many to be a key to higher level thinking and learning)—*moving to music via group parachute activity.*

Musical Play

Development of Musical Understanding—The Pillsbury Study. In 1937, the Pillsbury Foundation School was opened in Santa Barbara, California. Led by Gladys Evelyn Moorhead, director of the school, and Donald Pond, the school's music director, the facility was designed to study the development of musical understanding in young children from age 2 to early elementary school age. Throughout the day, the children were free to explore instruments representative of various cultures, listen to recordings that covered an extensive array of musical eras and genres, and take part in activities of their own choosing. Older children received formal instruction in reading; however, there was minimal emphasis placed on adult intervention during the rest of the day's schedule. Moorhead and Pond hypothesized that given the appropriate environment and opportunity, each stage of a young child's life would develop its own unique expression that would become the root of later musicality.

For seven years, the children were studied as they spontaneously sang, chanted, and played instruments. Moorhead and Pond observed that:

1. the children experimented with vocalizations and songs and did not organize their music in conventional tonalities as adults do;
2. the children's songs were plaintive compared to the songs adults would have them sing;
3. chanting took place under conditions of solitary free play as well as in group play;
4. physical activity was directly related to rhythmic chanting;
5. solo chanting resembled heightened speech with music conforming to the words, whereas group chanting usually was in duple meter and the words conformed to the rhythmic structure;
6. the children explored instruments before melodic and rhythmic patterns emerged; and
7. instrumental improvisation was characterized by asymmetrical meter, followed by duple and triple meters, then steady beat. (Burton, 2002)

Very little music research or research with young children was being conducted in the 1940s. Furthermore, qualitative music research was not widely recognized at the time. It was not until 1978 that all of the studies of Moorhead and Pond were compiled and published as *Music of Young Children*. This book remains a testimony that all children are naturally musical and that they will develop musical as well as technical skills if they are immersed in a free and favorable environment (Jordan-DeCarbo, 1997).

A Developmental Sequence of How Young Children Develop Musically. Briggs (1991) notes that that all children seem to pass through a developmental sequence for acquiring musical skills. Her model, based on others from developmental psychology, includes musical milestones in four areas: (1) auditory, (2) vocal/tonal, (3) rhythmic, and (4) cognitive. Musical skill development is divided into four phases: the Reflex Phase, the Intention Phase, the Control Phase, and the Integration Phase. These stages are characterized below:

- *Reflex Phase* (ages 0–9 months): Children are absorbing sensory information from their world and using their vocal and rhythmic skills to communicate. During this time they develop the ability to react to changes in musical elements, use their voice to play with sounds, and move to music with their whole body.

- *Intention Phase* (ages 9–18 months): Children begin to develop the concept of self and are learning to use the early components of language. Musically, they localize sound sources, recognize familiar songs, and move to music with individual body parts.

- *Control Phase* (ages 18–36 months): Characterized by children's need to be in control of their environments. They develop a more accurate pitch perception, begin to sing recognizable pitches and pitch contours, remember lyrics, and show a large increase in rhythmic/motor control.

- *Integration Stage* (ages 36–72 months): Children develop the set of characteristics that becomes the basis for personality. Their musical growth includes the ability to discriminate dynamics, the refinement of listening skills, a large growth in song repertoire, steady improvement in eye-hand coordination, an understanding of musical concepts, and the beginning of the ability to conserve musical elements.

For a basic, general overview of music characteristics of young children, see Figure 31.

CHARACTERISTICS OF YOUNG CHILDREN					
	Infants (6–18 months):	Toddlers (18–36 months):	3 year olds:	4 year olds:	5 year olds:
Singing	Participate in musical baby talk.	Create their own songs. Can sing simple songs or sections of songs.	Can sing a recognizable song (do it best when they start on their own pitch).	Enjoy singing with a group.	Have a large song repertoire.
Moving	Enjoy being rocked, stroked, patted, and bounced.	Can perform basic gross motor movements. Move spontaneously to music.	Begin to have the ability to keep a steady beat.	Move expressively to music (not yet inhibited).	Can follow movement directions in simple dances. Enjoy props and costumes for movement.
Listening	Enjoy being sung to. Enjoy sounds such as tongue fluttering.	Are aware of musical and nonmusical sounds.	Enjoy listening to lively music.	Begin to acquire musical vocabulary.	Respond to listening selections through movement or playing instruments.
Playing	Explore sound sources.	Play rhythm instruments by striking, shaking, and patting.	Are developing eye-hand coordination to play barred instruments.	Can identify and correctly play basic rhythm instruments.	Can follow symbols to play simple melodies on bells.
Comments	Love repetition.	Often display a delayed response to music.	Are able to sit with a group for music time.	Enjoy being the group leader. Will make up motions for the group to follow.	Enjoy musical drama.

Figure 31. Characteristics of Young Children. (Tweedle, 1999)

● ●

Effective Clinical Practice, Methods and Techniques

Music for young children is not an option, but is a part of the curricula "best practices." (Bayless & Ramsey, 1991)

Effective Clinical Practice

Developmentally Appropriate Practice

Currently, play is at the root of Developmentally Appropriate Practice, a philosophy set forth by NAEYC. The play-based approach is two-dimensional, advocating a curriculum that is age-appropriate as well as individually appropriate. In 1987, Bredekamp noted NAEYC's guidelines for D.A.P.:

- provide for all areas of a child's development;
- focus planning on observations and recordings of each child's interests and developmental progress;
- plan the environment to facilitate learning through *interactive play* with adults, peers, and materials;
- provide for a wide range of interests and abilities;

Re-examining the original principles of D.A.P., Bredekamp and Copple (1997) authored a second edition of guidelines for developmentally appropriate practice that further addressed these areas:

- children at risk and/or with special needs (the second edition examines how the guidelines apply to *all* children, looking at how these children develop and learn);
- a more flexible definition of the word "appropriate";
- infant brain research (and implications for the first three years of life); and
- insight into community building among young learners.

The increasing emphasis on inclusion and the demand for specialized programs for young children may seem to be on a philosophical collision course. A main goal of early intervention is to remediate as well as prevent other disabling conditions from occurring. However, specialized instruction does not require special or separate settings, materials, or activities. Sandell, Schwartz, and Joseph (2001), developed a Building Blocks Model for effective instruction in inclusive early childhood settings. This model builds upon a high quality early childhood program. To this program is added modifications and adaptations to classroom activities and routines. Learning centers include all children and enhance their participation in the classroom. Learning opportunities thus are embedded throughout the learning environment. If necessary, explicit child-directed instruction lets the adult transform opportunities for learning into successful learning interactions. This model recognizes that Developmentally Appropriate Practice for young children with disabilities may require varying, yet appropriate, levels of support and actual instruction across activities and settings.

Developmentally Appropriate Music Experiences

Musical experiences for young children should be both developmentally and individually appropriate. MENC: the National Association for Music Education, recognized the importance of D.A.P when it adopted its *Position Statement on Early Childhood Education.* This document states in part that all children have musical potential and they

- bring their own unique interests and abilities to the music learning environment;
- can develop critical thinking skills through musical ideas *[the authors note that we can expand this position statement to include communication, motor, social/ emotional skills]*;
- come to early childhood music experiences from diverse backgrounds; and
- should experience exemplary musical sounds, activities, and materials. (MENC, 1992)

Furthermore, young children should not be expected to meet performance goals. They learn best in pleasant physical and social environments that are diverse in nature with effective adult models (MENC, 1995).

Developmentally Appropriate Music Therapy

Though the above was written from a music education point of view, its principles can be comfortably aligned with models of music therapy service delivery to young children. Music therapy procedures can be assimilated with early intervention goals (Furman & Furman, 1993). Music therapy offers optimal individualization within group instruction, the development of meaningful communication skills, socially appropriate interactions between children with disabilities and their typically developing peers, and techniques for early childhood curricular instruction in academic/pre-academic, communication, motor, and social/emotional domains (Humpal, 1990). A study by Standley and Hughes (1996) documented a variety of developmentally appropriate activity components of a music therapy program for early intervention. Results of this study indicate that the music therapy sessions effectively implemented the D.A.P. philosophy of instruction.

Methods

Methodologies and Approaches

Many music approaches and methodologies that currently are used with young children incorporate some aspects of play.

Dalcroze (Eurhythmics). Jacque-Dalcroze, the creator of this approach, believed in child centered learning and age- as well as ability-appropriate experiences. There are three main components to this methodology: (1) *solfege* (ear training using a fixed *do*); (2) improvisation; and (3) the eurhythmics themselves (good rhythm, proportion, and symmetry). All three components are taught together (Frego, Liston, Hama, & Gillmeister, 2004).

Gordon's Theory of Audiation. The ability to hear and understand music without the presence of physical sound is to music what thought is to language. Gordon (1990) stresses that parents and caregivers must sing and make music with their children in order to help them learn to think in music. Much of a child's learning to audiate occurs through play. Babbling and exploring tonal and rhythm patterns, both vocally and through unrestricted free flowing movement, are types of such play (Valerio, 1997).

Kodaly. Zoltan Kodaly established his methodology, a developmental approach that utilizes multisensory experiences, to cultivate music literacy. Four key elements are embedded in his work: (1) singing, (2) folk music, (3) solfege, and (4) the movable *do*. John Curwen developed a series of hand signals to be used with the Kodaly method. Each signal corresponds to a pitch syllable and also indicates the rising and falling of the musical line (Brownell, Frego, Kwak, & Rayburn, 2004).

Nordoff-Robbins. The Nordoff-Robbins approach utilizes instrumental improvisation to focus on the child's movements, sounds, or sound making. The adult supports and builds on the child's responses and often follows the child's lead as they make music together. Music is viewed as a vehicle for self-actualization that can overcome emotional, physical, or cognitive difficulties (Nordoff-Robbins Center for Music Therapy, 2001).

Orff. In the Orff method, "play" movements such as running and jumping are incorporated into the activities, emphasizing the use of creativity within a structure. Children are encouraged to explore the sounds of words, melodies, and instruments. Certain elements of Orff-Schulwerk are fundamental to Orff Music Therapy: (a) a sense of music in its broadest sense, (b) improvisation (very compatible with a play-based approach), and (c) instrumentarium (not only quality instruments but also nonmusical materials that encourage participation in the musical experience) (Voight, 2003).

Other Approaches. In addition to classes that follow the above methodologies, many commercial music programs are available for young children and their families. Some offer training for those interested in teaching the particular method or in becoming part of a franchise.

Music therapists working with young children may use a variety of approaches or methodologies and most definitely will find they assume many different roles. At times they will be *entertainers*, serving as *models*. At other times, they will become *facilitators* or *directors*, and at other times *designers of the environment*. Finally, they should always be *analytic observers*. Music therapists can deliver services in a manner that is highly compatible with developmentally appropriate practices, since music therapy traditionally uses the music as a means to *nonmusical* as well as *musical* ends. The philosophy guiding developmentally appropriate practice and the basic constructs of music itself lend support to using music to develop the "whole child."

Music Service Delivery Settings That May Enhance Play

Regularly Scheduled Classes and Individual Sessions. Music therapy services may be delivered on a regular basis in the children's classrooms, in a music room, or wherever empty space can be found. Children may be seen on an individual basis or in inclusion, reverse mainstream, integrated, or self-contained classes (see Chapters 6 and 7 for further discussion of classroom settings).

The physical environment of the session definitely affects the opportunities for and types of musical play that can be facilitated. Know in advance if and how the room can be engineered to best enhance productive musical play experiences.

Family/Child Programs. These programs offer socialization with other young children and provide opportunities for families to share concerns and experiences. Besides furnishing enjoyable means for enhancing the developmental skills and behaviors of the children, music programs can help teach key parent interaction and play strategies as well as provide a fun playtime experience for caregivers and children.

Consultation. Music therapists often function as part of a team approach. Teachers and other related service personnel may request ideas for the use of music beyond the scheduled music sessions.

Music will enrich the lives of the children and also can be a rewarding, effective part of the teacher's day. So, in addition to giving direct service, music therapists often find themselves in the role of team member or consultant, demonstrating how music play can enhance and reinforce the goals and efforts of other professionals. Since classroom teachers and other staff members often have more interaction opportunities with the children, musical growth is enhanced because children learn through repetition.

However, for consultation to be most effective, the music therapist must do more than simply provide materials and resources to staff. Kern (2004, 2005) successfully designed

The philosophy guiding developmentally appropriate practice and the basic constructs of music itself lend support to using music to develop the "whole child."

and implemented a music therapy *collaborative consultative* approach for the inclusion of young children with autism in a childcare program. In this model, the teacher and the music therapist were equal partners in defining the problem, identifying goals, and planning interventions. The music therapist trained the staff to use specific music therapy techniques, then supported them during the implementation and took part in follow-up discussion. Kern concluded that the collaborative consultation method allowed for expansion of music therapy services and promoted effective program sustainability. Likewise, a study by Register (2004) indicated that providing a model for implementation and support may increase the amount of music used by personnel in early childhood classroom settings. MENC, in its *Position Statement on Early Childhood Education* (1992), calls for a combined effort among parents, music specialists, and early childhood professionals to ensure that music becomes a natural and important part of every young child's growth and development. Music therapists can consult with and offer suggestions and strategies to *parents* and *families* of young children (see Figure 32). There is no better place to instill the joys of musical play than within the minds of those who will make the most difference in the lives of these little ones.

All young children love music.
They experience music by *hearing* it, by *moving* to it, by *banging* to it, and by *playing with their voices*.
Little ones enjoy being sung to:
<ul><li>*With a quiet lullaby at nap time and bedtime as you rock. Keep the beat slow and steady. Many young children will find this special time very calming.*</li><li>*About activities of her day—no need to use the same words each time. Making up words that describe her activity is fun for both of you.*</li><li>*With children's songs that are familiar to him (such as "Row, Row, Row Your Boat"). Sing them over and over. Young children love repetition!*</li><li>*With your favorite songs. She will enjoy seeing you enjoy music, too.*</li><li>*As you change activities. The music will help your child accept and anticipate change.*</li></ul>
Little ones enjoy fingerplays, finger wiggles, tickles, and bounces:
<ul><li>*While holding onto your finger and feeling the beat as you bounce them on your lap.*</li><li>*Or hearing you sing simple finger play songs (like "Eensy Weensy Spider").*</li><li>*Or being part of chanting and rhyming games or songs that end with a tickle.*</li></ul>
Little ones enjoy sounds:
<ul><li>*That have surprises (like "Pop! Goes the Weasel!").*</li><li>*That rattle or ring.*</li><li>*That come from music boxes or musical toys.*</li><li>*That they can make on small instruments such as bells or rattles . . .*</li><li>*Or from things found around the house (such as pots and pans).*</li><li>*That are in their environment—such as trains or birds singing.*</li><li>*That they can make with their bodies (like clapping, tapping or patting).*</li></ul>
A few tips for using music with your little one:
<ul><li>*Don't be shy about singing—your child will respond to the rhythm, melody and the joy with which you sing... and he will welcome the chance to share this time with you.*</li><li>*Make music a part of the whole day.*</li><li>*Match your child's energy level—upbeat songs when she's ready for play and lullabies when she's tired.*</li><li>*Repeat, repeat, repeat . . . do it again, and again, and again. Children learn through repetition.*</li><li>*Expose your little one to many different types of music. Borrow tapes and CDs from the library before purchasing them to find the ones that you and your child like most.*</li><li>*By making music with your child, you can share traditions of your culture.*</li><li>*Relax and enjoy this special time for interacting and sharing with your little one.*</li></ul>
Compiled by the Cuyahoga Co. Bd. of MR/DD Early Childhood Music Therapy Dept., Cleveland, OH (1999) *Cuyahoga County Board of Mental Retardation and Developmental Disabilities* *Living, learning, working and playing in the community.*
Figure 32. Music and Your Little One. *(Reprinted with permission.)*

Types of Musical Play Within Settings

Music sessions may be conducted in many ways within the aforementioned settings. Hallquist and Wishon (2003) studied the development and evolution of developmentally appropriate practices. They developed an early childhood music education model that sets forth their view of appropriate learning environments as well as roles of teachers. The authors see both of these areas as existing on a continuum. They note that music circle time can appropriately include both directed learning and participatory play that leads to integration of learning. Likewise, music therapists may find that a combination of the following types of play opportunities present appropriate methods for facilitating goals and objectives for both individuals and groups.

Individual Exploratory Play. This musical play provides musical books, instruments, objects or props that give children the opportunity to freely explore and create. The music therapist facilitates play through arranging the environment.

Permeable Learning Settings. Music is embedded into transition times, resting, welcoming and goodbye times and throughout other aspects of the curricula.

Guided Group Play (e.g., "Circle Time"). Children are gathered together, though not always in a circle in chairs. They may gather on a rug or a blanket on the floor. Although the session may be structured and the play more adult-directed, spontaneity and the children's responses are an important part of the session. Children are encouraged to explore and investigate in a type of improvisation. They are presented with a wide variety of ways to *play with sound* and *respond to sound.* The abilities of all children are considered. Adaptations for instruments, augmentative ways to use the voice, and alternate ways to move are present so that *all* children can be successful in experiencing and making music.

Realistically, not all facilities serving young children will be able to have music therapists on staff to do this. The classroom teacher may conduct Guided Group Play.

Programmatic versus Goal driven. Regardless of whether music therapy is driven by a specific goal or objective on the IFSP or IEP or is programmatic in nature, music therapists working with young children should conduct ongoing assessment and be guided by the children's responses and their levels of play. A Music Therapy Matrix (Welch & Humpal, 2003) may help organize the large amount of information that the music therapist must remember, as well as help the therapist plan sessions that embed programmatic concerns and individual goals into an established format (see Figure 33). Additional information on programmatic service delivery may be found in Chapter 7.

MUSIC THERAPY CLASSROOM ACTIVITY & INDIVIDUAL GOAL MATRIX										
CHILD'S NAME										
Gathering Activity										
Greeting Song										
Singing/Using "Voice"										
Instrumental Play										
Movement/Motor										
Centers/Exploratory Musical Play										
Listening										
Good-bye										
Other Considerations										
Play/Interaction										
Transitions										
Communication										
Sensory										

* to mark goal area

CLASS: _____ YEAR: _____

Figure 33. Music Therapy Matrix (Welch & Humpal, 2003).

●

Techniques

Facilitating Musical Play

Play is a natural activity for most children who are developing typically. However, we cannot assume that all children will acquire play skills naturally. Furthermore, by adhering to certain consistent guidelines, music therapists may facilitate play for all children in a more effective manner. Linder (1990) recommends six ways to facilitate play:

- Follow the child's lead and the child's choices.
- Parallel play with the child and comment about the play action.
- Encourage any mode of communication the child has.
- Let the activity govern the interaction/turn-taking.
- Limit questioning and wait for the child to pause before commenting (this conveys that the child's comments are valuable).
- When the child is comfortable, try to "bump up" the level of play via modeling/expanding.

Firugre 34 gives examples of how these steps can be musically facilitated.

FACILITATING PLAY-BASED INSTRUCTION	
Facilitation skill	Musical example
Follow the child's lead and the child's choices.	Put out instruments and allow total freedom in playing. Imitate the actions of the child.
Parallel play with the child; occasionally comment about the play action.	Play an instrument next to the child; sing a simple phrase describing the playing.
Encourage any mode of communication the child may use by imitating or responding in a turn-taking manner.	Play instruments and imitate both motor and vocal actions, echoing dynamic, pitch, and tempo levels. Pause and offer child another turn (via eye gaze, gesture, words, etc.).
Let the activity govern the interaction; limit talking.	Hum along with the instrumental play or sing a nonsense syllable to draw attention to the play.
Limit questioning; wait— convey that the child's comments are valued.	Wait until the child pauses then sing a comment ("John played the blue bell") or play an answering phrase.
Once the child is comfortable at play, try to "bump up" the level of play.	Observe the music skill the child is performing. Model the next step on a task analysis or show the child another way to do the skill.
Figure 34. Facilitating Play-based Instruction (Humpal, 1999).	

Music therapists also must keep in mind typical developmental milestones and characteristics that apply to the ages of the children with whom they work. For instance, babies and toddlers should not be expected to sit in a circle for guided group play. The national organization Zero to Three has published several brochures that succinctly explain development of very young children. Their *Getting in Tune: The Powerful Influence of Music on Young Children's Development* (2002) is an excellent resource that tells what to expect of young children in the areas of bonding, using the voice, moving, and creating music. Of course, factors that are specific to the individual child as well as disabilities that affect normal development must also be considered when planning musical play strategies.

Setting Up and Utilizing the Environment

The place where children will be making music should be inviting, but not overwhelming. Compartmentalize instruments and musical play items and make them readily accessible. For guided group experiences, some children may need carpet squares or a blanket to mark the area where they are to sit. Such items provide visual reminders and help set up boundaries. Consider sensory needs of the children, too. For instance, some children may need to bounce on a therapy ball while sitting on a staff person's lap during a group activity, or may be calmed by holding something in their hands. Be aware of hyperacuity; notice how children react to volume and specific frequencies and adjust the environment accordingly. If you are traveling from room to room delivering music therapy service, develop some portable music play centers that can easily and quickly be set up yet kept out of sight until needed.

Think *structured* in a seemingly unstructured environment. The music therapist can use the music to structure the play. For example, if children are to pick a partner by tapping the person they are closest to at a certain point in the song, sing more slowly or more quickly to control who will be chosen when.

Know the needs of the children and their current levels of play. Have enough of the same instrument so that parallel play can exist, or use an instrument that requires sharing (such as xylophones and mallets, or triangles and beaters). In this way, the play levels of the children can be bumped up to a higher level.

Effective Strategies

Repetition, Repetition, Repetition, Repetition. Children learn through repetition. They will love doing a favorite song or activity over and over again (long after the adult is *very* tired of it!). A good guideline to follow is to do at least four repetitions of the song each time it is used. This helps the children internalize the information, practice it, and make it part of their musical play repertoire. Review songs or activities the next time you see the children. Eventually, bump up the song to another level (i.e., use it in a more complex way).

- Repeat the song but do it "another way." Systematically change one attribute (e.g., *words* or the *instrument used*) at a time. The following chant was originally taught as follows:

Friend Chant

Introduce by tapping tambourine and saying:
 Tap, tap, tap, tap

Then begin chanting to the beat:
 Say hello, say hello! Now it's time to say hello!

Shake the tambourine while saying:
 All---

Stop shaking and quickly thrust the tambourine in front of one child. The child should hit the tambourine once as the chant is finished with the word:
 ---- right!

- On another day, repeat the chant, presenting it in the same way but using different words, keeping the "*tap, tap, tap, tap*" as a bridge point:

Variations on the chant:

Friend of mine, friend of mine, (name) is a friend of mine

 All--------------right!

- Interrupt and do it another way.

Interrupting predictable play increases tolerance, teaches acceptance of change, and engages students who may be distracted. For children on the autism spectrum, this is a particularly useful strategy. Use the previously mentioned chant. Immediately prior to having the child strike the tambourine, set the tambourine aside and substitute a drum. The child will more readily accept the change in routine because the chant and the beat keep going and are familiar components to the activity that has been changed in some way.

Use Control Objects and Attention Grabbers. Music can be used to get the attention of children and re-direct them away from undesirable behavior. Strike a tambourine. Play a chord on the piano. Tap or clap a rhythm and teach the children to immediately respond by repeating it back to you. Wave both hands in the air, singing and holding one note until all are looking at you. Remember—repeat, repeat, repeat, repeat until these strategies and the expectations they bring become predictable to the children.

Pause and Wait. An extremely effective strategy is to pause. This active silence gives times for those with latency of response to process the information (see box below). Waiting without talking or singing gets children's attention and reminds them of expectations.

Lorna was a very passive child with significant developmental delays. During circle time and in her group music therapy sessions, she stared blankly and never participated. Her free play skills were extremely limited. If toys were placed in front of her, she might glance at them, but never explored them or her environment without assistance or prompting. Lorna preferred to just "sit there" . . . for hours and days at a time.

It was Halloween time, and we had been using rhythm sticks in a chant-like song. The objectives for the group were to increase fine motor skills at midline, increase vocalization, and to play as part of a group activity. Lorna's objectives were to stay within the area of the activity and to explore instruments that were presented to her.

Every child held two ridged sticks. They tapped and followed my lead as we sang:
> *All the little ghosts so spooky and neat,*
> *Said, "Let's tap a Halloween beat!"*
> *So they took their sticks and they hit the ground*

(at this point, all the children were to stop tapping and begin loudly hitting their sticks on the floor).

> *And went,*

(the clicking stopped and sticks were raised and circled overhead)

> *"OOOOOOOOOOOOOOO!" That's a mighty scary sound!*

After several repetitions of this song, all the children but Lorna were participating at some level. Without physical prompting, Lorna just sat there. As we were doing the song one last time, I needed to stop and get a drink to ward off a cough . . . right before the last line of the song. As I returned to continue the activity, Lorna looked at me, raised her sticks in the air, and smiled. To everyone's amazement, she uttered a quiet, "OOOOO." By accident, I had discovered that Lorna had needed a longer time to respond . . . she had needed us to wait for her to do so.

Stop/Go. Young children love stop and go musical games. These activities build anticipation and encourage children to communicate their readiness for the activity to begin again. Stop/go play is actually an extension of pausing and waiting for a response.

Up/Down. Activities using up and down movements also encourage children to anticipate and communicate. Pair an upward movement with a rising vocal inflection, and a downward movement with a falling vocalization. Use gestures to indicate direction. Give children fabric, scarves, ribbons, and parachutes and let them lead the activity.

Pace. Increasing the pace of an activity may entice children to try something they might otherwise resist. Slowing down the pace may give necessary response time. The pace of the session may change at a moment's notice. Part of using a play-based approach is being able to adjust to factors that are unplanned. The activity may head in an entirely different direction than you had anticipated, or children may not be at all interested in what you may present to them. The music therapist must constantly assess how and when to change activities as well as the pace of how they are being presented.

Contagion. Use music or music activity to engage children or bring them to the group. This can bump them up to a higher level of play. For example, start musical group play by shaking a parachute or putting out a gathering drum with several mallets. Lure a child who is usually content to play alone.

Partial Participation and Peer Assistants. All children will not play at the same level. Structure the musical environment and musical activities in the session so that each child, whether alone or with support, will be able to take part in some aspect of the musical play. Peers often like to help classmates who might need assistance. Avoid "babying" the child with more significant needs.

Cues and Transitions

Too much talk may crowd my head . . . try a little cue instead!

Cues and Prompts. Cues quickly and often quietly tell the child what is expected. A few examples of effective cuing strategies are:

- Looking/nodding;
- Gesturing, signing, or prompting;
- Touching;
- Showing a picture;
- Giving the child an object or representation of an object;
- Using an instrument sound.

Verbal cues should be clear and concise, using words that are in the child's receptive vocabulary. Often pairing the word with a nonverbal cue is highly effective. In cuing, the less said, the better.

Likewise, think before prompting. Use as few prompts as possible, thinking along a continuum or system of least prompts.

Transitions

Young children live in the here-and-now and do not have a good concept of time. For some children, especially those with autism or pervasive developmental disorders, change is especially difficult. Preparing children for what comes next helps the transition go much more smoothly.

Many children respond well to picture schedules and are calmed by knowing the structure of upcoming events. Using a picture schedule teaches pre-academic skills such as recalling a sequence or recalling what comes first, next, or last. Laminate photographs of instruments and objects commonly used in the music therapy session and pair these with the actual instrument or object when first introducing the activity. There are commercially available picture/icon systems that can be used, or therapists can download clipart, photographs, or other images off the web. Eventually, an entire schedule of what is planned or what will be available to explore can be shown to the children or attached with Velcro to a schedule board. The music therapist can remove one picture as the activity ends and immediately refer to the next.

Another extremely effective strategy with young children is to use music for transitioning. Simple messages can be given in music (often with a melody that can be quickly recalled). Children respond well to transition songs for many reasons:

- The song itself is predictable.
- A message via music is nonthreatening and does not turn into a control issue.
- It helps establish trust ("If I do this, something predictable will happen").

The same rules apply to transition strategies as they do to cues—the less said, the better. Transition songs should be sung repeatedly while the desired behavior is being modeled (such as cleaning up toys). A gentle physical assist may be necessary initially; remember to keep calmly singing as you both continue the transition action. Transitions also function well to provide familiarity and security when used repeatedly across sessions.

When using transition songs, aim for "seamless" transitions. Be ready to have the next song or activity ready as soon as the transition song ends. Don't give the child time to think about what he or she had to give up.

Other Considerations

Choice of Music
- Music used in sessions and within music centers should offer rich and varied experiences.
- Be familiar with music from a wide range of ethnic influences.
- Be able to include songs in the families' native language and employ instruments from a wide variety of cultures. Likewise, the choice of music should include both novel and traditional children's songs.

Using the Voice
Especially with very young children, the unaccompanied voice is a wonderful tool. Try to sing in a register that is compatible with that of the child. Expressive chanting and rhythmic speech captures children's attention and helps them develop better speech. Ascending vocal inflection tends to be energizing; descending inflection usually is more calming. Use the simple but effective tones of the universal children's chant (*sol, mi, la, sol, mi*) to capture a child's attention or to comment on his or her play.

Proximity, Eye Contact and Expression
When conducting musical play with young children, the music therapist should be highly expressive. When the play is emphatically personal, the child will usually become more engaged. Be near enough to the children to establish definite eye contact. Be at the child's level. Be playfully dramatic in your facial expressions, your gestures, and in your speech. Children learn to read and then imitate our expressions; this is an important social as well as communication skill.

Instruments

- Have different types of each instrument (such as wrist bells, sleigh bells, etc.). Many companies produce high quality instruments in small sizes. Test these out before you buy them. Make sure they will not break easily and do not have small parts.
- Rhythm sticks can be cut in half and sanded to make shorter versions that are safer for exuberant little hands.
- Have instruments that draw children to group play, such as a gathering drum.
- Use high quality, inviting pentatonic instruments such as the 11-note marimba (C pentatonic) from Music for Little People. This company also offers a steel drum (G pentatonic) that is a good size for small children.
- Facilitate instrumental play in a manner that gives children as much independence and active participation as possible. For example, help a child with limited fine motor ability play sticks by positioning the sticks in the child's hands, molding a grasp. Then remove your hands and hold the sticks behind the child's hands to help activate them.

Adapted or Augmentative Equipment

Using special equipment or modifying instruments or objects provides children with a way to freely play, helps promote intrinsic motivation, and gives them control of their environment. Many commercial items are available for these purposes. However, everyday items can be creatively used. For example, rubber shelf liner placed under a tambourine helps stabilize it on the floor or on a hard surface. This material also can be wrapped around mallets to make grasping easier. See Chapter 13 for more information on this topic.

Multisensory Opportunities

Employ many different senses when conducting musical play. Information that is processed in many ways builds mental muscles.

- Use instruments and objects that meet a variety of needs. Ocean drums, rain sticks, hanging chimes, afuches, clatterpillars, Chinese therapy balls, and ridged sticks give multisensory input and can be played with others, thus encouraging social interaction or turn taking. Many instruments can be used to enhance group improvisation activities so that each member of the group will be an active participant at his or her own level.
- Attach a wrist bell to a handle of a parachute. When children move the parachute to music, they will see the parachute, feel the movement in their arms and joints, and also hear an additional sound.
- "Fling-Its" are large nets that can be used like parachutes, though Fling-Its are especially easy to manipulate because fingers can slip into the openings in the net and need not be able to grasp. Children can get proprioceptive input to their joints as well as visual and auditory information as they take part in activities such as shaking the net and making small bee puppets fly

to the music of the "Flight of the Bumblebee." Be sure that the child is able to tolerate this type of range of motion.

- Transparent fabric (such as scarves or large "Canopies of Color") promote touching soft material. These can be used to embed the concept of object permanence because you can see through them.
- Hanging orchestra chimes can be activated by the slightest touch and give immediate auditory input.
- Likewise, diatonic desk bells are easy to play and remain secure when placed on a solid surface.
- Bubbles provide visual and tactile experiences and can give exercises in lip closure and blowing.
- Beanbags give heavy input for proprioception as well as tactile exploration.
- Stuffed animals that "talk" present children with many different play options that use many senses.
- Use conventional items in unconventional ways. A vibrating pen (e.g., the Squiggle Wiggle Writer), with the tip removed, makes a wonderful "mallet" that can be placed in a child's hand to play a drum or tambourine. Long pieces of plastic drainpipe make fun-sounding "guiros" that can be scraped by an entire group of children. Shorter pieces can be placed over an arm to invite cooperative play that gives wonderful sensory input.

Take into account any possible sensory issues the child may have when setting up instrumental play or choosing body percussion activities. You may want to consult with other members of the child's team before introducing new sensory activities to ensure the experiences will be appropriate.

Other Modalities

- Books with repetitive musical refrains teach both musical elements as well as literacy skills.
- Props such as cutout shapes, puppets, and "found sounds" (objects found in the environment that make sound, such as a wooden spoon and a bucket) encourage discovery and creative musical play.
- Pretend microphones inspire vocalization as well as turn taking and pretend play.
- A repertoire of short rhymes, wiggles, tickles, and bounces are good resources for babies and very young children.

A collection of picture cues can be used for choice making as well as telling or showing a schedule of activities.

•

Summary

Working with young children in an educational setting requires knowledge of each child's goals and needs as well as an understanding of general child development and also of various disabilities and how they present. A key concept in the play-based, child-directed approach is flexibility. Music therapists need to be skilled in conducting ongoing assessment and developing effective programming that is both age- and ability-appropriate yet may be accomplished through play. Since play permeates the world of the young child, it is only logical that music therapists embed a play-based philosophy and utilize play strategies in their work with children of this age group.

•

References

Bayless, K., & Ramsey, M. (1991). Music: A way of life for the young child. *New York: Macmillan.*

Bredekamp, S. (Ed.). (1987). Developmentally appropriate practice in early childhood programs serving children from birth through age 8. *Washington, DC: National Association for the Education of Young Children.*

Bredekamp, S., & Copple, C. (Eds.). (1997). Developmentally appropriate practice in early childhood programs *(Rev. ed.). Washington, DC: National Association for the Education of Young Children.*

Brett, A. (1997). *Child's play: Making the most of what children do best.* Early Childhood Connections, 3(3), 24–29.

Briggs, C. (1991). *A model for understanding musical development.* Music Therapy, 10(1), 1–21.

Brownell, M., Freg, R., Kwak, E. & Rayburn, A. (2004). The Kodaly approach to music therapy. In A. Darrow (Ed.), Introduction to approaches in music therapy *(pp. 25–33). Silver Spring, MD: American Music Therapy Association.*

Burton, S. (2002). *An exploration of preschool children's spontaneous songs and chants.* Visions of Research in Music Education, 2, 7–16.

Cuyahoga County Board of Mental Retardation and Developmental Disabilities (CCBMR/DD). (1999). Music and your little one. *Cleveland, OH: Author.*

Frego, R., Liston, R., Hama, M., & Gillmeister, G.. (2004). The Dalcroze approach to music therapy. In A. Darrow (Ed.), Introduction to approaches in music therapy *(pp. 15–24). Silver Spring, MD: American Music Therapy Association.*

Frost, J., & Klein, B. (1984). Children's play and playgrounds. *Austin, TX: Playgrounds International.*

Furman, A., & Furman, C. (1993). Music for children with special needs. In M. Palmer and W. Sims (Eds.), Music in prekindergarten *(pp. 33–36). Reston, VA: Music Educators National Conference.*

Gordon, E. (1990). A music learning theory for newborn and young children. *Chicago: G.I.A.*

Hallquist, M., & Wishon, P. (2003). *Rethinking developmentally appropriate practice: An early childhood music education model.* Early Childhood Connection, 9(3), 7–24.

Hughes, F. (1999). Children, play, and development. *Boston: Allyn and Bacon.*

Humpal, M. (1990). *Early intervention: The implications for music therapy.* Music Therapy Perspectives, 8, 30–35.

Humpal, M. (1999). Facilitating play-based instruction. Handout for M. Humpal & R. Tweedle, Play—It's fundamental. *Presentation at the World Congress of Music Therapy, Washington, DC.*

Humpal, M., & Dimmick, J. (1996). Music therapy for learners in an early childhood community interagency setting. In B. Wilson (Ed.), Models of music therapy interventions in school settings: From institution to inclusion *(pp. 277–311). Silver Spring, MD: National Association for Music Therapy.*

Jordan-DeCarbo, J. (1997). *Characteristics of young children's play and musical play.* Early Childhood Connections, 3(3), 43–48.

Kern, P. (2004). Using a music therapy collaborative consultative approach for the inclusion of young children with autism in a childcare program. *Unpublished doctoral dissertation, University of Witten-Herdecke, Germany.*

Kern, P. (2005). The use of single case designs in an interactive play setting. In D. Aldridge (Ed.), Case study designs in music therapy *(pp. 119–144). Bristol, PA: Jessica Kingsley.*

Linder, T. (1990). Transdisciplinary play-based assessment: A functional approach for working with young children. *Baltimore: Paul H Brankes.*

McCracken, J. (1997). Play is fundamental. *Washington, DC: National Association for the Education of Young Children.*

Music Educators National Conference. (1992). MENC Position Statement on Early Childhood Education. *Reston, VA: Author.*

Music Educators National Conference. (1995). Strategies for teaching prekindergtarten music. *Reston, VA: Author.*

O' Brien, L. (2000). Engaged pedagogy—One alternative to "indoctrination" into D.A.P. Childhood Education, *76(5), 283–288.*

Moorhead, G. E., & Pond, D. (1978). Music of young children. *Santa Barbara, CA: Pillsbury Foundation for Advancement of Music Education.*

Nordoff-Robbins Center for Music Therapy. (2001). Introduction. *Retrieved from http://www.nyu.edu/education/music/nrobbins/*

Parten, M. (1932). Social play among preschool children. Journal of Abnormal and Social Psychology, *27, 243–269.*

Register, D. (2004). Teaching child-care personnel to use music in the classroom: A comparison of workshop training versus on-site modeling. Music Therapy Perspectives, *22(2), 109–115.*

Sandell, S., Schwartz, I., & Joseph, G. (2001). A building blocks model for effective instruction in inclusive early childhood settings. Young Exceptional Children, *4(3), 3–9.*

Standley, J., & Hughes, J. (1996). Documenting developmentally appropriate objectives and benefits of a music therapy program for early intervention: A behavioral analysis. Music Therapy Perspectives, *14(2), 87–94.*

Tweedle, R. (1999). Musical characteristics of young children. Handout for M. Humpal & R. Tweedle. Play—It's fundamental. Presentation at the World Congress of Music Therapy, Washington, DC.

Valerio, W. (1997). Surprise! Music development means music play for adults as well as children. Early Childhood Connections, *3(3), 7–14.*

Voight, M. (2003). Orff music therapy—An overview. Voices: A world forum for music therapy. *Retrieved January 14, 2004, from http://www.voices/no/mainissues/mi40003000129.html*

Welch, M., & Humpal, M. (2003). Music therapy goal matrix. *Cleveland, OH: Cuyahoga County Board of Mental Retardation and Developmental Disabilities.*

Zero to Three. (2002). Getting in tune—The powerful influence of music on young children's development. *Washington, DC: Author.*

Chapter 13

Using Technology, Adaptations, and Augmentative Tools

Beth McLaughlin, MS, MT-BC

The author would like to thank the following people for contributing their time and expertise in the development of this chapter: Cindy Chioleno, Educational Consultant; Mark Aholo, MT-BC; Jason Rafalak, MT-BC; John Rafalak, Media and Technology Specialist; and Linda Benton, Assistant Director of Wildwood School.

As the demand for music therapy in schools increases, so does our responsibility to maximize the learning opportunities for our students using all the resources we have available to us.

We are living in an age of technology today that invites us to sink or swim. While our students are surfing the net and configuring their hard drives, some of us (in the over 40 crowd) are still struggling to find the "on" button for our computers. The good news is the hardware and software that is available to us today is becoming increasingly user friendly with a learning curve that is no longer the mountainous climb it used to be. Moreover, the benefits of technology to both our students and to music therapy in general make the challenges of learning about it a worthwhile adventure.

Why is technology important to the music therapist today? As the demand for music therapy in schools increases, so does our responsibility to maximize the learning opportunities for our students using all the resources we have available to us. As music therapists, we learn how to meet the needs of our students or clients by being sensitive to and respectful of their learning style, musical preferences, cultural background, and social relationships. Computers, augmentative communication devices, and electronic music all have a prominent place in the education and everyday lives of our students. Technology is constantly changing and growing, challenging us to do likewise. Moreover, The National Association of Schools of Music (NASM) requires that all music students be educated in both the "understanding of how technology serves the field of music as a whole . . . [and] the working knowledge of the technical developments applicable to their area of specialization" (Crowe & Rio, 2005). Technology in music therapy can be defined as the use of "any equipment, device, or method that systematically fosters the production of or response to music" (Crowe & Rio, 2005).

In this chapter, we will learn how technology can be successfully integrated into a special education setting to achieve specific student focused goals, meet educational standards, and enhance the overall quality of the music therapy program. Specific areas of technology will be discussed, followed by examples from clinical applications of the programs and tools. Finally, this author wishes to emphasize that these examples were chosen for discussion based on successful clinical experience and are in no way inclusive of all the technology-based resources available that may further enrich the music therapy practice.

●

Specific Areas of Technology

Electronic Keyboard

The electronic keyboard (such as a Casio or Yamaha) is a multifaceted tool for music therapy practice in a school setting. This type of keyboard or piano synthesizer has a wide variety of programmed sounds and accompaniment styles to choose from and can be used to promote independence while teaching visual sequencing skills, motor planning, color or letter recognition, bilateral coordination, and leisure skills. Moreover, it can be used to provide a full accompaniment to the songs used in therapy classes.

Most keyboards today have a song bank as well as style and tone banks. Additionally there are "break" and "fill-in" buttons that add a short percussion break as well as "bridge" buttons that create an instrumental bridge to a slight change of instrumentation within the musical style. All of these options offer many opportunities for creative arranging as well as visual sequencing steps for students to learn, leading to independent use of the equipment.

Assistive Technology

Assistive technology (AT) refers to the use of adaptations, including one-touch switches, computers, and a variety of alternative and augmentative communication (AAC) devices. These adaptations enable and empower people with physical and cognitive disabilities to communicate and actively participate in the learning environment. The simplest type of AAC allows one to record approximately one minute of voice or other sound input that is then accessible to the student by depressing a single switch. Switches come in different sizes and angles to accommodate various physical needs of the student. More complex AAC devices enable the development of complete pages of song or instrument choices with voice output with which students may interact. These devices are adaptable for use in the music therapy environment, but it is important that ideas for their use are implemented with input and direction from the educational team (L. Benton, personal communication, September 9, 2004; C. Shioleno, personal communication, August 26, 2004).

Compositional Tools

While many compositional tools are available today, the two programs discussed in this chapter include GarageBand™ and Band-in-a-Box™ (BiaB). Both these programs allow the student to create simple arrangements with musical styles and rhythmic grooves that have been pre-recorded in the applications. The sequencing technology built into these programs contain both MIDI data and/or digitally recorded audio in multi-track format that allows for complex compositions to be built up one part at a time. Original melodies (vocal or instrumental) can be added to the arrangements and saved as a new song. Music generated by these programs can also be arranged and recorded for movement, instrumental, or singing activities used in music therapy sessions.

Band-in-a-Box™ is an accompaniment program that automatically generates professional quality solos and full arrangements that can be heard on any instrument or in any style that the user chooses. The program includes a built-in sequencer, allowing the user to record a melody or chord progression into the program, which BiaB will then play back with any chosen style or instrumentation. For instance, the students can hear "Mary Had a Little Lamb" played as a Blues or a Reggae song on a guitar or a steel drum. Tempo is easily adjusted to allow students to play along. While being played, the music can be viewed as notation, on a piano keyboard, or on a guitar fret board. Any music generated by this program can be saved as a MIDI file and shared by other programs such as Finale, a music notation program designed to create and customize printed music as well as convert audio files to sheet music. Biab is available in both PC and Macintosh format.

GarageBand™ is a free application for Macintosh users only. It allows the students to choose from a variety of loops (a repeated rhythmic pattern called "riffs" or "grooves") to layer a multitude of instrumental tracks and sound effects into a musical arrangement. GarageBand™ includes virtually thousands of loops that have been pre-recorded into the program and includes styles ranging from hip hop to 80's dance grooves to alternative jazz. Loops that have been recorded in one key will automatically adjust to match the key of the current arrangement. After assigning instruments and styles to specific tracks, the students are able to vary the length, volume, and other musical elements to their choosing. Once the basic rhythmic feel has been established, the user may then plug in a microphone or instrument to record vocals, real instrumental, or MIDI instruments to add solo and harmony. Cakewalk Home Studio is a similar program that can be used with PC computers.

Recording

Studio quality recording has become more accessible with developments in recording technology, and the benefits to music therapy practice are immeasurable. Multi-track recording allows the clinician to pre-record instrumental tracks then add student voices in layers that can be edited and mixed separately. Large numbers of students can contribute to a recording project in groups of manageable size. Recorded music can be imported onto a track and edited for specific purposes. For instance, deleting repeated sections or fading out the music after a selected verse may shorten a song. MIDI files of songs can be downloaded and specific instrumental or vocal sections deleted to allow students to add their own parts. Recording applications range from free downloadable utilities (such as Audacity) to commercial hardware and software that includes both integrated MIDI sequencing and digital to audio capabilities.

Graphics

Providing visuals for students in a special education setting is critical to helping them develop both receptive and expressive language skills. There are several programs that are compatible with both Mac and PC computers. The Mayer-Johnson Boardmaker™ symbols are probably the most familiar and widely used, but others such as Picture This and EyeCons are also available. EyeCons include graphics that are specific to music therapy, including instruments, props, and directions. Boardmaker™ offers the most flexibility by letting users custom design their icons or arrangement of icons in the assigned boxes on the page.

Picture graphics also are available by doing a search within word processing programs. In Word, a selection of clipart is available under "Picture" in the "Insert" menu. In AppleWorks, find "Picture Clippings" in the "File" menu, then type in the name of the image for which you are looking. If you are connected to the Internet, the computer will do an automatic search and a number of pictures will appear. Any of these can be dragged onto a document page using the selection  tool. Once in the document, the image can be resized or manipulated around the page. Using Internet search engines can also access graphics.

MIDI Technology

MIDI (Musical Instrument Digital Interface) is a language that allows computers, synthesizers, and other devices to share information. It is:

> an international standard developed that specifies how musical instruments with microprocessors can communicate with other microprocessor-controlled instruments or devices. The first synthesizer to speak MIDI was the Sequential Prophet 600 in 1983, played by some of the greatest keyboard players in jazz and rock. (Bove, 2004, p. 6)

A standard MIDI file (SMF) is a format that can be accessed by any computer, synthesizer, or music software program. MIDI files are readily available on the web and can be downloaded at no cost. Information communicated by MIDI is not represented by a waveform but by discrete bits of information that indicate pitch and duration. These bits, when displayed on a recording track, can be easily manipulated by moving them up or down to change pitch, or by shortening or elongating to adjust the note duration.

> With practice, the aesthetic qualities of music (e.g., dynamic and harmonic elements) can be approached. Meeting the [students'] abilities and needs is a significant advantage of MIDI formatted music. In addition to increasing or decreasing tempo and modulating key areas, the therapist can change the form, arrangements, and instrumentation to support [student] performance." (M. Ahola, personal communication, September 1, 2004)

Any computer has the capability to play MIDI files. In order to be edited, the musical parts must be imported into a sequencing program such as Cakewalk Home Studio, Emagic Logic Education, or Pro-tools Digidesign. Once imported, adjustments can be made to adapt the music to your students' needs and preferences.

MIDI files can be purchased or downloaded for free. Songs are easily found by title using a web browser. The copyright protection of these files should be respected as any other recorded medium. The Resources at the end of the chapter provides lists of sites for MIDI files, links to musical archives, and other information about MIDI basics.

Applications for Music Therapy Practice

The suggestions described in this section include applications of technology that are student-focused and illustrate ways to enrich the music therapy environment. The content areas and achievement standards from the *National Standards for Arts Education* are included in the discussion of the activities in order to demonstrate the relationship between music therapy and music education. For music therapists working in a school setting, understanding the relationship between music therapy goals and music education standards is important. Reflecting this connection in our communication demonstrates that, while our goals may be nonmusical in nature, our activities support the standards through appropriately designed programs that support the needs and range of musical responses of students in special education.

Keyboard/Synthesizer

As previously mentioned, using electronic keyboards for adapted piano instruction helps students develop a variety of skills. They can learn about musical styles while choosing preferred accompaniments to their favorite songs. They can learn the steps for independently programming the keyboard and preparing the environment to include practice as a free time or leisure activity. Finally, they can take pride in their performance by sharing the songs that they have learned with their peers and family.

Preparing the Environment

Choose a familiar 2- or 3-chord song and arrange it using a programmed musical style and tempo setting. Have lyrics with visual cues printed out in advance (as described in Figure 35). To teach the steps for programming, write out the sequence for the student to follow using simple drawn illustrations to represent the buttons, or written instructions, depending on the reading level of student. The following steps for programming a Casio keyboard were illustrated using the drawing option in AppleWorks.

Reflecting this connection in our communication demonstrates that while our goals may be non-musical in nature, our activities support the standards through appropriately designed programs that support the needs and range of musical responses of students in special education.

Workin' on the Railroad		
on → FINGERED CASIO CHORD off NORMAL		1. piano on
RHYTHM		2. rhythm
⑦⑧⑨ ④⑤⑥ ①②③		3. #64
TEMPO ▽ △ ◀ ▶		4. 125
START/STOP		5. start
"Beth, I'm ready for you to sing."		
Ⓡ Ⓨ Ⓖ Ⓑ		6. Follow color dots
Figure 35. Visual Cues for "Workin' on the Railroad."		

Model the sequence, then have the student repeat following the written directions. As the student becomes more familiar with this procedure, songs can be added to his/her repertoire with the programming codes indicated on the page of music (e.g., tempo 90; rhythm 36). Depending on the type of keyboard being used, break buttons, bridge buttons, and endings can be added into the arrangement as well.

Setting Goals and Implementing the Plan

The lesson that follows outlines goals for following a color-coded sequence to indicate chord changes. Included in the procedure are instructions for color-coding lyrics using Word or AppleWorks.

Content Standard 2 (K–4):

Performing on instruments, alone and with others, a varied repertoire of music.

Achievement Standards:

• Students perform on pitch, in rhythm, with appropriate dynamics and timbre, and maintain a steady tempo.

- Students perform easy rhythmic, melodic, and chord patterns accurately and independently on rhythmic, melodic, and harmonic classroom instruments.
- Students perform expressively a varied repertoire of music representing diverse genres and styles.

Goal:

Student will develop language, cognitive, motor, and music skills through adapted keyboard instruction.

Objectives:

- Given visual cues, student will sequence steps for starting and stopping keyboard.
- Given visual cues, student will program rhythm bank and tempo for specific songs.
- Given visual cues, student will play with correct harmonic rhythm, a harmonic sequence by following color-coded chord progression above lyrics as song accompaniment up to 3 chords per song.
- Student will acquire a repertoire of songs from varied music genre including traditional, patriotic, and contemporary; 2 songs from each category.
- Student will perform 1 song at an all school event 1x annually.

Materials Needed:

- Programmable keyboard (e.g., Casio or Yamaha)
- Printed lyrics with adapted chord notation

Procedure:

- Using AppleWorks (Mac), open a document and type your lyrics.
- Open the tool bar and click on the oval. (If using Word, go to the "View" menu and then to "Toolbar" that will take you to a drawing program and give you the oval option there).
- Insert an oval for every one or two beats of music.
- Determine the colors needed to correspond with colored stickers that have been put on the chording keys and color the dots accordingly above the lyrics.
- Model the song for the student.
- Have student play with single finger without the accompaniment while you point to the dots on the page or to the colored keys, depending on their attention to the medium.
- Add programmed music to introduce external rhythm to performance.

Extensions:

- Substitute letter names for colors dots.
- Add color dots to corresponding notes an octave above to encourage bilateral accompaniment.

- Add color dots to the third to introduce 2 finger chords.
- Play song with bi-lateral accompaniment without programmed music.
- Arrange instrumentation by deleting instrument sounds.

Assistive Technology

Preparing the Environment
The following lesson is designed to elicit simple responses from students who are in the initial stages of language development. Through the cause-and-effect feature of a simple switch, this activity will teach the students that they can impact their environment through self-initiated behavior. The goals and implementation plan have been determined with input from various members of the child's educational team, including the speech language therapist, occupational therapist, music therapist, and teacher. The BIGmack® switch has been introduced in a 1-1 setting with eventual inclusion in the music therapy class described below. The BIGmack® switch is a communication tool that allows the user to record a single message or song of up to 75 seconds in length. It is a single round switch with a 5-inch activation surface (C. Shioleno, personal communication, August 26, 2004).

Setting Goals and Implementing the Plan
Content Standard 1 (K–4):
> Singing alone and with others, a varied repertoire of music.

Achievement Standard:
> Students sing in groups, blending vocal timbres, matching dynamic levels, and responding to the cues of a conductor.

Goal:
> Student will develop attending behaviors, motor control, and language skills through participating in group singing activities.

Objectives:
- Given physical prompts, student will initiate use of a BIGmack® switch to complete a song phrase ("e-i-e-i-o") 2 out of 3 times by 2nd quarter.
- Given gestural cues, student will initiate use of a BIGmack® switch to complete a song phrase ("e-i-e-i-o") 2 out of 3 times by 3rd quarter.
- Independently, student will initiate use of a BIGmack® switch to complete a song phrase ("e-i-e-i-o") at appropriate time in the song, 3 out of 3 times by 4th quarter.

Materials Needed:
- BIGmack® Communicator (Ablenet, Inc.)
- Snap cap to secure picture on switch
- Boardmaker™ pictures for song choices
- Step by Step Communicator (allows for 3 sequential messages to be recorded)

Procedure:

- Record the phrase "e-i-e-i-o" into the BIGmack® Communicator.
- Sing the song "Old McDonald" and model the switch use to complete the phrase.
- Repeat, prompting the student to initiate switch use to complete the song phrase.
- Repeat, fading the prompts until child is independent.
- Include student in class with peers, instructing him/her to sing the song while waiting for the song phrase to be completed by the child and the switch.

Extensions:

- Have picture representations of 2 different songs that the student has learned, allowing the child to make a choice. Place picture chosen on switch with a snapcap and proceed with activity.
- Using a Step by Step Communicator, record a song in 3 phrases and have student "sing" the whole song by hitting the switch 3 times in succession. For example:
    1. "Twinkle, twinkle little star, how I wonder what you are."
    2. "Up above the world so high, like a diamond in the sky."
    3. "Twinkle, twinkle little star, how I wonder what you are."
- Have student 'sing' "Twinkle, Twinkle" as a solo for her class.

Using Visuals

When determining how and when to use visuals, make the distinction between using pictures to illustrate a story sequence or language concept and teaching the students to use pictures for their own communication. Often the term *PECS* is incorrectly used in a general sense to refer to the use of visuals for any purpose in a teaching environment. P.E.C.S. (Picture Exchange for Communication System) is a very specific approach designed to teach children how to initiate communication by removing a picture icon from a strip or a book page and handing it to an adult to indicate a particular need or choice of an item such as food or a toy. The activity suggested here is intended to give a visual representation of a direction given in a music activity using some creative editing options in Mayer-Johnson's Boardmaker™ program.

Preparing the Environment

In this activity, you will need 4 cards with fish pictured on them corresponding to numbers 1 through 4. When you have opened a Boardmaker™ page, create 4 boxes and size them to about a 2-inch square. Go to the Preferences menu and click on Re-size option. This "un-checks" the option and allows you to manipulate the picture in the square. Once you have your fish in the box, add the number "1" using the text tool. Copy the fish into the next square and resize to make it slightly smaller. Copy and paste another one into the box. Repeat this process with all 4 boxes until you have 1, 2, 3, and 4 fish pictured on the 4 cards. Print the page on card stock and laminate. Cut into individual cards.

 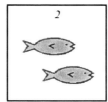 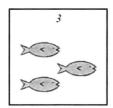

To create quarter note flash cards, draw a quarter note by simply grouping a circle and a line in a drawing program to make a single graphic. Cut and paste the image into Boardmaker™ squares. Remember to uncheck the re-size tool in order to copy the new image into a box. Follow the procedure as above.

  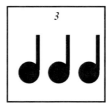

Setting Goals and Implementing the Plan

Content Standard 5 (K-4):
Reading and notating music.

Achievement Standard:
> Students read whole, half, dotted half, quarter and eight notes and rests in 2/4, 3/4, and 4/4 meter signatures.

Goal:
> Student will develop motor, management and academic (math) skills through drumming activities.

Objectives:
- Given visual cues, student will play correct number of beats on a drum as indicated by the number of objects on a picture card.
- Given visual prompt, student will stop playing after a designated number of beats.

Materials Needed:
- Hand drum or ocean drum
- Picture cards and paper clips
- Magnet, short string and rhythm stick

Procedure:
- Put a paper clip on each card and place them in a hand drum or on top of an ocean drum.
- Tie a magnet on the end of a thick string that's attached to a rhythm stick or mallet.

- Repeat the chant:

  How many fish in the deep blue sea?

  How many fish can you catch for me?

  One fish, two fish, I fish, you fish.

  How many fish in the deep blue sea?

- Have each student take a turn to "catch" a number of fish by aligning the magnet to the paper clip on the card and pulling it off the drum.
- Have student count the number of fish on the card and play the correct number on the drum.

Extensions:

- Substitute quarter notes for the fish to provide another extension to this activity.
- Have students play correct number of quarter notes on a variety of instruments.

Recording

Music therapy programs that include a studio recording component can motivate students to practice a wide range of skills. The examples that follow illustrate experiences that promote cooperative learning, brainstorming, decision making, and performance, helping students to build self-esteem and gain confidence in their abilities. The first example illustrates how recording technology was used as a component to successfully enrich and support the educational program through music therapy in a school in upstate New York for children with autism and complex learning disabilities. The second example describes how the recording studio helped to provide the adaptations and support needed for an individual to achieve her music therapy goals with competence and confidence.

Preparing the Environment (Example 1)

Four classes of students ages 8 to 16 were involved in a social studies unit on the Revolutionary War. Because of the geographical location of the school, the Battle of Saratoga was a primary focus of the study. Chris Shaw, a local storyteller and songwriter, was invited to come for a week and teach the students about this time and place in history through story and song. The classes were divided into two large groups. Each day, in addition to the lesson, Chris would brainstorm with the students, giving them the opportunity to reflect on what they had learned and to offer their own ideas about what Saratoga and the Adirondacks meant to them today. Through these brainstorming sessions, two original songs emerged that were completely authored by the students. Chris discussed with the students various styles of music that fit the lyrics, arranged them, and recorded his vocal and instrumental tracks using the recording facilities at the school. At the end of the week, a performance was held for families at which students sang both songs. In the weeks that followed, small groups of 4 to 5 students recorded 3 to 4 separate tracks on top of Chris's guitar and vocals tracks. A CD-ROM was created, complete with video that was accompanied by the two songs. The art therapist helped a student design the cover, and copies were sent home with all who had participated.

Besides enriching the social studies curriculum for these classes, this program had multiple benefits. Students were motivated to work cooperatively in a large group setting towards a common goal. Various members of the educational team staffed the sessions, allowing participation to be individualized and paced for success. All those who had contributed to the recording felt a great sense of pride and accomplishment. There were a few students who were unwilling to sing but demonstrated enthusiasm about the project by asking to play percussion during the performance. Some were assigned as technicians and assisted in setting up the equipment for the recording session.

Setting Goals and Implementing the Plan (Example 1)

Standard 1 (K–4):
Singing alone and with others, a varied repertoire of music.

Performance Standard:
Students sing in groups, blending vocal timbres, matching dynamic levels, and responding to the cues of a conductor.

Standard 7 (5–8):
Evaluating music and music performance.

Performance Standard:
Students explain, using appropriate music terminology, their personal preferences for specific musical works and styles.

Annual Goal:
Students will develop language, social, academic and music skills through an integrated curriculum based arts-in-education project.

Objectives:
- Student will sing songs from traditional, contemporary, and thematic repertoire.
- Student will extend expression of classroom concepts through participating in song writing and performance tasks with peers.
- Student will indicate qualities of preferred musical accompaniment style.
- Student will participate with peers in creating an audio-recording of song.

Preparing the Environment (Example 2)

M. is a young lady of 17 who is highly anxious and afraid of failure. She requires a great deal of support to process through difficulties and can be very distractible. She prefers to seek out adult support rather than complete a task independently in spite of her abilities.

M. has a lovely voice, learns songs easily, and enjoys a wide range of songs and musical styles. She has been receiving voice lessons for 3 years. Her music therapist had taken a modified academic approach to her instruction to increase her confidence and age-appropriate behavior. Early in the year she chose the song "Don't It Make My Brown Eyes

Blue" to sing at an annual school concert. In preparation for this performance, the therapist recorded a piano track accompaniment, using Pro-tools recording software, at a tempo appropriate to M. with which she could practice. A second recording of M. singing with the piano accompaniment was made as well. Both recordings were burned onto a CD for her to take home. A copy of the CD was given to her teacher as well. When played in the classroom, M. received positive recognition and encouragement for her singing ability. Given the opportunity to practice at a comfortable tempo in the home environment as well as at school assured her a successful performance experience.

Setting Goals and Implementing the Plan (Example 2)

Content Standard 1:

Singing alone and with others a varied repertoire of music.

Achievement Standard:

Students sing accurately and with good breath control throughout their singing ranges, alone and in small and large ensembles.

Annual Goal:

Student will develop independence and self-esteem through adapted vocal instruction.

Objectives:

- Given a model, student will sing with dynamics and timbre appropriate to music material.
- Given verbal prompts, student will record 1 new song per quarter.
- Give song selections, student will independently choose preferred music to work on.
- Student will participate in annual music performance with staff support.

GarageBand™

Preparing the Environment

L. is a young man of 18 who has severe learning disabilities. He is able to read but has difficulty processing information and often will misinterpret what he hears. He lacks motivation to attend to or participate in activities unless they are of interest to him. He enjoys music and poetry and has a strong preference for hip hop. He is a very talented rapper but shy about demonstrating this skill. When his music therapist introduced him to GarageBand™, he was enthusiastic about creating some background grooves for a rap he had improvised. He quickly learned how to navigate the program, experiment with various loops, and compose a piece to his liking. He asked to have the program installed on the classroom computer, which he would then use with his peers during free time. Using an external microphone (iMic), L. recorded his rap song with the pre-recorded loops that he had arranged. The song was then imported into the iTunes application of the Mac and burned onto a CD for his keeping.

Setting Goals and Implementing the Plan

Content Standard 4:

Composing and arranging music within specified guidelines.

Achievement Standard:

Students create and arrange shorts songs and instrumental pieces within specified guidelines (e.g., particular style, form, instrumentation, compositional technique).

Annual Goal:

Student will develop self-esteem and appropriate leisure skills through music compositional activities.

Objectives:

- Given categories of instruments, student will identify preferred instrumentation for an original song.
- Independently, student will volunteer to share original poem or song lyrics with therapist.
- Given verbal prompts, student will participate in group compositional activity using GarageBand™ software, taking turns building a song arrangement.
- Given a model, student will give appropriate feedback to peers concerning their choices.
- Independently, student will participate in a recording of his original work.

Creating Original Music for the Music Therapy Classroom

The programs and applications described above offer the music therapist creative opportunities for developing original arrangements of music designed to address some very specific goals. The following is a description of music that has been created for this purpose in a variety of therapy settings.

Synthesizer

Using a Yamaha synthesizer, an instrumental piece of music was arranged in ABA form to teach the concept of fast and slow. A musical style was chosen and programmed at a tempo of 90 with full instrumentation. Six bars of music were recorded at this tempo. As the tempo was increased to 145, the therapist added a preprogrammed bridge button that initiated a change in instrumentation. The next six bars were played with the new tempo and instrumentation that transitioned back to the initial tempo and style. This sequence was repeated twice with the music ending with the A section. This arrangement was recorded on a track into a Pro-tools recording program. A vocal track was added with the therapist counting to "8" during the tempo changes to cue the students to listen for the change and respond appropriately. This music was used with instrumental and movement activities.

GarageBand™

In an activity designed to teach the concept of "stop," four tracks of instrumental grooves were recorded using GarageBand™. Eight bars of music were arranged in the tracks, followed by two measures of solo percussion loops. This sequence was repeated four times. The file was imported to an iTunes application and burned to CD. The students were instructed to play or move during the musical section and rest during the percussion solo.

MIDI Files

A collaborative project involving occupational therapy and music therapy was designed to use passive listening to help children learn to calm and ground themselves when in a state of sensory defensiveness. Several selections of popular and classical music were chosen and downloaded from available MIDI files on the web. The files were downloaded into Pro-tools and manipulated in the following ways to help teach the children to self regulate:

1. The tempo was gradually slowed to entrain the student physiologically.
2. The form was simplified so that the structural changes were symmetrical and predictable.
3. The instrumentation was edited so that the melodies were apparent and the harmonic qualities of the music soothing.

A voice track was layered over the music to structure the relaxation experience with brief, affirming statements such as "I like to feel calm and relaxed." As individual responses to the music are assessed, further adjustments to the tracks can be made to address individual needs and preferences. Future adaptations may include the deletion of the vocal track as independent, self-regulated behavior increases.

●

Conclusion

Technology can be a powerful tool and highly motivating, but it can also be a solitary experience. It's very easy for students to become immersed in the features of a synthesizer or the options in a sequencing program to the exclusion of people in the learning environment. Technology should support but never supersede the relationship that develops through the music experience. Without this relationship, there is no therapy. However one chooses to integrate technology into music therapy practice, it must remain "goal directed, organized, knowledge-based, and regulated" (Bruscia, 1998).

Music therapy and technology offer the greatest benefits to students when the following elements are present:

*   The project has relevance to the students' world and life experiences.
*   The technology empowers the student to make decisions and be actively involved in the learning process.
*   There is opportunity for interaction and discovery.
*   The experience is open-ended and allows individuals to work at their own pace.

- Students are allowed and encouraged to interact while working with the programs.

Music therapy is a unique modality in that it relies "on music experience as an agent of intervention" (Bruscia, 1998). What makes any music therapy intervention unique is that both the music and the therapist are partners in the process. The clinical context of our work helps to define "music experience" for our students and clients. The tools and approaches used with one population may not always be the most appropriate interventions with another. For this reason, we are challenged to meet the needs of our respective populations by being responsive to their interests and skills as well as to their cultural and social circumstances. As we work to keep pace with the developments in music and technology, we become our own active learners, stimulating our practice and developing skills that offer both personal and professional benefit.

●

References

Bove, T. (2004) Kick out the jams: GarageBand overview. Retrieved August 27, 2004, from http://www.rockument.com/bove_books/02tutorgb_over.htm

Bruscia, K. E. (1998). Defining music therapy (2nd ed.). Gilsum, NH: Barcelona Publishers.

Crowe, B., & Rio, R. (2005). Implications of technology in music therapy practice and research for music therapy/education: A review of literature: Journal of Music Therapy, 41(4), 282–230.

LaVine, S. (2004, August). Digital Audio for beginners. Paper presented at the NYSSMA Technology Mini-Conference, Buffalo, New York.

●

Resources

Early connections: Technology in early childhood education. Retrieved August 25, 2004, from http://www.netc.org/earlyconnections/primary/development.html

Kersten, F. (2004, March). Using MIDI accompaniments for music learning at school and at home. Music Educators Journal, 90, 44–49.

McCord, K., Reese, S., & Walls, K. (Eds.). (2001). Strategies for teaching technology. Reston, VA: MENC: The National Association for Music Education.

Picture Communication Symbols (PCS). (1981–2004). Solana Beach, CA: Mayer-Johnson, Inc.

Standards for Arts Education. (2004). ArtsEdge: Standards. Retrieved August 25, 2004, from http://artsedge.kennedy-center.org/teach/standards.cfm

Wilson, B. (Ed.). (2002). Models of music therapy interventions in school settings (2nd ed.). Silver Spring, MD: American Music Therapy Association.

● ●

Glossary of Terms

Analogue Recording: Sound waves are captured and recorded with a microphone or directly from any appropriate electronic signal such as a synthesizer or electric guitar. The microphone converts variations in sound pressure to voltage. The voltage changes are sent to a tape recording where magnetic particles on the tape are altered to correspond to the voltages. The process is called analog recording, as the "picture" on the tape is analogous to the original sound wave (LaVine, 2004).

Assistive Technology: Any equipment that is designed, modified, or customized to promote independence for individuals with disabilities by increasing, maintaining, or improving their functional communication or physical capabilities.

Digital Recording: Taking measurements of the voltages created by the microphone or line level source and assigning a series of binary digits to each measurement create digital recording—a "snapshot" or "sample" of the sound. The process of measuring the voltages several thousand times a second is called "sampling" (LaVine, 2004).

General MIDI: A standard within the MIDI standards for the order of voices in the first 128 sounds of a synthesizer. By making these a common list, it is possible to create MIDI files that will use the same voice sounds as they are played on different synthesizers.

MIDI: An acronym for Musical Instrument Digital Interface; a digital signal system (a system of number signals) used to communicate performance information to and from musical instruments making music (J. Rafalak, personal communication, September 1, 2004).

MIDI Sequencer: A computer program that can record and playback MIDI data in such a way to control the performance of MIDI-controlled musical instruments or devices in a series of timed steps.

Sampler: Also called a digital sampler. A type of synthesizer which derives its sounds from recording actual sounds (instruments or nonmusical sounds) and then storing them in computer memory, either floppy discs, hard drive, or recorded onto CD-ROM. Samplers are used extensively for generating sound effects. There are both hardware samplers and software samplers. They work the same; however, one is free standing while the other is a program on a computer that emulates a hardware sampler.

Sound Sample: The smallest unit of a digitized sound that represents the audio signal at a particular moment, several thousand of which are needed to digitize a sound; the complete set of samples that make up a digitized sound that is available as a file.

Sequencer: Hardware or software that allows a sequence of notes to be put together to create music. They range in complexity from 16-note sequencers found in synthesizers to 256-track audio sequencers found in computer programs such as Cakewalk or Pro-tools. Sequencers today allow you to use a mix of both MIDI and/or Digital Audio tracks.

Synthesizer: A device (or computer-based program), with or without an integrated keyboard or other controller, which uses various electronic means to generate musical sounds. Most synthesizers either have a built in keyboard or are "rack mounted" (just a synth module with no built in controller) and have a large number of built in patches (sounds) designed to imitate the waveform (sound) of existing acoustic instruments (J. Rafalak, personal communication, September 1, 2004).

• •

Useful Websites

Assistive Technology:

>   http://www.aacintervention.com/
>
>   http://ablenetinc.com
>
>   http://www.creative-comm.com
>
>   http://www.donjohnston.com/
>
>   http://www.lburkhart.com
>
>   http://www.mayer-johnson.com/

Band-in-a-Box™:

>   http://www.alisdair.com/gearsoftware/biablinks.html
>
>   http://www.pgmusic.com/review10.htm

Copyright:

>   http://fairuse.stanford.edu/
>
>   http://www.menc.org/information/copyright/copyr.html#recording
>
>   http://www.pdinfo.com/list.htm
>
>   http://www.reach.net/~scherer/p/copyrit1.htm

Definitions/Glossary:

>   http://www.fortunecity.com/tinpan/faithfull/379/glossary.html
>
>   http://www.recordingeq.com/GlosPubPT.htm
>
>   http://www.scala.com/definition/

GarageBand™:

>   http://www.rockument.com/bove_books/02tutor-gb_over.htm

MIDI Sites:

> *http://www.harmony-central.com/MIDI*
>
> *http://www.kunstderfuge.com/midi.htm*
>
> *http://www.manythings.org/midi*
>
> *http://www.midi.com*
>
> *http://midiworld.com*
>
> *http://virtual.xs4all.nl/world/index.html*

Music Therapy in Technology:

> *http://www.rolandus.com/musictherapy/index.asp*

National Standards for Arts Education:

> *http://artsedge.kennedy-center.org/teach/standards.cfm*

Chapter 14

Noteworthy Examples

The following music therapists contributed to the content of this chapter: Ruthlee Figlure Adler, MT-BC; Nicole Allgood, MSEd, MT-BC; Amy Furman, MM, RMT; Marcia Humpal, MEd, MT-BC; Ronna Kaplan, MA, MT-BC; Beth McLaughlin, MS, LCAT, MT-BC; Jean Nemeth, MA, MT-BC; Elizabeth Schwartz, LCAT, MT-BC; Glenn Sonoda, RMT; and Rebecca Tweedle, MEd, MT-BC

●

Sessions That Work

Creative Solutions in a School Setting

Somebody forgot to tell the kids in Pam's class that music therapy was a fun, nonthreatening, motivating, and rewarding experience. By the time they arrived at the music therapy room, they were disorganized and distraught with shoes flying and tears flowing... if they made it at all.

These students had been diagnosed with autism and ranged in age from 8 to 10 years of age. Individually, they each loved music but had difficulty bringing that love to the group. They were nonverbal but used gestures, pictures, or augmentative communication devices to get their needs met. Their behavior clearly communicated that we were not meeting their needs in their music therapy sessions.

Perhaps the transition from the classroom to the music therapy room was contributing to their disorganized behavior. The change in the routine was disruptive to their need for consistency. A few of the students were sensitive to the noise, and the lights in the hall added to their distress. If they were going to benefit from music therapy, a change of course was required.

Therefore, music therapy would come to them. Morning Circle was a 30-minute routine that occurred daily in the classroom. The music therapy staff developed songs for each concept that was being taught and facilitated the routine 4 days a week. The structure of the routine was illustrated by picture symbols developed by the classroom staff to give the students a visual representation of the activity sequence. As each activity was completed, the picture was removed from the Velcro board on the wall. The sequence was as follows:

Routine:	Example:
Joining Activity	"Hi! How Are Ya?"
Pledge of Allegiance & Patriotic Song	"Grand Old Flag"
Attendance	"Who is Here?"
Days of the Week	"Today is _____"
Date	"What's the Number on the Calendar"
Weather	"We're Gonna Have Weather, Whether or Not"
Movement or Instrumental Activity	This would vary but was intended to be an all group activity
Song Choice	Students would take turns choosing a song from a picture board
Goodbye Song	"You Did a Good Job"

A few of the music therapy activities are described below in more detail.

Joining Activity

> ### Hi! How Are Ya?
> ### by Beth McLaughlin
> (sung to the tune of the old Rice-a-Roni commercial)
>
> [start clapping and wait for all to join in before singing]
> *Hi! How are ya? It's nice to see you here.*
> *Hi! How are ya? Let's give a great big cheer.*
> *I'll raise my hands and then I'll say* (lift hands above head)
> *A great big "Hip, Hip, Hip Hooray!"* (pump arms as in a cheer)
> *Hi! How are ya? It's nice to see you here.* (resume clap)
> [Repeat with stamp, patschen, or a wave hello]

During this activity, students are encouraged to imitate movements, wave to their friends, and approximate vocalization for "*Hip, Hip, Hip Hooray!*" This phrase could also be programmed into a communication device for student-initiated response.

Pledge of Allegiance

Students are instructed to stand and put their right hands over their hearts. One student is selected to pass out flags to the peers. Students begin marching to initiate the playing of the song, "Grand Old Flag."

Date

> ### What's the Number?
> ### by Beth McLaughlin
> (sung to the tune of Clementine)
>
> *What's the number on the calendar?*
> *What's the number for today?*
> *We will start from the beginning,*
> *Number 1 will lead the way.*

Procedure: Give a mallet to all the students and have them gather around a large drum. Point to the numbers on the calendar as they play the drum. If they can follow the pulse of your count, great! However, this is not the goal. At the end of the counting, instruct students to "rest" their mallets on their shoulder to signal that counting is finished.

> *Number 10, number 10 is the number for today.*
> *Now we're finished with our counting*
> *Everybody shout "Hooray!"* (students raise their arms up to cheer)

Movement or Instrumental Activity

While the foregoing activities are short, students are taking turns and having to wait while the staff allows time for processing and independent, self-initiated response. Now it's time for everyone to move! The music chosen for this activity should have a simple ABA form with 3 to 4 repetitions of a theme. The students are given the opportunity to work together using a theraband, hula hoop, or simple rhythm instruments following a 2- to 3-movement sequence. This is also an opportunity for students to help pass out instruments or practice getting their own instrument in response to a group direction.

Song Choice

It's time to bring Morning Circle to a close. Each day a different student gets a turn to choose a song from a set of picture cues representing favorite songs. One song is sung leading into the final closing song.

Several goals were addressed through these activities:

Management (behavior)
- increase tolerance for waiting during music activities
- assume rest position when music stops
- participate in music activities as modeled
- use instruments appropriately
- sit appropriately with group
- follow directions

Academic (cognitive, language)
- increase attending and focusing behaviors
- increase repertoire of picture/song associations
- use sign language within the context of a song
- extend expression of academic concepts (weather, calendar) by choosing correct picture associated with activity
- extend expression of concepts through movement and instrument play
- repeat word or sound in a recurring song phrase

Physical (motor)

- stand to take a turn
- self-initiate participation
- imitate body percussion and non-locomotor movement
- maintain grasp on hoop or theraband in movement activity
- walk in a circle while holding a prop
- perform 2–3 step movement sequence with or without instruments

Social

- raise hand to be recognized
- wait appropriately for turn to play
- engage in a reciprocal gestural exchange during hello or goodbye song
- distribute instrument or prop to peer
- identify peers by matching their picture or name

> *To avoid problems that arise when students are rigid about playing only their favorite color of instrument, place a group of colored instruments such as egg shakers in a canvas bag. Ask each student to guess what color(s) he will pull out. Have him remove the shaker(s) and determine if his guess was correct (the rule here is that you must play the ones you take out, thus avoiding lengthy searching for a favorite color or negative reaction to being given the "wrong" color!).*
>
> *A variation on this that can assuage feelings is to have each student pull one shaker as described above. After all the students have one each, go around again with the bag open and ask each student if the next one they choose will be the "same" or "different" from the color they already have. Thus, they can choose to match their color or take a favorite color.*

Music Therapy and Role Playing

The next activity is representative of those that address social interaction as well as verbal and nonverbal pragmatic communicative functions. Especially effective for students with autism spectrum disorders, those with other social difficulties, or those with language delays, social story songs teach behavior that is appropriate and acceptable. For students in an educational setting, learning how to act and react is a necessary part of classroom survival. Role playing and practicing are important components of this type of activity.

Excerpts from "Use Your Words"
by Ronna Kaplan (©1997)

Chorus
Use your words, use your words,
You've got to use your words.

1. *If someone is bothering you,*
And you just don't know what to do,
Say "Please stop," but don't yell,
Or find a grown-up to tell,
But you've got to use your words.

Chorus

2. *If something's not working just right,*
Don't sit while the day turns to night.
You can say, "Help me, please,"
And then someone sees
That you have just used your words.

Chorus

Procedure:
* *Put numeral cards in a large drum or tambourine.*
* *Ask one student to choose a card and announce the number.*
* *Instruct the children to listen to or read the verse about to be sung and played.*
* *Sing and play the verse number selected.*
* *After the verse, ask student what it was about using:*
  1. *open-ended questions, to encourage answers,*
  2. *choice verbal prompt questions, such as, "Was it about asking for a turn or about saying 'Hello'?" or "Look at the third line. What does it say?",*
  3. *paraphrasing topic.*
* *Praise good listening and answering.*
* *Role play topic of that verse.*
* *Repeat above steps for other verses.*

Role-play suggestions:
* *Either adult or another student is given the task of "bothering" someone (e.g., pulling his carpet square or taking an object from him). If the student who is being bothered protests and uses words appropriately, offer praise. If the appropriate actions or words are not evident, ask the rest of the class what the student should do. Verbally prompt as needed for the student to be successful. Continue until everyone has had a turn.*
* *Take the batteries out of an instrument such as a Q-chord or disconnect an adapter. Act out asking for help inserting batteries, plugging in instrument, etc.*

Musical Material and Songs—Considerations for Early Intervention and Early Childhood

Original Compositions. Sometimes music therapists may compose much of the material used in sessions with young children. Often the material will begin through improvisation and then become a structured song.

For early intervention and preschool, the importance of the song form, as well as the importance of the unaccompanied singing voice, must not be overlooked. When using harmony, consider the diatonic, pentatonic, and mixolydian scales. In creating lyrics to songs, the focus may adhere to directional concepts or contrasting ideas (e.g., up/down) or "power words" such as: Yes, No, Stop, Go, Me, More and Please.

Traditional Tunes. On the other hand, when the music therapist uses traditional songs in the educational setting, the young children are exposed to information that is very normalizing. Try to become familiar with the music education curriculum that will be used in the next mainstream learning experience for the student. By using songs found within the music curriculum while focusing on the IEP goals and objectives, we provide our students with incidental learning that becomes very applicable in their next educational environment.

Especially at the beginning of the school year, young children who previously were part of special education programs will be coping with the need to generalize skills previously learned. Having a new teacher, room, classmates, as well as perhaps being expected to walk and transition to a music room make the educational experience very overwhelming to some students.

If some of the music in the new setting is familiar, children may become more confident and more willing to participate, thereby gaining positive attention and increased independence. Furthermore, teach essential classroom skills such as play and stop, look at the teacher, hold instruments quietly, pass safely, as well as how to hold hands and stand or sit next to peers without invading their space.

By using songs found within the music curriculum while focusing on the IEP goals and objectives, we provide our students with incidental learning that becomes very applicable in their next educational environment.

It was the second week of school, so it was only the second time the kindergarten class had come to the music room. Omar, who had received music therapy as part of his early intervention program for two years, smiled and waved hello as the class came. Everyone was pretending to be a train, as they practiced walking in a line.

After singing the hello songs he already knew, Omar joined in on "Down at the Station," a song in the kindergarten book of the Macmillan series used by the music education department. He raised his hand and asked, "Can we play shakers and drums?" The rest of the class looked at him with amazement and waited to see what would happen. "What a creative idea—let's get them out!" It was a creative idea—he had taken an activity previously performed in the early intervention setting and now asked to do it in a new situation. When the teacher came to pick up the class, the children excitedly told her about what a special opportunity they had thanks to Omar, who was creative—and well prepared to be an active part of this new educational environment.

Songs for Guided Group Play, Circle Time, and Concept Development. In the educational setting, music therapy strategies that are introduced by the music therapist often are repeated throughout the week by the classroom staff. This is a highly desirable outcome of successful music therapy service delivery. Using a mix of original and traditional music allows others to feel comfortable with replicating at least part of your session. Try to give children concrete and multisensory information through the musical experience.

Traditional children's song: "Twinkle, Twinkle Little Star"

Targeted Concept: *Up*

Procedure:

1. *Sing the song, emphasizing the word "up" (perform a vocal glissando as you ascend to the word).*
2. *Repeat the song and sweep your hands upwards.*
3. *Put out enough small flashlights for each child and darken the room.*
4. *Sing again, and this time emphasize the word "UP" and demonstrate by sweeping the flashlight upward to the ceiling.*
5. *Repeat as children join in on this musical play. You may wish to add a xylophone accompaniment that demonstrates the concepts:*

Variation:
Have everyone shine a light on one child at a time (only one rule . . . NOT in the eyes!) Suggest body parts: "Let's all shine our stars on Lakisha's foot."

Likewise, using piggyback songs (traditional tunes with parodied lyrics that emphasize targeted concepts) helps children remember the information contained therein. In addition, adult staff may more readily remember a familiar tune.

We Can Play with Our Hammers
—variation on traditional *Johnny Works with One Hammer*

Targeted Concepts: *Stop and Go*

Procedure:
1. *Use plastic hammers, wooden spoons, or just pretend to hammer with your fist.*
2. *Capture the attention of all the children by holding your hands or the "hammer" high over your head and singing, "Ooooooohhhhhhhhh . . ."*
3. *Be very dramatic as you pound to the beat or tap your knees with your fists. Emphasize the word stop.* **Pause** *before starting the song again, adding, "Ready, set . . . . .GO!"*
4. *Let children determine when to "go".*

> *We can play with our hammers,*
> *Our hammers, our hammers.*
> *We can play with our hammers,*
> *Then we STOP!*

Variation:
Make the song a turn-taking activity. Sing the child's name and let the child hammer. Substitute your name on the next verse and have the child wait while you take your turn.

Systematic Variations

To help children accept change, and to expand their musical and play skills, initially vary only one attribute at a time. Use a "musical hook" (such as chanting while playing, "*tap, tap, tap, tap*") as a bridge into the song in the example that follows:

Figure 36. M. Humpal

Systematically change one attribute (e.g., *instrument, name*) at a time. This really helps establish flexibility. Often students with special needs, especially those with autism spectrum disorders, become locked into a routine that becomes difficult to change. For instance, if a classroom teacher or music specialist needs to conserve time and therefore sings **Three** Little Monkeys Jumping on the Bed instead of the more typical five, the child might find this difficult to handle. Prepare your students for change and surprises.

Interruption

Another technique that helps children accept change and act on anticipation is interruption. This chant is accompanied on a hand drum or tambourine.

Little Miss Muffet

Little Miss Muffet sat on a tuffet eating her curds and whey.
When along came a spider who sat down beside her and...
FRIGHTENED Miss Muffet away!

Procedure:
1. *Initially, the music therapist chants the nursery rhyme while tapping the beat on the instrument.*
2. *Model playing one loud tap on the word, "frightened," and continue the chant, tapping the beat quietly.*
3. *Repeat the chant, but this time, quickly extend the instrument to the child on the word, "frightened." Remove the instrument and immediately continue the chant, after the child hits the instrument once.*
4. *Continue repeating the experience for other children.*

Variation:
 Expand the activity by making instruments available to each child. Interrupt play by taking the tambourine away after loud "frightened" and then return it after the end of the chant.

Weaving Music Therapy Into Music Standards

School districts may require that music therapy sessions address established music education standards, as well as nonmusical goals implemented via music. Note the many music components of form as well as composition that are embedded in this lesson.

The traditional spiritual "I'm On My Way" can be the basis for a multifaceted musical experience for older students. The four phrases (I'm on my way; And I won't turn back (3x); I'm on my way, oh yes, I'm on my way) are each broken in half and performed in Call and Response (e.g., I'm on my way, I'm on my way, and I won't turn back, and I won't turn back). The heavy repetition affords extended practice of the words.

An excellent outgrowth of this song is to make up an imaginary journey, such as "I'm on my way . . . to the beach today." Extend this with ideas from the group about how the trip will go, what to bring, what you do, see, or eat as well as how you get there. Weave all of this information into the second parts of each phrase. The students play their responses on an instrument that can then be passed to the next person. The repetitive practice is woven within a story that taps imagination and thinking skills and awakens recognition of how music may be organized.

•

Equipment, Strategies, Techniques, and Tips

Musical Instruments You Can Create

Numerous companies offer a large variety of instruments and equipment that may be used in an educational setting. Examine these resources before purchasing to determine if they (a) produce high quality sound, (b) are sturdy enough to withstand use by a large number of students, and (c) have small parts that could be dangerous.

Students, colleagues, and families may enjoy making instruments with the students. Instructions for doing so follow. (Adapted from R. Adler's *Target on Music* (1988), Rockville, MD: Ivymount School, unless otherwise noted.)

Percussion Instruments

Castanets or Finger Clappers. Fold a piece of cardboard in half. Glue two or more items (e.g., flattened lids, bottle caps, empty walnut shells, or seashells) inside the ends, facing each other. Play by striking the two sides together. Adapt for students lacking fine motor coordination by running a string through the top of the folded side of the cardboard. The instrument can then be shaken. Bottle caps or shells may also be loosely nailed to one side of a 1" × 1" dowel or piece of wood, and played by striking the handle against one's knee or palm of the hand.

Drum Sticks (Mallets or Beaters). Dowels, 3/8" thick, chopsticks, unsharpened pencils, or cocktail mixers may be used as drum sticks. If necessary, sand the ends. Drumstick heads or knobs may be made from stuffed squares of material, twine, cotton, paper spools, or super balls. Use tape or rubber bands to secure the head to one end of the stick. A basting brush or wire whisk may be used as a brush.

Tambourines. Position two paper plates or aluminum pie pans, facing each other. Tape, sew, or staple them together and make holes around the outside rim. Attach small bells, buttons, shells, or bottle caps to the holes with string. Shake to play.

Ocean Drum (designed by G. Sonoda)

1. Cut 1" x 2" fir wood into four equal lengths for a square or sets of different lengths to make a rectangle shape.
2. Pound 2 nails into each corner to make square or rectangle.
3. Paint or decorate wood.
4. Place the drum frame over a catch tray or container.
5. Wrap wood frame with clear packing tape with the STICKY SIDE OUT going around and around both sides overlapping in a diagonal direction. Just before sealing drum, insert bells, BB's, rice, or beans. Close drum up, still with the sticky side out.
6. Run tape around flat edge of drum, sealing in objects so they don't fall out.
7. Now begin wrapping in a perpendicular direction with the tape sticky side down pulling very hard to put tension on the drum face.
8. Push down on tape to seal sticky sides together so that the objects inside don't fall out.
9. Shake drum or hit with some type of mallet.

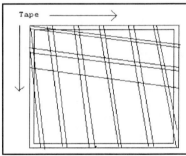

Figure 37. Ocean Drum.

PVC Shaker (designed by R. Tweedle)

Materials: 1/2" or 3/4" PVC pipe, four 90° elbows, or eight 45° pieces, PVC glue.
Instructions: Cut PVC pipe to desired length. Glue pieces and elbows together and add one film cap full of BB's before gluing last piece. Decorate.
Variations:
*   Use only one piece of PVC with caps on each end.
*   Tape vibrator to hoop.
*   Add texture to PVC to change grip edge.

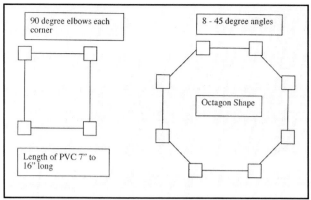

Figure 38. Two Types of PVC Shakers.

String Instruments

Picks for Autoharp (and Other String Instruments). In addition to using plastic or felt guitar picks, use plastic spoons, door stops, small margarine tub covers (may be cut in half), or spatulas.

Washtub Bass

Materials:

1.   A metal washtub or basin
2.   Broom or mop handle (or a 3' dowel)
3.   Sturdy twine, heavy cord, a bass string or piece of thin clothesline
4.   Small block of wood, screw, or nut and bolt to secure the string

Directions: Invert the washtub and drill a hold through its center, large enough for the string to easily pass through. Saw a notch in the end of the stick so it can fit over the rim of the washtub. Drill a hole, or make a groove, for the string to pass through at the top of the pole (or wherever the height will be most convenient for you or your students). You may wish to drill several holes.

Wrap or tie the string around the small block of wood, or attach the string to the bolt. Thread the free end of the string through the hole in the washtub so the wooden block remains on the inside. Invert the washtub. Place the notched end of the pole on the rim of the washtub and hold it up. Thread the free end of the string through the stick and tie it as taut as you can. Be sure the knot is facing away from the washtub (this takes two people).

To play: Stand up and place one foot on top of the washtub. Hold the pole with your left hand and strum or pluck the string with your right hand. To change pitch, tilt the pole down toward the washtub, or tighten the string (the tighter the string, the higher the pitch). You also may move your left hand down the string, grasping and shortening it to change the pitch.

Wind Instruments

Horn. Cover one end of an empty paper towel holder with wax paper. Secure the paper in place with a rubber band. Using a sharp pencil, nail, or screwdriver, punch a row of holes along one side of the roll. Hum or sing a song into the open end of the horn. If you have long, dry bamboo sticks, you may make flutes in the same manner.

Jugs or Bottles. Blow across the mouth of a jug or bottle. Add water to change the sound (the more water, the higher the pitch; the less water, the lower the pitch).

General Strategies and Considerations

- Establish rapport—understand the student's world. Set realistic goals/objectives.
- Identify and structure the necessary steps to complete the task/situation at hand. Give clear, concise directions. Remember that motivation and attention go hand-in-hand.
- Design music instruction proceeding from skills/strengths. Proceed from known to unknown in small steps and "chunks" (this builds confidence).
- Raise the bar but teach in small steps and be patient—your students' success is always worth the wait.
- Use a variety of approaches; give as many multisensory cues as possible. However, avoid overstimulation. Indications of this vary from escalating responses and nondifferentiated movement (i.e., overactive full body movement) to cessation of responding altogether (i.e., "shut-down").
- Communicate with more than words (include visual, auditory, tactile, and kinesthetic senses). Combine gestures or signs with verbal directions. Add puffy paint to props or cut them out of sandpaper to give tactile reinforcement and provide an avenue for information for students with vision impairments. Added cues will benefit all group members.
- Pace the session appropriately—remember the importance of repetition and review. Allow the students to ask questions, plan, and lead activities.
- Provide opportunities for your students to demonstrate their skills. Reinforce learning experiences through activities—listening, observing, and imitating.
- Set clear limits, giving effective, specific, consistent feedback and reinforcement.
- Consult with specialists, therapists, and related professionals about the strengths, learning strategies, and goals of individual students.
- Be positive: provide for success. Believe in each student's capabilities and strive for optimum potential.
- Examine your own skills, thoughts, feelings, and reactions to others.

More Specific Music Therapy Tips and Techniques

- Use sound as a focusing agent.
- Utilize props and visuals as focusing agents, too.
- Capture attention and help students focus by playing catchy rhythms.
- Keep the beat slow (e.g., use a hand drum) and follow the child's natural rhythm. Walk or move to the beat.

- Select activities that initially require only one or a few movements or movement concepts.
- Do not expect correct responses to "right" or "left." Say, "the other side."
- Use modified notation such as circles of different sizes to show beat and accent.
- When practicing sound production or articulation skills, sing a song with extended or intermittent syllable sections in the lyrics. By substituting different consonant-vowel combinations with each new verse, a range of sounds can be addressed within the context of one song activity. When appropriate, end each verse by asking the students to identify the letter(s) they have just sung.
- Teach correct hand placement on recorders, by adding hole reinforcers and a red dot for right hand.
- Include pop standards or "oldies." Many students are familiar with these songs from TV and movie culture and often are eager to use them in sessions. The block structure and repetitive nature of this music lends itself well to all types of activities.
- Revisit previously learned music and music activities to give the students security and enjoyment.

Group Management Tips

- When working in the group setting, consider the differing skills levels of individual children and design activities that will simultaneously address these disparities.
- Play music as the students enter the room. This sets the mood for the session as well as gives the students an auditory cue about the environment they are entering.
- Set a session structure that can include slight variations. A definitive opening and closing should frame the session with a somewhat predictable flow of activities throughout. Students come to rely on this format and learn what to expect. Use a "Today in Music" schedule chart and remove a picture or name of activity as it is completed.
- Use a circle format to ensure a clear line of vision between all group members and foster peer modeling and cohesiveness of the group.
- Emphasize and shape eye contact and listening skills through repeated reinforcement of these skills (e.g., have students play an instrument only when the therapist looks at them and they return the eye contact).
- Keep the entire group actively involved, even when the therapist is working on individual responses. Students can keep the beat via knee tapping or some other repetitive response throughout the activity.
- When seating issues arise, try using a "magic mix-up" technique. Stop suddenly and call "magic mix-up" along with 2 students' names. These

students must switch seats as quickly as possible. Applaud quick response. This game should be introduced prior to any problems and used as a fun activity. Once established, a technique such as this can be called upon to avert potential disruption or problems between group members.

- Establish an effective means of keeping instruments quiet. The students must consistently practice set responses when not playing the instruments they are given. Egg shakers in the "nest" (the space created in the lap by cross-legged sitting) or the "stick garage" ("parking" sticks, one on each shoulder) are examples of using a simple phrase to elicit an effective response for managing instruments during group activities.

- Keep instruments and equipment in the mysterious depths of a rolling suitcase or other closed, portable storage container. Introduce only what will be used next to keep the focus on the activity at hand, avoid distraction and impulse control issues, and heighten interest (as well as ensure the safety of both students and equipment!).

- Have a set space for instruments and props in the music room. Attach pictures and names of instrument to mark the location. Involve the students in cleaning up at the end of the session.

- Alter activities within session sequence to vary the responses and avoid fatigue, overload, or boredom. Shift between movement, listening, singing, and instrument play responses at 3–5 minute intervals with younger groups. Older groups may be able to sustain an activity for longer periods. The therapist must judge according to the group response.

- Overplan and have a bank of extra activities. Even the best plan will not work at times. Having a group of high probability, back-up activities ready is essential.

Secrets to Effectiveness and Contentment in a Special Education Setting

- When working in school settings, keep abreast of legislative and municipal changes that affect the work setting.

- Become familiar with the national standards set for music education (available from MENC at www.menc.org) as well as educational benchmarks set by individual states or municipalities.

- Participate in the school system's continuing education offerings or attend conference offerings in these areas whenever possible. Acquire information that will justify music therapy and program choices within the context of the school's mission of meeting educational standards.

- Serve on a committee at school (but not too many!).

- Learn the education system's inherent terminology and jargon. Having this common understanding will provide comfort and credibility if you are called upon to discuss a particular case or situation with other professionals or parents.

- Demonstrate music therapy's alliance with the mandate to move toward least restrictive environment (LRE) by promoting the skills necessary for success in the classroom social group setting.
- Be a proactive member of the educational team; learn about curricula and develop integrated activities. By consulting with the classroom teacher or simply using good observational skills (e.g., perusing bulletin boards or examining students' work), the music therapist can create a very timely tie-in to the class curricula during session activities. For example, use a "dinosaur" song for a movement or instrument play activity when the science unit deals with prehistoric animals. This may springboard a discussion of dinosaurs for rhythmic drumming or speech patterning work.
- Be nice to the custodian and school secretary.
- Use your resources; invite other specialists to be part of your sessions and ask to be a part of theirs.
- Be generous with your music; write an appreciation song for the teacher assistants and have the teachers sing it.
- Find ways to collaborate with artists and musicians in the community. They love to learn about the power of music therapy.
- Listen to the parents. They know their children best, and are usually right!
- Get to know your students before reading their files.
- Embrace the joy of making music with your students.
- Buy a lamp with a 40-watt bulb and begin and end your sessions with low light and 90 seconds of quiet music. The classroom staff will love you for returning their students to them in a more relaxed state (plus *you* will be more relaxed, too).

Resources

Articles Published in Music Therapy Journals Through 2005 Categorized by Special Education Topics
Beth Swaney, MS, MT-BC

●

ADHD/Other Health Impairment

Cripe, F. F. (1986). *Rock music as therapy for children with ADD: An exploratory study.* Journal of Music Therapy, *23(1),* 30–37.

Jackson, N. A. (2003). *A survey of music therapy methods and their role in the treatment of early elementary school children with ADHD.* Journal of Music Therapy, *40(4),* 302–323.

●

Assessment

Bixler, J. (1968). *Musical aptitude in the educable mentally retarded.* Journal of Music Therapy, *5(2),* 41–43.

Brunk, B. K., & Coleman, K. A. (2000). *Development of a special education music therapy assessment process.* Music Therapy Perspectives, *18(1),* 59–68.

Chase, K. (2004). *Music therapy assessment for children with developmental disabilities: A survey study.* Journal of Music Therapy, *41(1),* 28–54.

Cotter, V. W., & Toombs, S. (1966). *A procedure of determining the music preference of mental retardates.* Journal of Music Therapy, *3(2),* 57–64.

Gfeller, K., & Baumann, A. A. (1988). *Assessment procedures for music therapy with hearing impaired children: Language development.* Journal of Music Therapy, *25(4),* 192–205.

Gordon, E. (1968). *The use of the musical aptitude profile with exceptional children.* Journal of Music Therapy, *5(2),* 37–40.

Griggs-Drane, E. R., & Wheeler, J. J. (1997). *The use of functional assessment procedures and individualized schedule in the treatment of autism: Recommendations for music therapists.* Music Therapy Perspectives, *15(2),* 87–93.

Hunter, L. L. (1989). *Computer-assisted assessment of melodic and rhythmic discrimination skills.* Journal of Music Therapy, *26(2),* 79–87.

Jones, R. E. (1986). *Assessing developmental levels of mentally retarded students with the musical-perception assessment of cognitive development.* Journal of Music Therapy, *23(3),* 166–173.

Layman, D. L., Hussey, D. L., & Laing, S. J. (2002). *Music therapy assessment for severely emotionally disturbed children: A pilot study.* Journal of Music Therapy, *40(3),* 164–187.

Maranto, C. D., Decuir, A., & Humphrey, T. (1984). *A comparison of digit span scores, rhythm span scores, and diagnostic factors or mentally retarded persons.* Music Therapy, *4(1),* 84–90.

VanWeelden, K., & Whipple, J. (2005). *Preservice teachers' predictions, perceptions, and actual assessment of students with special needs in secondary general music.* Journal of Music Therapy, *42(3),* 200–215.

Wigram, T. (2000). *A method of music therapy assessment for the diagnosis of autism and communication disorders in children.* Music Therapy Perspectives, *18(1),* 13–22.

Wilson, B. L., & Smith, D. S. (2000). *Music therapy assessment in school settings: A preliminary investigation.* Journal of Music Therapy, *37(2),* 97–117.

●

At-Risk

Goolsby, T. M., Jr., Frary, R. B., & Rogers, M. M. (1974). Observational techniques in determination of the effects of background music upon verbalizations of disadvantaged kindergarten children. Journal of Music Therapy, 11(1), 21–32.

Wolfe, D. E. (1982). The effects of interrupted and continuous music on bodily movement and task performance of third grade students. Journal of Music Therapy, 19(2), 74–85.

●

Early Intervention

Baird, S. (1969). A technique to assess the preferences for intensity of musical stimuli in young hard-of-hearing children. Journal of Music Therapy, 6(1), 6–11.

Davis, R. K. (1990). A model for the integration of music therapy within a preschool classroom for children with physical disabilities or language delays. Music Therapy Perspectives, 8, 82–84.

Galloway, H. F., & Bean, M. F. (1974). The effects of action songs on the development of body-image and body-part identification in hearing-impaired preschool children. Journal of Music Therapy, 11(3), 125–134.

Gfeller, K. E. (1990). A cognitive-linguistic approach to language development for the preschool child with hearing impairments for music therapy practice. Music Therapy Perspectives, 8, 47–51.

Gunsberg, A. (1988). Improvised musical play: A strategy for fostering social play between developmentally delayed and nondelayed preschool children. Journal of Music Therapy, 25(4), 178–191.

Gunsberg, A. S. (1991). A method for conducting improvised musical play with children both with and without developmental delays in preschool classrooms. Music Therapy Perspectives, 9, 46–51.

Harding, C., & Ballard, K. D. (1982). The effectiveness of music as a stimulus and as a contingent reward in promoting the spontaneous speech of three physically handicapped preschoolers. Journal of Music Therapy, 19(2), 86–101.

Hoskins, C. (1988). Use of music to increase verbal response and improve expressive language abilities of preschool language delayed children. Journal of Music Therapy, 25(2), 73–84.

Hughes, J. E., Robbins, B. J., McKenzie, B. A., & Robb, S. S. (1990). Integrating exceptional and nonexceptional young children through music play: A pilot program. Music Therapy Perspectives, 8, 52–56.

Humpal, M. E. (1990). Early intervention: The implications for music therapy. Music Therapy Perspectives, 8, 30–35.

Humpal, M. (1991). The effects of an integrated early childhood music program on social interaction among children with handicaps and their typical peers. Journal of Music Therapy, 28(3), 161–177.

Kern, P., & Wolery, M. (2001). Participation of a preschooler with visual impairments on the playground: Effects of music adaptations and staff development. Journal of Music Therapy, 38(2), 149–164.

Kramer, S. A. (1978). The effects of music as a cue in maintaining handwriting in preschool children. Journal of Music Therapy, 15(3), 138–144.

Monti, R. (1985). Music therapy in a therapeutic nursery. Music Therapy, 5(1), 22–27.

Register, D. (2001). The effects of an early intervention music curriculum on prereading/writing. Journal of Music Therapy, 38(3), 239–248.

Register, D. (2004). The effects of live music groups versus an educational children's television program on the emergent literacy of young children. Journal of Music Therapy, 41(1), 2–27.

Seybold, C. D. (1971). The value and use of music activities in the treatment of speech delayed children. Journal of Music Therapy, 8(3), 102–110.

Standley, J. M., & Hughes, J. E. (1996). Documenting developmentally appropriate objectives of a music therapy program for early intervention: A behavioral analysis. Music Therapy Perspectives, 14(2), 87–94.

Standley, J. M., & Hughes, J. E. (1997). Evaluation of an early intervention music curriculum for enhancing prereading/writing skills. Music Therapy Perspectives, 15(2), 79–86.

Wilson, C. V. (1976). The use of rock music as a reward in behavior therapy with children. Journal of Music Therapy, 13(1), 39–48.

Wolfe, D. E., & Hom, C. (1993). Use of melodies as structural prompts for learning and retention of sequential information by preschool students. Journal of Music Therapy, 30(2), 100–118.

●

Emotional, Social, and Behavioral Disorders

Burleson, S. J., Center, D. B., & Reeves, H. (1989). The effect of background music on task performance in psychotic children. Journal of Music Therapy, 26(4), 198–205.

Eidson, C. E., Jr. (1989). The effect of behavioral music therapy on the generalization of interpersonal skills from sessions to the classroom by emotionally handicapped middle school students. Journal of Music Therapy, 26(4), 206–221.

Giacobbe, G. A., & Graham, R. M. (1978). The responses of aggressive emotionally disturbed and normal boys to selected musical stimuli. Journal of Music Therapy, 15(3), 118–135.

Gibbons, A. C. (1983). Rhythm response in emotionally disturbed children with differing needs for external structure. Music Therapy, 3(1), 94–102.

Grossman, S. (1978). An investigation of Crocker's music projective techniques for emotionally disturbed children. Journal of Music Therapy, 1(4), 179–184.

Haines, J. H. (1989). The effects of music therapy on the self esteem of emotionally disturbed adolescents. Music Therapy, 8(1), 78–91.

Hanser, S. B. (1974). Group-contingent music listening with emotionally disturbed boys. Journal of Music Therapy, 11(4), 220–225.

Jorgenson, H. (1974). The use of a contingent music activity to modify behaviors which interfere with learning. Journal of Music Therapy, 11(1), 41–46.

Kivland, M. J. (1986). The use of music to increase self-esteem in a conduct disordered adolescent. Journal of Music Therapy, 23(1), 25–29.

Krout, R. E. (1986). Use of a group token contingency with school-aged special education students to improve a music listening skill. Music Therapy Perspectives, 3, 13–16.

Krout, R. E., & Mason, M. (1988). Using computer and electronic music resources in clinical music therapy with behaviorally disordered students, 12 to 18 years old. Music Therapy Perspectives, 5, 114–118.

Larson, B. A. (1981). Auditory and visual rhythmic pattern recognition by emotionally disturbed and normal adolescents. Journal of Music Therapy, 18(3), 128–136.

Madsen, C. K., Smith, D. S., & Feeman, C. C., Jr. (1988). The use of music in cross-age tutoring within special education settings. Journal of Music Therapy, 25(3), 135–144.

Merle-Fishman, C. R., & Marcus, M. L. (1982). Musical behaviors and preferences in emotionally disturbed and normal children: An exploratory study. Music Therapy, 2(1), 1–11.

Michel, D. E., & Martin, D. (1970). Music and self-esteem research with disadvantaged, problem boys in an elementary school. Journal of Music Therapy, 7(4), 124–127.

Miller, D. M., Dorow, L., & Greer, R. D. (1974). The contingent use of music and art for improving arithmetic scores. Journal of Music Therapy, 11(2), 57–64.

Montello, L., & Coons, E. E. (1998). Effects of active versus passive group music therapy on preadolescents with emotional, learning, and behavioral disorders. Journal of Music Therapy, 35(1), 49–67.

Rickson, D. J., & Watkins, W. G. (2003). Music therapy to promote prosocial behaviors in aggressive adolescent boys—A pilot study. Journal of Music Therapy, 40(4), 283–301.

Underhill, K. K., & Harris, C. M. (1974). The effect of contingent music on establishing imitation in behaviorally disturbed retarded children. Journal of Music Therapy, 11(3), 156–166.

Wilson, A. (1964). Special education for the emotionally disturbed child. Journal of Music Therapy, 1(1), 16–18.

Wilson, C. V. (1976). The use of rock music as a reward in behavior therapy with children. Journal of Music Therapy, 13(1), 39–48.

●

Information and Professional Surveys

Aigen, K. (1995). Cognitive and affective processes in music therapy with individuals with developmental delays: A preliminary model for contemporary Nordoff- Robbins practice. Music Therapy, 13(1), 18–46.

Alley, J. M. (1977). Education of the severely handicapped: The role of music therapy. Journal of Music Therapy, 14(2), 50–59.

Alley, J. M. (1979). Music in the IEP: Therapy/education. Journal of Music Therapy, 16(3), 111–127.

Bennis, J. A. (1969). The use of music as a therapy in the special education classroom. Journal of Music Therapy, 6(1), 15–18.

Briggs, C. (1991). A model for understanding musical development. Music Therapy, 10(1), 1–21.

Cassity, M. D. (1977). Nontraditional guitar techniques for the educable and trainable mentally retarded residents in music therapy activities. Journal of Music Therapy, 14(1), 39–42.

Chester, K. K., Holmberg, T. K., Lawrence, M. P., & Thurmond, L. L. (1999). A program-based consultative music therapy model for public schools. Journal of Music Therapy, 17(2), 82–91.

Cohan, R. D. (1984). Auditory mental imagery in children. Music Therapy, 4(1), 73–83.

Cooke, R. K. (1969). The use of music in play therapy. Journal of Music Therapy, 6(3), 66–75.

Darrow, A. A. (1989). Music therapy in the treatment of the hearing-impaired. Music Therapy Perspectives, 6, 61–70.

Darrow, A. A. (1999). Music educators' perceptions regarding the inclusion of students with severe disabilities in music classrooms. Journal of Music Therapy, 36(4), 254–273.

Edgerton, C. D. (1990). Creative group songwriting. Music Therapy Perspectives, 8, 15–19.

Furman, C. E., & Steele, A. C. (1982). Teaching the special student: A survey of independent music teachers with implications for music therapists. Journal of Music Therapy, 19(2), 66–73.

Gfeller, K. E. (1984). Prominent theories in learning disabilities and implications for music therapy methodology. Music Therapy Perspectives, 2(1), 9–13.

Grant, R. E. (1989). Music therapy guidelines for developmentally disabled children. Music Therapy Perspectives, 6, 18–22.

Hadsell, N. A., & Coleman, K. A. (1988). Rett syndrome: A challenge for music therapists. Music Therapy Perspectives, 5, 52–56.

Hedden, S. K. (1971). N = 4: A small-sample statistical technique for use in music therapy research. Journal of Music Therapy, 8(4), 146–151.

Hilliard, R. (2001). The effects of music therapy-based bereavement groups on mood and behavior of grieving children: A pilot study. Journal of Music Therapy, 38(4), 291–306.

Hughes, J. E., Robbins, B. J., & King, R. J. (1988). A survey of perception and attitudes of exceptional student educators toward music therapy services in a county-wide school district. Journal of Music Therapy, 25(4), 216–222.

Isern, B. (1964). Music in special education. Journal of Music Therapy, 1(4), 139–142.

James, M. R. (1987). Implications of selected social psychological theories on life-long skill generalization: Considerations for the music therapist. Music Therapy Perspectives, 4, 29–33.

Jellison, J. A. (1979). The music therapist in the educational setting: Developing and implementing curriculum for the handicapped. Journal of Music Therapy, 16(3), 128–137.

Jellison, J. A., & Duke, R. A. (1994). The mental retardation label: Music teachers' and perspective teachers' expectations of children's social and music behaviors. Journal of Music Therapy, 31(3), 166–185.

Jones, L. L., & Cardinal, D. N. (1998). A descriptive analysis of music therapists' perceptions of delivering of services in inclusive settings: A challenge to the field. Journal of Music Therapy, 35(1), 34–48.

Kennedy, R. (2005). A pilot study: The effects of music therapy interventions on middle school students' ESL skills. Journal of Music Therapy, 42(4), 244–261

Kessler, J. (1967). Therapeutic methods for exceptional children. Journal of Music Therapy, 4(1), 1–2.

LaFon, D. (1989). Music therapy with developmentally disabled: Will we continue to be unique? Music Therapy Perspectives, 6, 23–25.

Lathom, W. (1982). Report on the Office of Special Education Grant, Special Project: A national in-service training model for educational personnel providing music education/therapy for severely/profoundly handicapped children. Music Therapy Perspectives, 1(1), 27–29.

Loewy, J. (1995). The musical stages of speech: A developmental model of pre-verbal sound making. Music Therapy, 13(1), 47–73.

Luce, D. (2004). Music learning theory and audiation: Implications for music therapy clinical practice. Music Therapy Perspectives, 22(1), 26–33.

McCormick, J. L. (1988). Report: Status of public school music therapy. Music Therapy Perspectives, 5, 73–77.

Metzler, R. K. (1973). Music therapy at the behavioral learning center, St. Paul Public School. Journal of Music Therapy, 10(4), 177–183.

Michel, D. E., & May, N. H. (1974). The development of music therapy procedures with speech and language disorders. Journal of Music Therapy, 11(2), 74–80.

Pfeifer, M. (1989). A step in the right direction: Suggested strategies for implementing music therapy with the multihandicapped child. Music Therapy Perspectives, 6, 57–60.

Register, D. (2004). Teaching child-care personnel to use music in the classroom: A comparison of workshop training versus on-site modeling. Music Therapy Perspectives, 22(2), 109–115.

Rogers, P. J. (1995). Childhood sexual abuse: Dilemmas in therapeutic practice. Music Therapy Perspectives, 13(1), 24–30.

Siegel, S. L., Cartwright, J. S., & Katz, E. (1986). Where's the research? Journal of Music Therapy, 23(1), 38–45.

Smith, D. S., & Hairston, M. J. (1999). Music therapy in school settings: Current practice. Journal of Music Therapy, 36(4), 274–292.

Steele, A. L. (1979). A report on the First World Congress on Future Special Education. Journal of Music Therapy, 16(1), 43–47.

Steele, A. L. (1984). Music therapy for the learning disabled: Intervention and instruction. Music Therapy Perspectives, 1(3), 2–7.

Steele, A. L., Vaughan, M., & Dolan, C. (1976). The school support program: Music therapy for adjustment problems in elementary schools. Journal of Music Therapy, 13(2), 87–100.

Thaut, M. H. (1984). A music therapy treatment model for autistic children. Music Therapy Perspectives, 1(4), 7–13.

Thresher, J. M. (1972). A music workshop for special class teachers. Journal of Music Therapy, 9(1), 40–43.

VanWeelden, K., & Whipple, J. (2005). Preservice teachers' predictions, Perceptions, and actual assessment of students with special needs in secondary general music. Journal of Music Therapy, *42(3)*, 200–215.

Wheeler, B. L. (1999). Experiencing pleasure in working with severely disabled children. Journal of Music Therapy, *36(1)*, 56–80.

Wolfe, D., & Jellison, J. (1995). Interviews with preschool children about music videos. Journal of Music Therapy, *32(4)*, 265–285.

Wolfe, D., & Stambaugh, S. (1993). Musical analysis of Sesame Street: Implication for music therapy practice and research. Journal of Music Therapy, *30(4)*, 224–235.

●

Learning Disabilities

Colwell, C. M., & Murlless, K. D. (2002). Music activities (singing vs. chanting) as a vehicle of reading accuracy of children with learning disabilities: A pilot study. Music Therapy Perspectives, *20(1)*, 13–19.

Eisenstein, S. R. (1974). Effect of contingent guitar lessons on reading behavior. Journal of Music Therapy, *11(3)*, 138–146.

Gfeller, K. E. (1983). Musical mnemonics as an aid to retention with normal and learning disabled students. Journal of Music Therapy, *20(4)*, 179–189.

Gfeller, K. E. (1984). Prominent theories in learning disabilities and implications for music therapy methodology. Music Therapy Perspectives, *2(1)*, 9–13.

Krout, R. E. (1986). Use of a group token contingency with school-aged special education students to improve a music listening skill. Music Therapy Perspectives, *3*, 13–16.

Larson, B. A. (1978). Use of the motorvator in improving gross-motor coordination, visual perception and IQ scores: A pilot study. Journal of Music Therapy, *15(3)*, 145–149.

Madsen, C. K., Smith, D. S., & Feeman, C. C., Jr. (1988). The use of music in cross-age tutoring within special education settings. Journal of Music Therapy, *25(3)*, 135–144.

Montello, L., & Coons, E. E. (1998). Effects of active versus passive group music therapy on preadolescents with emotional, learning, and behavioral disorders. Journal of Music Therapy, *35(1)*, 49–67.

Roskam, K. (1979). Music therapy as an aid for increasing auditory awareness and improving reading skill. Journal of Music Therapy, *16(1)*, 31–42.

Shehan, P. K. (1981). A comparison of mediation strategies in paired-associate learning for children with learning disabilities. Journal of Music Therapy, *18(3)*, 120–127.

Steele, A. L. (1984). Music therapy for the learning disabled: Intervention and instruction. Music Therapy Perspectives, *1(3)*, 2–7.

●

Mental Retardation

Bellamy, T., & Sontag, E. (1973). Use of group contingent music to increase assembly line production rates of retarded students in a simulated shelter workshop. Journal of Music Therapy, *10(3)*, 125–136.

Bixler, J. (1968). Musical aptitude in the educable mentally retarded. Journal of Music Therapy, *5(2)*, 41–43.

Bokor, C. R. (1976). A comparison of musical and verbal responses of mentally retarded children. Journal of Music Therapy, *13(2)*, 101–108.

Cassity, M. D. (1977). Nontraditional guitar techniques for the educable and trainable mentally retarded residents in music therapy activities. Journal of Music Therapy, *14(1)*, 39–42.

Cassity, M. D. (1978). Social development of TMRs involved in performing and nonperforming groups. Journal of Music Therapy, *15(2)*, 100–105.

Decuir, A. A. (1975). Vocal responses of mentally retarded subjects to four musical instruments. Journal of Music Therapy, *12(1)*, 40–43.

Dileo, C. L. (1975). The use of a token economy program with mentally retarded persons in a music therapy setting. Journal of Music Therapy, *12(3)*, 155–160.

Dorow, L. G. (1976). Televised music lessons as educational reinforcement for correct mathematical responses with the educable mentally retarded. Journal of Music Therapy, *13(2)*, 77–86.

Edenfield, T. N., & Hughes, J. E. (1991). The relationship of a choral music curriculum to the development of singing ability in secondary students with Down syndrome. Music Therapy Perspectives, *9*, 52–55.

Flowers, E. (1984). Musical sound perception in normal children and children with Down syndrome. Journal of Music Therapy, *21(3)*, 146–154.

Grant, R. E., & LeCroy, S. (1986). Effects of sensory mode input on the performance of rhythmic perception tasks by mentally retarded subjects. Journal of Music Therapy, *23(1)*, 2–9.

Grant, R. E., & Share, M. R. (1985). Relationship of pitch discrimination skills and vocal ranges of mentally retarded subjects. Journal of Music Therapy, 22(2), 99–103.

Gregoire, M. A. (1984). Music as a prior condition to task performance. Journal of Music Therapy, 21(3), 133–145.

Hair, H. I., & Graham, R. M. (1983). A comparison of verbal descriptions used by TMR students and music therapists. Journal of Music Therapy, 20(2), 59–68.

Humphrey, T. (1980). The effects of music ear training upon the auditory discrimination abilities of trainable mentally retarded adolescents. Journal of Music Therapy, 17(2), 70–74.

Jellison, J. A., & Gainer, E. W. (1995). Into the mainstream: A case-study of a child's participation in music education and music therapy. Journal of Music Therapy, 32(4), 228–247.

Johnson, J. M., & Zinner, C. C. (1974). Stimulus fading and schedule learning in generalizing and maintaining behaviors. Journal of Music Therapy, 11(2), 84–96.

Jones, R. E. (1986). Assessing developmental levels of mentally retarded students with the musical-perception assessment of cognitive development. Journal of Music Therapy, 23(3), 166–173.

Jorgenson, H., & Parnell, M. K. (1970). Modifying social behaviors of mentally retarded children in music activities. Journal of Music Therapy, 7(3), 83–87.

Larson, B. A. (1977). A comparison of singing ranges of mentally retarded and normal children with published songbooks used in singing activities. Journal of Music Therapy, 14(3), 139–143.

Lathom, W. (1964). Music therapy as a means of changing the adaptive behavior level of retarded children. Journal of Music Therapy, 1(4), 132–134.

Leland, H. (1964). Adaptive behavior as related to the treatment of the mentally retarded. Journal of Music Therapy, 1(4), 129–131.

Lienhard, M. E. (1976). Factors relevant to the rhythmic perception of a group of mentally retarded children. Journal of Music Therapy, 13(2), 58–65.

Maranto, C. D., Decuir, A., & Humphrey, T. (1984). A comparison of digit span scores, rhythm span scores, and diagnostic factors or mentally retarded persons. Music Therapy, 4(1), 84–90.

Miller, L. L., & Orsmond, G. (1994). Assessing structure in the musical explorations of children with disabilities. Journal of Music Therapy, 31(4), 248–265.

Myers, E. G. (1979). The effect of music on retention in a paired-associate task with EMR children. Journal of Music Therapy, 16(4), 190–198.

Orsmond, G. I., & Miller, L. K. (1995). Correlates of musical improvisation in children with disabilities. Journal of Music Therapy, 32(3), 152–166.

Peters, M. L. (1970). A comparison of the musical sensitivity of mongoloid and normal children. Journal of Music Therapy, 7(4), 113–123.

Saperston, B. (1973). The use of music in establishing communication with an autistic retarded child. Journal of Music Therapy, 10(4), 184–188.

Soraci, S., Jr., Deckner, C. W., McDaniel, C., & Blanton, R. L. (1982). The relationship between rate of rhythmicity and the stereotypic behaviors of abnormal children. Journal of Music Therapy, 19(1), 46–54.

Spencer, S. L. (1988). The efficiency of instrumental and movement activities in developing mentally retarded adolescents' ability to follow directions. Journal of Music Therapy, 25(1), 44–50.

Staples, S. M. (1968). A paired-associates learning task utilizing music as the mediator: An exploratory study. Journal of Music Therapy, 5(2), 53–57.

Steele, A. L. (1967). Effects of social reinforcement on the musical preference of mentally retarded children. Journal of Music Therapy, 4(2), 57–62.

Steele, A. L. (1968). Programmed use of music to alter uncooperative problem behaviors. Journal of Music Therapy, 5(4), 103–107.

Stubbs, B. (1970). A study on the effectiveness of an integrated, personified approach to learning with trainable mental retardates. Journal of Music Therapy, 7(3), 77–82.

Talkington, L. W., & Hall, S. M. (1970). A musical application of Premack's hypothesis to low verbal retardates. Journal of Music Therapy, 7(3), 95–99.

Velásquez, V. (1991). Beginning experiences in piano performance for a girl with Down syndrome: A case study. Music Therapy Perspectives, 9, 82–85.

Wingert, M. L. (1972). Effects of a music enrichment program in the education of the mentally retarded. Journal of Music Therapy, 9(1), 13–22.

●

Multiple Disabilities

Ayres, B. R. (1987). The effects of a music stimulus environment versus regular cafeteria environment during therapeutic feeding. Journal of Music Therapy, 24(1), 14–26.

Colwell, C. M. (1995). Adapting music instruction for elementary students with special needs: A pilot. Music Therapy Perspectives, 13(2), 97–103.

Dorow, L. G. (1975). Conditioning music and approval as new reinforcers for imitative behaviors with the severely retarded. Journal of Music Therapy, 12(1), 30–39.

Ghetti, C. M. (2002). Comparison of the effectiveness of three music therapy conditions to modulate behavior states in students with profound disabilities: A pilot study. Music Therapy Perspectives, 20(1), 20–30.

Herman, F. (1985). Music therapy for the young child with cerebral palsy who uses blissymbols. Journal of Music Therapy, 5(1), 28–36.

Herron, C. J. (1970). Some effects of instrumental music training on cerebral palsied children. Journal of Music Therapy, 7(2), 55–58.

Holloway, M. S. (1980). A comparison of passive and active music reinforcement to increase preacademic and motor skills in severely retarded children and adolescents. Journal of Music Therapy, 17(2), 58–69.

Jorgenson, H. (1974). The use of a contingent music activity to modify behaviors which interfere with learning. Journal of Music Therapy, 11(1), 41–46.

Krout, R. (1987). Music therapy with multi-handicapped students: Individualizing treatment within two group settings. Journal of Music Therapy, 24(1), 2–13.

Larson, B. A. (1977). A comparison of singing ranges of mentally retarded and normal children with published songbooks used in singing activities. Journal of Music Therapy, 14(3), 139–143.

Moore, R., & Mathenius, L. (1989). The effects of modeling, reinforcement, and tempo on imitative rhythmic responses of moderately retarded adolescents. Journal of Music Therapy, 24(3), 160–169.

Rainey Perry, M. M. (2003). Relating improvisational music therapy with severely and multiply disabled children to communication development. Journal of Music Therapy, 40(3), 227–246.

Reid, D. H., Hill, B. K., Rawers, R. J., & Montegar, C. A. (1975). The use of contingent music in teaching social skills to a nonverbal, hyperactive boy. Journal of Music Therapy, 12(1), 2–18.

Ritholz, M. S., & Turry, A. (1994). The journey by train: Creative music therapy with a 17-year-old boy. Music Therapy, 12(2), 58–87.

Werbner, N. (1966). The practice of music therapy with psychotic children. Journal of Music Therapy, 3(1), 25–31.

Wylie, M. E. (1983). Eliciting vocal responses in severely and profoundly mentally handicapped subjects. Journal of Music Therapy, 20(4), 190–200.

●

Pervasive Developmental Disorders

Allgood, N. (2005). Parents' perceptions of family-based group music therapy for children with autism spectrum disorders. Music Therapy Perspectives, 23(2), 92–99.

Boxill, E. H. (1981). A continuum of awareness: Music therapy with the developmentally handicapped. Music Therapy, 1(1), 17–23.

Brownell, M. D. (2002). Musically adapted social stories to modify behaviors in students with autism: Four case studies. Journal of Music Therapy, 39(2), 117–144.

Buday, E. M. (1995). The effects of signed and spoken words taught with music on sign and speech imitation by children with autism. Journal of Music Therapy, 32(3), 189–202.

Cartwright, J., & Huckaby, G. (1972). Intensive preschool language program. Journal of Music Therapy, 9(3), 137–146.

Edgerton, C. L. (1994). The effect of improvised music therapy on the communicative behaviors of autistic children. Journal of Music Therapy, 31(1), 31–62.

Goldstein, C. (1964). Music and creative arts therapy for an autistic child. Journal of Music Therapy, 1(4), 135–138.

Hadsell, N. A., & Coleman, K. A. (1988). Rett syndrome: A challenge for music therapists. Music Therapy Perspectives, 5, 52–56.

Hairston, M. J. P. (1990). Analyses of responses of mentally retarded autistic and mentally retarded nonautistic children to art therapy and music therapy. Journal of Music Therapy, 27(3), 137–150.

Hoelzley, P. D. (1991). Reciprocal inhibition in music therapy: A case study involving wind instrument usage to attenuate fear, anxiety, and avoidance reactivity in a child with pervasive developmental disorders. Music Therapy, 10(1), 58–76.

Hollander, F. M., & Juhrs, P. D. (1974). Orff-Schulwerk, an effective treatment tool with autistic children. Journal of Music Therapy, 11(1), 1–12.

Kaplan, R. S., & Steele, A. L. (2005). An analysis of music therapy program goals and outcomes for clients with diagnoses on the autism spectrum. Journal of Music Therapy, 42(1), 2–19.

Kostka, M. J. (1993). A comparison of selected behaviors of a student with autism in special education and regular music classes. Music Therapy Perspectives, 11(6), 57–60.

Mahlberg, M. (1973). Music therapy in the treatment of an autistic child. Journal of Music Therapy, 10(4), 189–193.

Nelson, D. L., Anderson, V. G., & Gonzales, A. D. (1984). Music activities as therapy for children with autism and other pervasive developmental disorders. Journal of Music Therapy, 21(3), 100–116.

North, E. F. (1966). Music therapy as an important treatment modality with psychotic children. Journal of Music Therapy, 3(1), 22–24.

Orsmond, G. I., & Miller, L. K. (1995). Correlates of musical improvisation in children with disabilities. Journal of Music Therapy, 32(3), 152–166.

Saperston, B. (1973). The use of music in establishing communication with an autistic retarded child. Journal of Music Therapy, 10(4), 184–188.

Staum, M. J., & Flowers, P. J. (1984). The use of simulated training and music lessons in teaching appropriate shopping skills to an autistic child. Music Therapy Perspectives, 1(3), 14–17.

Stevens, E., & Clark, F. (1969). Music therapy in the treatment of autistic children. Journal of Music Therapy, 6(4), 98–104.

Thaut, M. H. (1984). A music therapy treatment model for autistic children. Music Therapy Perspectives, 1(4), 7–13.

Whipple, J. (2004). Music in intervention for children and adolescents with autism: A meta-analysis. Journal of Music Therapy, 41(2), 90–106.

Wylie, M. E. (1996). A case study to promote hand use in children with Rett syndrome. Music Therapy Perspectives, 14(2), 83–86.

●

Physical Disabilities

Cassity, M. D. (1981). The influence of a socially valued skill on peer acceptance in a music therapy group. Journal of Music Therapy, 18(3), 148–154.

Davis, R. K. (1990). A model for the integration of music therapy within a preschool classroom for children with physical disabilities or language delays. Music Therapy Perspectives, 8, 82–84.

Ford, S. C. (1984). Music therapy for cerebral palsied children. Music Therapy Perspectives, 1(3), 8–13.

Harding, C., & Ballard, K. D. (1982). The effectiveness of music as a stimulus and as a contingent reward in promoting the spontaneous speech of three physically handicapped preschoolers. Journal of Music Therapy, 19(2), 86–101.

Howell, R. D., Flowers, P. J., & Wheeler, J. E. (1995). The effects of keyboard experiences on rhythmic responses of elementary school children with physical disabilities. Journal of Music Therapy, 32(2), 91–112.

Josepha, M. (1964). Therapeutic values of instrumental performance for severely handicapped children. Journal of Music Therapy, 1(3), 73–79.

Thaut, M. H. (1985). The use of auditory rhythm and rhythmic speech to aid temporal muscular control in children with gross motor dysfunction. Journal of Music Therapy, 22(3), 108–128.

●

Sensory Impairments

Baird, S. (1969). A technique to assess the preferences for intensity of musical stimuli in young hard-of-hearing children. Journal of Music Therapy, 6(1), 6–11.

Darrow, A. A. (1979). The beat reproduction response of subjects with normal and impaired hearing: An empirical comparison. Journal of Music Therapy, 16(2), 91–98.

Darrow, A. A. (1984). A comparison of rhythmic responsiveness in normal and hearing impaired children and an investigation of the relationship of rhythmic responsiveness to the suprasegmental aspects of speech perception. Journal of Music Therapy, 21(2), 48–66.

Darrow, A. A. (1987). An investigative study: The effect of hearing impairment on musical aptitude. Journal of Music Therapy, 24(2), 88–96.

Darrow, A. A. (1989). Music therapy in the treatment of the hearing-impaired. Music Therapy Perspectives, 6, 61–70.

Darrow, A. A. (1990). The effect of frequency adjustment on the vocal reproduction accuracy of hearing impaired children. Journal of Music Therapy, 27(1), 24–37.

Darrow, A. A. (1991). An assessment and comparison of hearing impaired children's preference for timbre and musical instruments. Journal of Music Therapy, 28(1), 48–59.

Darrow, A. A. (1992). The effect of vibrotactile stimuli via the SOMATRON™ on the identification of pitch change by hearing impaired children. Journal of Music Therapy, 29(2), 103–112.

Darrow, A. A., & Cohen, N. (1991). The effect of programmed pitch practice and private instruction on the vocal reproduction accuracy of children with hearing impairments: Two case studies. Music Therapy Perspectives, 9, 61–65.

Darrow, A. A., & Gfeller, K. (1991). A study of public school music programs mainstreaming hearing impaired students. Journal of Music Therapy, 28(1), 23–39.

Darrow, A. A., & Goll, H. (1989). The effect of vibrotactile stimuli via the SOMATRON™ on the identification of rhythmic concepts by hearing impaired children. Journal of Music Therapy, 26(3), 115–124.

Darrow, A. A., & Starmer, G. J. (1986). The effect of vocal training on the intonation and rate of hearing impaired children's speech: A pilot study. Journal of Music Therapy, 23(4), 194–201.

Ford, T. A. (1988). The effect of musical experiences and age on the ability of deaf children to discriminate pitch. Journal of Music Therapy, 25(1), 2–16.

Galloway, H. F., & Bean, M. F. (1974). The effects of action songs on the development of body-image and body-part identification in hearing-impaired preschool children. Journal of Music Therapy, 11(3), 125–134.

Gfeller, K. (1987). Songwriting as a tool for reading and language remediation. Music Therapy, 6(2), 28–38.

Gfeller, K. E. (1990). A cognitive-linguistic approach to language development for the preschool child with hearing impairments for music therapy practice. Music Therapy Perspectives, 8, 47–51.

Gfeller, K. E. (2000). Accommodating children who use cochlear implants in music therapy or educational setting. Music Therapy Perspectives, 18(2), 122–130.

Gfeller, K., & Baumann, A. (1988). Assessment procedures for music therapy with hearing impaired children: Language development. Journal of Music Therapy, 25(4), 192–205.

Kern, P., & Wolery, M. (2001). Participation of a preschooler with visual impairments on the playground: Effects of music adaptations and staff development. Journal of Music Therapy, 38(2), 149–164.

Korduba, O. M. (1975). Duplicated rhythmic patterns between deaf and normal hearing children. Journal of Music Therapy, 12(3), 136–146.

Madsen, C. K., & Darrow, A. A. (1989). The relationship between music aptitude and sound conceptualization of the visually impaired. Journal of Music Therapy, 26(2), 71–78.

Robb, S. L. (2003). Music interventions and group participation skills of preschoolers with visual impairments: Raising questions about music, arousal, and attention. Journal of Music Therapy, 40(4), 266–282.

Staum, M. J. (1987). Music notation to improve the speech prosody of hearing impaired children. Journal of Music Therapy, 24(3), 146–159.

Stordahl, J. (2002). Song recognition and appraisal: A comparison of children who use cochlear implants and normally hearing children. Journal of Music Therapy, 39(1), 2–19.

•

Speech/Language Delays

Braithwaite, M., & Sigafoos, J. (1998). Effects of social versus musical antecedents on communication responsiveness in five children with developmental disabilities. Journal of Music Therapy, 35(2), 88–104.

Cohen, N. S. (1994). Speech and song: Implications for therapy. Music Therapy Perspectives, 12(1), 8–14.

Davis, R. K. (1990). A model for the integration of music therapy within a preschool classroom for children with physical disabilities or language delays. Music Therapy Perspectives, 8, 82–84.

Lathom, W., Edson, S., & Toombs, M. R. (1965). A coordinated speech therapy and music therapy program. Journal of Music Therapy, 2(4), 118–120.

Michel, D. E., & May, N. H. (1974). The development of music therapy procedures with speech and language disorders. Journal of Music Therapy, 11(2), 74–80.

Seybold, C. D. (1971). The value and use of music activities in the treatment of speech delayed children. Journal of Music Therapy, 8(3), 102–110.

•

Technology

Krout, R. (1987). Evaluating software for music therapy applications. Journal of Music Therapy, 24(4), 213–223.

Krout, R., Burnham, A., & Moorman, S. (1993). Computer and electronic music applications with students in special education from program proposal to progress evaluation. Music Therapy Perspectives, 11(1), 28–31.

Krout, R. E., & Mason, M. (1988). Using computer and electronic music resources in clinical music therapy with behaviorally disordered students, 12 to 18 years old. Music Therapy Perspectives, 5, 114–118.

Hunter, L. L. (1989). Computer-assisted assessment of melodic and rhythmic discrimination skills. Journal of Music Therapy, 26(2), 79–87.

Spitzer, S. (1989). Computers and music therapy: An integrated approach. Music Therapy Perspectives, 7, 51–54.

Annotated Bibliography of Articles from Music Therapy Journals (1990–2005) Specifically Relating to Music Therapy with Young Children in Educational Settings or Methodologies Pertaining to Young Children

Marcia E. Humpal, MEd, MT-BC; Ronna S. Kaplan, MA MT-BC

●

Journal of Music Therapy

Humpal, M. (1991). The effects of an integrated early childhood music program on social interaction among children with handicaps and their typical peers. Journal of Music Therapy, 28(3), 161–177.

> The purpose of this study was to examine the effects and benefits of a pilot inclusive preschool music program on both the children with disabilities and their typical peers. Interaction among the children increased following the music therapy intervention phase.

Wolfe, D., & Horn, C. (1993). Use of melodies as structural prompts for learning and retention of sequential verbal information by preschool students. Journal of Music Therapy, 30(2), 100–118.

> This study found that students learn information set forth within familiar melodies more quickly than when the information is presented via unfamiliar melody or spoken conditions.

Wolfe, D., & Stambaugh, S. (1993). Musical analysis of Sesame Street: Implication for music therapy practice and research. Journal of Music Therapy, 30(4), 224–235.

> The various ways music is employed in the production of Sesame Street are categorized and described.

Colwell, C. (1994). Therapeutic application of music in the whole language kindergarten. Journal of Music Therapy, 31(4), 238–247.

> Analyses indicated that both (a) song rehearsal of text set to music, and (b) spoken and song rehearsal of book text set to music facilitated greater text accuracy than (c) only spoken rehearsal of the book text.

Wolfe, D., & Jellison, J. (1995). Interviews with preschool children about music videos. Journal of Music Therapy, 32(4), 265–285.

> Results are discussed related to "intended" educational messages in commercially produced materials and to the factors that may influence children's recall of "educational material."

Register, D. (2001). The effects of an early intervention music curriculum on prereading/writing. Journal of Music Therapy, 38(3), 239–248.

> This study, which replicated that of Standley and Hughes (1997), using a larger sample, demonstrated that music sessions significantly enhanced the abilities of 4- to 5-year-old children enrolled in Early Intervention and Exceptional Student programs to learn prewriting and print concepts. The experimental group showed significantly higher results on logo identification posttest and word recognition tests. The author also offered implications for curriculum design and academic and social applications of music in Early Intervention programs.

Hilliard, R. (2001). The effects of music therapy-based bereavement groups on mood and behavior of grieving children: A pilot study. Journal of Music Therapy, 38(4), 291–306.

> This study found a statistically significant reduction in grief symptoms as evaluated in the home among subjects who participated in music therapy-based bereavement groups. Teacher and self-evaluations were less conclusive, indicating the recommendation for further research studying the effects of music therapy on grieving children.

Brownell, M. (2002). Musically adapted social stories to modify behaviors in students with autism: Four case studies. Journal of Music Therapy, 39(2), 117–144.

> This study's results indicated that both reading and singing conditions were significantly more effective in reducing target behaviors of 1st and 2nd grade students with autism than a no-contact condition. Furthermore, the findings suggested the use of a musically adapted, sung version of social stories as an effective and viable treatment option for modifying target behaviors with this population.

Layman, D., Hussey, D., & Laing, S. (2002). Music therapy assessment for severely emotionally disturbed children: A pilot study. Journal of Music Therapy, 39(3), 164–187.

> This article discussed a music therapy assessment instrument for children with severe emotional disturbances measuring behavioral/social functioning, emotional responsiveness, language/communication abilities, and music skills. Results of the pilot study demonstrated that subjects displayed significantly more behaviors in the disruptive/intrusive category than in the defensive/withdrawn or target behavior categories.

Perry, M. (2003). Relating improvisational music therapy with severely and multiply disabled children to communication development. Journal of Music Therapy, 40(3), 227–246.

A qualitative research project explored the issues of pre-intentional and early intentional communication of school-age children with severe and multiple disabilities, such as cerebral palsy, finding that turn taking and playing and singing together are important forms of communication during music therapy. The author denoted many communication problems related to disability and recommended further study of how music therapy may relate to general issues in communication for individuals with severe and multiple disabilities.

Robb, S. (2003). Music interventions and group participation skills of preschoolers with visual impairments: Raising questions about music, arousal, and attention. Journal of Music Therapy, 40(4), 266–282.

Statistical analysis of data collected in this study revealed that the attentive behavior of 4- to 6-year-old children with visual impairments was significantly higher during music-based sessions than during play-based sessions. Other group participation behaviors occurred more frequently in the music condition, but these differences were not statistically significant. Differential outcomes among participants, as well as an exploration of theories related to music, arousal, and attention, were discussed in an effort to guide future research.

Jackson, N. (2003). A survey of music therapy methods and their role in the treatment of early elementary school children with ADHD. Journal of Music Therapy, 40(4), 302–323.

Results of the survey indicated that music therapists often utilize a number of music therapy methods in the treatment of children with ADHD and address multiple types of goals, with treatment outcomes generally perceived to be favorable. Further implications of results and areas for continuing research into the use of music therapy with ADHD were identified.

Register, D. (2004). The effects of live music groups versus an educational children's television program on the emergent literacy of young children. Journal of Music Therapy, 41(1), 2–27.

This study confirmed that music increases students' on-task behavior. In addition, the combination of music and video enrichment showed gains in 4 of 8 tests used to measure students' progress, a pattern supporting the need for further investigation regarding benefits of enrichment programs, particularly those incorporating music, specifically designed to enhance curricula for students from low socioeconomic backgrounds.

Chase, K. (2004). Music therapy assessment for children with developmental disabilities: A survey study. Journal of Music Therapy, 41(1), 28–54.

Music therapists working with children with developmental disabilities responded to this survey, noting (a) major skill areas and subcategories they most frequently assessed, (b) how these areas are assessed, (c) common features of their current assessment tools, (d) positive and/or negative aspects of their current assessment tools, and (e) the 3 most important features desired in a standardized music therapy assessment for use in their clinical practice.

Whipple, J. (2004). Music in intervention for children and adolescents with autism: A meta-analysis. Journal of Music Therapy, 41(2), 90–106.

This meta-analysis of the dependent variables of theoretical approach; number of subjects; participation in and use, selection, and presentation of music; researcher discipline; published or unpublished source; and subject age from 9 quantitative studies, compared music to no-music conditions during treatment of children and adolescents with autism. The significant effect size, combined with the homogeneity of the studies, led to the conclusion that all music intervention, regardless of purpose or implementation, had been effective for children and adolescents with autism. Clinical implications as well as recommendations for future research were discussed.

Kaplan, R., & Steele, A. L. (2005). An analysis of music therapy program goals and outcomes for clients with diagnoses on the autism spectrum. Journal of Music Therapy, 42(1), 2–19.

The researchers investigated music therapy interventions, session types, and formats most frequently used with music therapy clients with diagnoses on the autism spectrum. Clients' ages ranged from 2–49 years. The authors also analyzed goals most frequently addressed and generalization of skills.

●

Music Therapy

Music Therapy was the official journal of the former American Association of Music Therapy. When this organization merged with the former National Association for Music Therapy and the two became the present American Music Therapy Association, *Music Therapy* ceased publication.

Briggs, C. (1991). A model for understanding musical development. Music Therapy, 10(1), 1–21.

This very thorough article is structured to begin placing the research related to musical development into a model that integrates musical research with accepted models of child development.

Aigen, K. (1995). Cognitive and affective processes in music therapy with individuals with developmental delays: A preliminary model for contemporary Nordoff-Robbins practice. Music Therapy, 13(1), 13–46.

The author, reaffirming Nordoff and Robbins' idea of "the music child within," describes a model that provides a description of hierarchical client processes as well as a system for understanding therapeutic interventions and scope of treatment.

Loewy, J. (1995). The musical stages of speech: A developmental model of pre-verbal sound making. Music Therapy, 13(1), 47–73.

This article presents a model for using the musical development of speech as a means of understanding the level of vocal activity that occurs in a pre-verbal context.

Music Therapy Perspectives

Gfeller, K. (1990). *A cognitive-linguistic approach to language development for the preschool child with hearing impairment: Implications for music therapy practice*. Music Therapy Perspectives, *8, 47–51*.

> This paper outlines the basic components of a cognitive-linguistic model for language rehabilitation: levels of representation, levels of operation, and core content area. Each of these components is discussed as they relate to music therapy practice.

Hughes, J., Robbins, B., McKenzie, B., & Robb, S. (1990). *Integrating exceptional and nonexceptional young children through music play: A pilot program*. Music Therapy Perspectives, *8, 52–56*.

> This article describes a pilot program that combined prekindergarten Exceptional Student Education (ESE) children with their typical peers in a public school music therapy program that provided structured interaction opportunities through traditional early childhood music and social activities.

Humpal, M. (1990). *Early intervention: The implications for music therapy*. Music Therapy Perspectives, *8, 31–34*.

> This article reviews the history of early intervention practices and the music therapy research pertaining specifically to this age group. Implications for utilizing music therapy in the early intervention setting are discussed in an attempt to facilitate understanding of its legitimate inclusion as a unique part of an interdisciplinary approach.

Gunsberg, A. (1991). *A method for conducting improvised musical play with children both with and without developmental delay in preschool classrooms*. Music Therapy Perspectives, *9, 46–51*.

> The author provides an analysis of the methodological steps involved in conducting Improvised Musical Play (IMP), a strategy for fostering social play among children both with and without developmental delays, including a detailed description of steps involved in implementing IMP activities with young children in mainstreamed settings.

Standley, J., & Hughes, J. (1996). *Documenting developmentally appropriate objectives and benefits of a music therapy program for early intervention: A behavioral analysis*. Music Therapy Perspectives, *14(2), 87–94*.

> This study documents the variety of developmentally appropriate activity components in the music therapy sessions, assesses responses of the young children, and evaluates teaching interactions using the standards of the National Association for Education of Young Children.

Wylie, M. (1996). *A case study to promote hand use in children with Rett Syndrome*. Music Therapy Perspectives, *14(2), 83–86*.

> This case study documents significantly increased hand usage following music therapy interventions with preschool girls with Rett Syndrome.

Standley, J., & Hughes, J. (1997). *Evaluation of an early intervention music curriculum for enhancing prereading/writing skills*. Music Therapy Perspectives, *15(2), 79–86*.

> This study evaluates the effects of music sessions designed to enhance prereading and writing skills in an early intervention setting. Results demonstrate that music significantly enhanced print concepts and prewriting skills.

Luce, D. (2004). *Music learning theory and audiation: Implications for music therapy clinical practice*. Music Therapy Perspectives, *22(1), 26–33*.

> This paper provides an overview of Gordon's music learning theory and audiation, as well as the types and stages of preparatory audiation. The author considers the model's distinctively musical vocabulary and notes the implications for music therapy clinical practice.

Register, D. (2004). *Teaching child-care personnel to use music in the classroom: A comparison of workshop training versus on-site modeling*. Music Therapy Perspectives, *22(2), 109–115*.

> Findings of this study indicated that provision of an implementation and support model may increase the amount of music used by early childhood teachers in their classrooms and that teachers are more likely to implement and follow through with new programs early in their careers. The author discussed suggestions for future research as well.

Allgood, N. (2005). *Parents' perceptions of family-based group music therapy for children with autism spectrum disorders*. Music Therapy Perspectives, *23(2), 92–99*.

> This study investigated parents' perceptions of family-based music therapy services for children aged 4–6 years old with diagnoses on the autism spectrum. Parents noted positive responses to music therapy intervention and articulated new insights about themselves and their children.

Representative Resources for Music Therapists Working in Educational Settings

Compiled by Rebecca Tweedle, MEd, MT-BC

•

Activity Guides and Books

Adamek, M., & Darrow, A. (2005). Music in special education. *Silver Spring, MD: American Music Therapy Association.*

Explains essential features of special education, characteristics of students with specific disabilities, and music education and music therapy approaches for these populations.

Adler, R., & Davis, L. R. (1988). Target on music. *Rockville, MD: The Ivymount School.*

A wealth of music activities for children, including original songs, movement, and using instruments.

Agay, D. (1975). Best loved songs of the American people. *Garden City, NY: Doubleday.*

Anthology of American songs from traditional to Broadway. Full accompaniment, guitar chords, and lyrics for approximately 200 songs.

Andress, B. (1989). Promising practices: Prekindergarten music education. *Reston, VA: Music Educators National Conference.*

Many models of early childhood music education as well as sample activities.

Andress, B. (1998). Music for the young child. *Fort Worth, TX: Harcourt Brace College. Publishers.*

An excellent resource that includes information on the overall development of the young child; musical behaviors of young children; and models, materials, and methods for singing, using instruments and movement.

Andress, B., & Walker, L. B. (Eds.). (1992). Readings in early childhood music education. *Reston, VA: Music Educators National Conference.*

Articles on early childhood music education by a variety of authors.

Beall, P. C., & Nipp, S. H. (1989). Wee sing fun and folk. *Los Angeles: Price/Stern/Sloan.*

Children's songs and folk songs with simple melodies and chords. Note: Several additional Wee Sing editions have also been published.

Birkenshaw-Fleming, L. (1982). Music for fun, music for learning. *St. Louis, MO: Magnamusic-Baton.*

Songs, dances, listening games, movement ideas, and ideas for adapting lessons.

Birkenshaw-Fleming, L. (1993). Music for all. *Toronto: Gordon V. Thompson Music.*

Information on disabilities and strategies for teaching students with disabilities.

Blood, R., & Patterson, A. (Eds.). (1992). Rise up singing: The group singing songbook. *Bethlehem, PA: The Sing Out Corporation.*

A compendium of 1,200 song lyrics with guitar chords and publication references. An excellent source for a wide range of familiar songs when lyrics and chords are needed.

Bredekamp, S., & Copple, C. (Eds.). (1997). Developmentally Appropriate Practice in early childhood programs. *Washington DC: National Association for the Education of Young Children.*

An overview of child development from birth through age 8. Contains examples of appropriate practices.

Brunk, B., Coleman, K., & Dacus, D. (1994). Learning through music: Music therapy learning strategies for special education. *Grapevine, TX: Prelude Music Therapy Products.*

Original songs that address academic, language, math, and social skills. Four volumes are now available.

Burton, L., & Kudo, T. (2000). SoundPlay: Understanding music through creative movement. *Reston, VA: Music Educators National Conference.*

Activities using movement to teach children ways to respond to music. Includes a CD.

Coleman, C., & Brunk, B. (1999). Special Education Music Therapy Assessment process handbook. *Grapevine, TX: Prelude Music Therapy Products.*

An assessment to determine if music therapy services are appropriate for a preschool or school-aged child.

Farnan, L., & Johnson, F. (1988). Music is for everyone. *New Berlin, WI: Jenson Publications.*

A collection of songs especially good for students with significant needs.

Feierabend, J. (1990). TIPS: Music activities in early childhood. *Reston, VA: Music Educators National Conference.*

A compilation of ideas for teaching music to young children.

Feierabend, J. (2000). The book of bounces; The book of lullabies; The book of wiggles and tickles. *Chicago: GIA First Steps.*

Traditional songs and rhymes to use with babies and toddlers.

Feierabend, J. (2000). First steps in music for infants and toddlers. *Chicago: GIA Publications.*

> *Lesson plans and activities for group music sessions for children ages birth to 3.*

Kleiner, L. (1998). Kids make music, babies make music, too! *Miami, FL: Warner Bros.*

> *Lesson plans for babies through primary age children using action songs, games, percussion instruments, movement, and many traditional songs and chants. Other books by this author are also available.*

McLaughlin, B. (1995). Songs for stories. *Albany, NY: PODS Music.*

> *A collection of original songs that coordinate with children's books. Audio version also available.*

Neeley, L., Kenney, S., & Wolf, J. (2000). Start the music strategies. *Reston, VA: Music Educators National Conference.*

> *Activities for early childhood music classes.*

Nordoff, P., & Robbins, C. (1971). Music therapy in special education. *New York: John Day.*

> *Classic book relating the authors' philosophy of using music as therapy with children who have special needs. Includes many activities.*

Palmer, M., & Sims, W. (Eds.). (1993). Music in prekindergarten—Planning and teaching. *Reston, VA: Music Educators National Conference.*

> *Descriptions of musical developmental characteristics of young children provide guidelines for devising musical experiences to meet various needs.*

Paperback songs series. (Various). *Milwaukee, WI: Hal Leonard.*

> *A series of upwards of 20 volumes including children's songs, the Beatles, classic rock, movie music, and country hits. Melody line, chords, and lyrics for at least 200 songs per volume. Very helpful both for finding lyrics and chords for a specific song.*

Regner, H. (1991). Music for children. *New York: Schott Music.*

> *Three volumes of Orff activities based on American folk songs. Chants, rhymes, games, singing, instruments, and movement activities.*

Richards, W. (1999). Time for music, Vol. 1. *Time for Music Publishing.*

> *This book, as well as other resources by the same author, contains many original fun songs that target a variety of goals. Some Orff arrangements are included.*

Reid, R. (1995). Children's jukebox: A subject guide to musical recordings and programming ideas for songsters ages one to twelve. *Chicago: American Library Association.*

> *Approximately 2,400 children's songs organized under some 50 popular themes. Each entry contains a song summary, age/grade levels, distributor information, and tested tips.*

Ritzholz, M. S., & Robbins, C. (1993). More themes for therapy. *New York: Carl Fischer.*

> *Songs suitable for preschool and early elementary that address various areas of development. Also consider an earlier edition, Themes for Therapy.*

Weikert, P. (1989). Movement plus music: Activities for children ages 3 to 7. *Ypsilanti, MI: High/Scope Press.*

> *Key experiences in movement for children.*

Weikert, P. (1989). Teaching movement and dance. *Ypsilanti, MI: High/Scope Press.*

> *A sequential approach to rhythmic movement. Includes dance steps to folk dances. Accompanying CDs available.*

Wilson, B. (Ed.). (2002). Models of music therapy intervention in school settings. *Silver Spring, MD: American Music Therapy Association.*

> *Theoretical issues and practical applications of music therapy in educational settings.*

Yurko, M. (1992). Music mind games. *Miami, FL: Warner Brothers.*

> *Beginning to advanced games for learning music theory and reading.*

●

Journals

Custodero, L. (Ed.). (2002). Musical lives of babies and families, *23(1). Washington, DC: Zero to Three.*

> *Special journal issue on the importance of music with young children.*

Hallquist, M. (Ed.). Early childhood connections: Journal of Music- and Movement-Based Learning. *Foundation for Music Based Learning, P.O. Box 4274, Greensboro, NC 27404-4274. www.ecmma.org/*

> *A quarterly publication of the Early Childhood Movement and Music Association featuring articles on music and movement education for young children. Future plans include discontinuing a quarterly format and possibly instituting topic monographs.*

MENC: The National Association for Music Education. Music Educators Journal and Teaching Music. *1806 Robert Fulton Dr., Reston, VA 20191.*

> *Both journals occasionally feature articles about effectively including students of all ability levels in school as well as early childhood programs.*

●

Music Textbook Series

The Music Connection

Silver Burdett Ginn

Glenview, IL

Spotlight on Music

MacMillan/McGraw-Hill

New York, NY

●

Audio Recordings

An immense number of excellent audio resources are available from various music suppliers. Preview these at a library or refer to web sites prior to purchasing. The following web site gives reviews of audio favorites as well as new releases for young people: http://www.bestchildrensmusic.com/. Note: Many of the performers listed here have made numerous audio recordings. Only one representative title is given.

A child's celebration of the world. *(1998). Redway, CA: Music for Little People.*

Berkner, L. (2000). Whaddaya think of that? *New York: Two Tomatoes Records.*

Campbell, D. (1997). The Mozart Effect for children, *Vol. 1. Ontario, Canada: Children's Group.*

Gill, J. (1993). Jim Gill sings the Sneezing Song and other contagious tunes. *Chicago: Jim Gill Music.*

Grammer, R. (1986). Teaching peace. *Brewerton, NY: Red Note Records.*

Greg and Steve. (Various). We all live together, *Vol. 1, 2, 3, 4, & 5. Cypress, CA: Youngheart Records.*

Jenkins, E. (1989). You'll sing a song and I'll sing a song. *Washington DC: Smithsonian Folkways.*

Lewis, B. (1997). A tisket a tasket a children's rhythm basket. *Joshua Tree, CA: Brent Lewis Productions.*

Palmer, H. (Various). Learning basic skills *(Series). Freeport, NY: Educational Activity Records.*

Parachute Express. (1998). Feel the music. *Glendale, CA: Trio Lane Records.*

Rebops. (Various). Oldies for kool kiddies. *Hollywood, CA: A & M Records.*

Sugar Beats. (1995). Everybody is a star. *New York: Sugar Beats Entertainment.*

Sweet Honey in the Rock. (1989). All for freedom. *Redway, CA: Music for Little People.*

They Might Be Giants. (2002). No! *Cambridge, MA: Idlewild/Rounder.*

Tickle Toon Typhoon. (1984). Circle around. *Seattle: Tickle Toon Typhoon Publishing.*

World playground. *(Various artists). (1999). Putamayo.*

●

Children's Literature with a Musical Theme

There are many children's books based on songs, orchestral music, or with a rhythmical text.
The following is a representative sample.

Baer, G. (1989). Thump, thump, rat-a-tat-tat. *New York: HarperCollins.*

Christelow, E. (1989). Five little monkeys jumping on the bed. *New York: Clarion.*

Dillon, L., & Dillon, D. (2002). Rap a tap tap: Here's Bojangles, think of that. *New York: Blue Sky Press.*

Gollub, M. (2000). The jazz fly. *Santa Rosa, CA: Tortuga Press.*

Mallett, D. (1995). Inch by inch: The garden song. *New York: Harper Collins.*

Martin, J., & Archambault, J. (1989). Chicka chicka boom boom. *New York: Simon and Schuster Books for Young Readers.*

Miller, J. P., & Greene, S. M. (2001). We all sing with the same voice. *New York: Harper Collins.*

Trapani, I. (1993). Itsy bitsy Spider. *Boston: Whispering Coyote Press.*

Turner, B. (1998). Carnival of the Animals by Saint Saens. *New York: Henry Holt.*

Weiss, G., & Thiele, B. (1995). What a wonderful world. *New York: Simon and Schuster.*

Westcott, N. B. (1980). I know an old lady who swallowed a fly. *Boston: Little Brown.*

Winter, J. (1988). Follow the drinking gourd. *New York: Knopf.*

●

Professional Organizations

American Orff-Schulwerk Association
http://www.aosa2.org
Information on resources and professional development

The Dalcroze Society of America
www.dalcrozeusa.org
Information on Dalcroze eurhythmics

Early Childhood Music and Movement Association
http://www.ecmma.org/
Organization of professional educators dedicated to teaching music and movement to children from birth to age 7

National Association for the Education of Young Children
http://www.naeyc.org/
Information, links, resources, and articles on early childhood education

The National Association for Music Education
www.menc.org
This site includes resources and publications for all areas of music education

Organization of American Kodaly Educators
www.oake.org
Home site for teaching the Kodaly method

Zero to Three
www.zerotothree.org
A resource for parents and professionals on the first years of life

●

Web Sites

Note that web sites change frequently. The following is a short list of web sites that are a starting point for information on early childhood education, music education, and music therapy resources (current as of 8/1/06).

Clearinghouse on Early Education and Parenting
http://ceep.crc.uiuc.edu/
Publications and information on early childhood education

Early Childhood Music Education Links
http://www.questionsink.com/Links/childhood.html

ECE Web Guide

http://www.ecewebguide.com/

Comprehensive list of online web resource related to early childhood education

Education Resources Information Center

www.eric.ed.gov

Sponsored by the U.S. Department of Education, this site is a database of more than 1.1 million citations going back to 1966.

The International Center for Disability Resources on the Internet

www.icdri.org

Kathy Schrocks's Guide for Educators

http://school.discovery.com/schrockguide/arts/artp.html

Contains over 2000 web links to performing arts resources for teachers

The Music Education Madness Site

http://www.musiceducationmadness.com/

Articles, lesson plans, product reviews, and more on music education

Appendix A

MUSIC THERAPY AND YOUNG CHILDREN FACT SHEET

What is Music Therapy?

Music Therapy is the clinical and evidenced-based use of music interventions to accomplish individualized goals within a therapeutic relationship by a credentialed professional who has completed an approved music therapy program. Music Therapy is a well-established allied health profession similar to occupational therapy and physical therapy. It consists of using music therapeutically to address physical, psychological, cognitive, behavioral and/or social functioning. Because music therapy is a powerful and non-threatening medium, unique outcomes are possible. With young children, music therapy provides a unique variety of music experiences in an intentional and developmentally appropriate manner to effect changes in a child's behavior and facilitate development of his/her communication, social/emotional, sensori-motor, and/or cognitive skills.

Music therapy enhances the quality of life. It involves relationships between a qualified therapist and child; between one child and another; between child and family; and between the music and the participants. These relationships are structured and adapted through the elements of music to create a positive environment and set the occasion for successful growth.

How Does Music Therapy Make a Difference with Young Children?

- Music stimulates all of the senses and involves the child at many levels. This "multi-modal approach" facilitates many developmental skills.
- Quality learning and maximum participation occur when children are permitted to experience the joy of play. The medium of music therapy allows this play to occur naturally and frequently.
- Music is highly motivating, yet it can also have a calming and relaxing effect. Enjoyable music activities are designed to be success oriented and make children feel better about themselves.
- Music therapy can help a child manage pain and stressful situations.
- Music can encourage socialization, self-expression, communication, and motor development.
- Because the brain processes music in both hemispheres, music can stimulate cognitive functioning and may be used for remediation of some speech/language skills.

Example Case Study:

A music therapist working in a community music school refers to one of her students as a "musical child." The six-year old girl, who has physical and developmental delays, is somewhat verbal and interacts in a limited way with others. When she began music therapy at age three, it quickly became obvious that she had exceptional innate musical ability. She could play the piano by ear when she was two, although her hands have only four fingers each. And even though she rarely spoke, she sang – and in tune.

The last three years have resulted in significant growth. Through weekly individual 45-minute and then 60-minute music therapy sessions, the child has made progress in the length of her attention span, degree of independence and ability to follow directions. She now speaks one and two word phrases spontaneously, and there is also marked improvement in her social skills. In addition to singing and playing keyboard and piano, the child now plays the omnichord, autoharp, bells, chimes, xylophones, drum set and various small percussion instruments. In her initial stages of music therapy, when she played the keyboard and piano, she would not allow anyone else to play with her. Now, however, she plays the melody and the therapist plays the accompaniment. The child's preschool teacher has asked her to play for other children in her class, thereby using her musical strength to draw her into the group.

What Do Music Therapists Do?

Music therapists involve children in singing, listening, moving, playing, and in creative activities that may help them become better learners. Music therapists work on developing a child's self-awareness, confidence, readiness skills, coping skills, and social behavior and may also provide pain management techniques. They explore which styles of music, techniques and instruments are most effective or motivating for each individual child and expand upon the child's natural, spontaneous play in order to address areas of need.

Often working as a part of an interdisciplinary team, music therapists may coordinate programming with other professionals such as early intervention specialists, medical personnel, child-life specialists, psychologists, occupational and physical therapists, speech/language pathologists, adapted physical education specialists and art and dance/movement therapists. Music therapists may also furnish families with suggestions and resources for using music with the child at home.

Music therapists develop a rapport with children. They observe the child's behavior and interactions and assess communication, cognitive/academic, motor, social/emotional, and musical skills. After developing realistic goals and target objectives, music therapists plan and implement systematic music therapy treatment programs with procedures and techniques designed specifically for the individual child. Music therapists document responses, conduct ongoing evaluations of progress, and often make recommendations to other team members and the family regarding progress. Music therapists will also often make recommendations to team members and the family regarding ways to include successful music therapy techniques in other aspects of the child's life.

Who is a Qualified Music Therapist?

Graduates of colleges or universities from more than 70 approved music therapy programs are eligible to take a national examination administered by the Certification Board for Music Therapists (CBMT), an independent, non-profit certifying agency fully accredited by the National Commission for Certifying Agencies. After successful completion of the CBMT examination, graduates are issued the credential necessary for professional practice, Music Therapist-Board Certified (MT-BC). In addition to the MT-BC credential, other recognized professional designations are Registered Music Therapists (RMT), Certified Music Therapists (CMT), and Advanced Certified Music Therapist (ACMT) listed with the National Music Therapy Registry. Any individual who does not have proper training and credentials is not qualified to provide music therapy services.

What Can One Expect from a Music Therapist?

Since music therapy may be listed on the child's IEP (Individualized Education Program) as a "related service" or may be provided to children under the age of three as part of the IFSP (Individualized Family Service Plan), music therapists must be able to assess the needs of the young child as well as those of the family. They design individualized programming, monitor progress, evaluate, and provide documentation related to the child's goals and objectives.

A music therapist who works with young children should possess a strong knowledge of relevant music and materials, early childhood development, specific needs of the child, and developmentally appropriate practices. A music therapist is accomplished in the use of instruments and voice. He/she is able to adapt strategies to a variety of settings and across disciplines, thus individualizing music therapy interventions to meet children's specific needs. In addition, he/she may provide structured or semi-structured opportunities for children with and without disabilities to interact together in a music setting. Music therapists are creative, energetic, and positive. They demonstrate strong oral and written communication skills and work well with families and other professionals.

Where do Music Therapists Work?

In addition to early intervention centers, preschools, and schools, music therapists offer services to individuals and groups in a variety of settings. These settings include, but are not limited to, mental health clinics, rehabilitation facilities, outpatient clinics, wellness programs, schools, nursing homes, senior centers, private practice, group homes, day care treatment centers, medical and psychiatric hopitals, substance abuse programs, hospice and bereavement programs, and correctional and forensic facilities. Some music therapists are self-employed and may be hired on a contractual basis to provide assessment, consultation, or treatment services for children and adults.

How Does Music Therapy Help Families?

Music therapy can provide enjoyable yet purposeful activities and resources for families to share with their children. Families can learn to use music through meaningful play and nurturing experiences. Music therapy may serve as a positive outlet for interaction, providing fun activities that can include parents, siblings, and extended family. Often music therapy allows a family to see a child in a new light as the child's strengths are manifested in the music therapy environment.

What Research and Resources are Available to Substantiate and Support Music Therapy?

Through *Journal of Music Therapy, Music Therapy Perspectives,* and other resources, AMTA promotes much research exploring the benefits of music therapy with young children. Furthermore, AMTA has an Early Childhood Network that disseminates additional information to interested parties.

Why Music Therapy?

Music therapy may address several needs simultaneously in a positive and exciting medium: it may provide pleasurable learning that promotes success. Furthermore, music therapy can greatly enhance the quality of life of the young child and his/her family. Music is often the first thing to which a child relates. It is a "universal language" that crosses all cultural lines. Music occurs naturally in our environment in many settings and is a socially appropriate activity and leisure skill. Music provides a predictable time-oriented and reality-oriented structure while offering opportunities for participation at one's own level of functioning and ability.

Not only may music activities be opportunities for a child to "shine," but they may also be used to reinforce nonmusical goals. Most people, especially children, enjoy music – therefore, music therapy can be the therapy that reinforces all other therapies.

A Director of Educational Services for a public school system affirms:

"The inclusionary preschool music therapy sessions gave children an opportunity to make new friends and learn things about themselves and others. I saw major gains in the children's social skills and in their attention spans. I wholeheartedly endorse the program and think that every child could benefit from music therapy."

An occupational therapist writes:

"I love having a music therapist on our interdisciplinary team. When we co-lead sessions, I notice that the children are much more motivated to push themselves when working with such things as fine motor control and range of motion activities."

The father of a 5 year old child diagnosed with Attention Deficit/Hyperactivity Disorder observes:

"Music therapy has helped my son to increase his concentration and attending. His eye contact has increased since participating in music therapy. Moreover, I believe that in part his increased use of language may be attributed to attending music therapy. Finally, he has developed an interest in music." (Child has participated in individual music therapy for 1 1/2 years.)

The mother of a 6 1/2-year-old child diagnosed with Down Syndrome states:

"Music therapy has helped my son to learn turn-taking, sharing, listening skills and some colors, animals, parts of the body and clothes." (Child participated in group music therapy for 2 years in preschool and then in individual music therapy for 1 year in kindergarten.)

The mother of 7 year old twin sons, one diagnosed with Tourette Syndrome and one diagnosed with Pervasive Developmental Disorder, comments:

"For one son music therapy seems to have reduced an extreme sensitivity to sound. For both boys, the therapy has been a catalyst for improved sociability. Much of the time the boys seem to exist on parallel universes, but on the drive home from therapy they usually have a conversation." (The boys have participated in small group or partner music therapy sessions for two years.)

The mother of an 8-year-old child with Apert Syndrome and Attention Deficit Behaviors notes:

"Music therapy has (1) helped with my daughter's spontaneous speech; (2) allowed her to use her hands with many different textures and independently of each other; (3) expanded on her natural musical ability; and (4) helped her learn to focus and develop patience with music as the motivator." (Child participated in small group music therapy for 1 1/2 years in preschool and in individual music therapy for 4 years.)

The parent of a hospitalized child undergoing treatment for cancer relates:

"Music therapy has been a tremendous benefit not only for my child, but also for our family. During music therapy time, my child is able to do fun things that help him forget about his pain. We are grateful to share some time with him doing things that bring back a smile to his face."

How Can You Find a Music Therapist or Get More Information?

American Music Therapy Association
8455 Colesville Road, Suite 1000
Silver Spring, MD 20910
(301) 589-3300 Fax (301) 589-5175
Email: info@musictherapy.org
Web: http://www.musictherapy.org

Appendix B

MUSIC THERAPY AND SPECIAL EDUCATION FACT SHEET

- Music Therapy is considered a related service under the Individuals with Disabilities Education Act (IDEA).

- When music therapy is deemed necessary to assist a child benefit from his/her special education, goals are documented on the Individualized Education Program (IEP) as a related service intervention.

- Music therapy can be an integral component in helping the child with special needs attain educational goals identified by his/her IEP team.

- Music therapy interventions can address development in cognitive, behavioral, physical, emotional, and social skills. Music therapy can also facilitate development in communication and sensori-motor skills.

- Music therapy can offer direct or consultant services as determined by the individual needs of the child.

- Music therapists can support special education classroom teachers by providing effective ways to incorporate music into their academic curriculum.

- Music therapy involvement can stimulate attention and increase motivation to participate more fully in other aspects of the educational setting.

- Music therapy interventions apply the inherent order of music to set behavioral expectations, provide reassurance, and maintain structure for children with special needs.

- Music therapy can adapt strategies to encourage a child's participation in the least restrictive environment.

Appendix C

MUSIC THERAPY AND MUSIC EDUCATION FACT SHEET
Meeting the Needs of Children with Disabilities

What is Music Therapy?

Music Therapy is the clinical and evidenced-based use of music interventions to accomplish individualized goals within a therapeutic relationship by a credentialed professional who has completed an approved music therapy program. Music therapy is a well-established allied health profession similar to occupational therapy and physical therapy. It consists of using music therapeutically to address physical, psychological, cognitive and/or social functioning. Because music therapy is a powerful and non-threatening medium, unique outcomes are possible. In music therapy, each individual is provided support and encouragement in the acquisition of new skills and abilities. Because music touches each person in so many different ways, participation in music therapy offers opportunities for learning, creativity and expression that may be significantly different from more traditional educational/ therapeutic approaches.

What is the Rationale for Providing Music Therapy Services in the School Setting?

According to Public Law 94-142 (Education for All Handicapped Children Act) subsequently renamed the Individuals with Disabilities Education Act (IDEA), students with special education needs are entitled to the same educational opportunities as their typically developing peers. The concept of providing education in the "least restrictive environment" is defined to mean that ALL students, regardless of disability, should have full access to the general education curriculum. As a result, students with more severe learning problems are now included in general education classrooms not only to meet academic needs but also to increase socialization opportunities.

Music therapists typically use music activities to foster the development of motor, communication, cognitive, and social abilities in students with special education needs. Music therapy can be used to address many of the goals targeted in the Individualized Education Program (IEP) such as the learning of academic concepts, increasing cooperation and appropriate social behavior, providing avenues for communication, increasing self-esteem and self confidence, improving motoric responses and agility, and encouraging exploration and examination of issues that impact the life of the student. By creating, singing, moving, and listening to music, a wide range of cognitive, emotional and physical abilities are brought into focus. Under the direction of a qualified music therapist, the new skills learned in the music therapy setting can be transferred to other areas of the student's life.

What is the IEP and Why is it Important for the Music Educator to be Involved in this Process?

The Individualized Education Program (IEP) is the legal document that results from the initial assessment and periodic reviews of students receiving special education services. Among other things, the IEP identifies the educational goals and suggested teaching strategies for each student along with what related services are required to meet those goals. Since placement in a music classroom may be a part of the student's IEP, the music educator needs to understand how the process works and what services may be available to the student in order to ensure a successful participation. A music therapist can assist the music educator in defining and developing the pre-requisite musical, behavioral, and social skills necessary for the student to be successful in the music classroom.

Are Music Therapists Employed in Public/Private Schools?

Nationwide, hundreds of credentialed music therapists are currently employed by local school districts and private educational centers. Music therapy is recognized as a related service that can be an integral component in helping the student receiving special education services reach his or her IEP goals. In many school districts, music therapists also offer support services for music educators in the form of direct service, consultation, or inservice training.

Specifically, How Can a Music Therapist be of Assistance to a Music Educator?

Published research studies indicate that music educators often report lacking adequate training regarding the educational needs of students with disabilities and limited knowledge of effective teaching strategies to meet those needs. Music therapists can assist the music educator in the following ways:

Consultant. Music therapists can assist the music educator in designing and implementing appropriate music education experiences for students with disabilities.

Direct Service.
- In the regular music education classroom: Music therapists may accompany the student to assess the skills needed for successful participation and to assist with development of those skills.

- In the self-contained classroom: The music therapist may work alone or in concert with a music educator who has been assigned to teach a self-contained class.
- Outside the classroom: In some cases, it may be necessary to provide individualized services outside the classroom in order to assist the student with to develop the skills needed to successfully participate in the classroom setting.

Inservice Education. Music educators frequently call upon music therapists to provide support in the development of techniques and strategies that will lead to successful inclusion. Specifically, music therapists can help the music educator with the development of augmentative devices, adaptation of equipment and instruments, simplification of musical arrangements, and various teaching strategies.

Why Music Therapy?

Music therapy, practiced by highly skilled and specially trained professionals, can profoundly affect the lives of the individuals participating in the therapy.

M. is 7 years old. She was diagnosed at birth with Tuberous Sclerosis, a neurological disorder that can result in autistic-like behavior and significant developmental delays. M. has a very limited use of language. While she appears to understand and receive language, she rarely talks or verbally communicates with others. However, M. loves to sing and play instruments. M. can recall and sing, with remarkably accurate pitch and rhythm, almost any song she hears. At times, the lyrics of the songs she sings can be clearly understood. Through music therapy, M. is learning to interact with her therapist, her family, and her surroundings. She has learned to follow directions, make requests, and organize herself through singing. After three years of work, M. is now responding to spoken language and is using words and music to communicate with the world around her. She has much more to learn, but music and music therapy will be a part of her life for a long time to come.

Who is Qualified as a Music Therapist?

Graduates of colleges or universities from more than 70 approved music therapy programs are eligible to take a national examination administered by the Certification Board for Music Therapists (CBMT), an independent, non-profit certifying agency fully accredited by the National Commission for Certifying Agencies. After successful completion of the CBMT examination, graduates are issued the credential necessary for professional practice, Music Therapist-Board Certified (MT-BC). In addition to the MT-BC credential, other recognized professional designations are Registered Music Therapists (RMT), Certified Music Therapists (CMT), and Advanced Certified Music Therapist (ACMT) listed with the National Music Therapy Registry. Any individual who does not have proper training and credentials is not qualified to provide music therapy services.

Where do Music Therapists Work?

Besides schools and other special education programs, music therapists offer services to individuals and groups from early intervention to the elderly in a variety of settings. These settings include, but are not limited to, mental health clinics, rehabilitation facilities, outpatient clinics, wellness programs, schools, nursing homes, senior centers, private practice, group homes, day care treament centers, medical and psychiatric hopitals, substance abuse programs, hospice and bereavement programs, and correctional and forensic facilities. Some music therapists are self-employed and may be hired on a contractual basis to provide assessment, consultation, or treatment services for children and adults.

What is AMTA?

The American Music Therapy Association (AMTA) represents over 5,000 music therapists, corporate members, and related associations worldwide. AMTA's roots date back to organizations founded in 1950 and 1971. Those two organizations merged in 1998 to ensure the progressive development of the therapeutic use of music in rehabilitation, special education, and medical and community settings. AMTA is committed to the advancement of education, training, professional standards, and research in support of the music therapy profession. The mission of the organization is to advance public knowledge of music therapy benefits and increase access to quality music therapy services. Currently, AMTA establishes criteria for the education and clinical training of music therapists. Professional members of AMTA adhere to a Code of Ethics and Standards of Practice in their delivery of music therapy services.

Resources for Music Therapists and Music Educators Available from AMTA.
- Music in Special Education; Written by Mary S. Adamek and Alice-Ann Darrow
- Models of Music Therapy Intervention in School Settings: From Institution to Inclusion

How Can You Find a Music Therapist or Get More Information?

American Music Therapy Association
8455 Colesville Road, Suite 1000, Silver Spring, MD 20910
T: (301) 589-3300 • F: (301) 589-5175
Web: http://www.musictherapy.org • Email: info@musictherapy.org